HIS DEEPER WORK IN US

HIS DEEPER WORK IN US

A further enquiry into New
Testament teaching on the
subject of Christian Holiness

J. SIDLOW BAXTER

ZONDERVAN PUBLISHING HOUSE OF THE ZONDERVAN CORPORATION GRAND RAPIDS, MICHIGAN 49506

HIS DEEPER WORK IN US
© J. Sidlow Baxter 1967

Library of Congress Catalog Card Number 74-4965

First Zondervan printing 1974
Eighth printing 1982
ISBN 0-310-20651-0

Printed in the United States of America

DEDICATION

These chapters on the Holy Spirit's deeper work
in believers are dedicated with deep esteem to
my dear friend, the Reverend Doctor

J. PALMER MUNTZ

known and loved by evangelical leaders in many
lands for his gifted and devoted ministry to our
dear Lord.

Although this penetrating exposition of New Testament teaching on Christian sanctification is complete in itself, it is the second volume in a trilogy on the subject from Dr. Baxter's pen.

It is a careful restudy and restatement of the New Testament teaching—and with good reason; for as Dr. Baxter urges, no subject can be of more vital concern to Christian believers than inwardly experienced holiness. Moreover, as Dr. Baxter rightly avers, there is much bondage engendered today through certain widely taught but misleading theories. These are firmly but courteously countered by appeal to exact Scripture statement.

This leads to some challenging surprises. The rival theories of "eradication" and "counteraction", as also the idea of "two natures" in the believer, come under keen scrutiny and are found fallacious. But the real, simple teaching of the New Testament breaks through the more clearly as shadowy errors are dispelled.

Dr. Baxter makes copious references to the testimony of Christian experience; but his final court of appeal is always the written Word. These studies will say little to the superficial; but to many a Christian heart "hungering and thirsting" after heart-holiness they can be a Jordan-crossing into a spiritual Canaan.

CONTENTS

SUPPLEMENTARY

FOREWORD

Some of the theological questions which were rifest twenty-five years ago are dead issues today. So quickly do human thought-currents change. It may be, also, that some of the older "strife of theories" which gathered round the subject of Scriptural holiness a generation or so ago has now spent itself into a rueful memory. But may God save us from ever thinking that holiness *itself* is a spent issue; for Christian holiness, by which I mean individual holiness *inwrought* by the Holy Spirit, and then *outwrought* through Christlike character, is a living issue, the importance of which nothing can ever eclipse. When the organized Church treats *that* as a spent issue, we may well write "Ichabod" over its doors.

Only a few evenings ago a college professor said to me over the telephone, "My wife and I want to talk with you about the matter of holiness. We want to be all that God would have us be in this present life, so we want to know what the teaching of Scripture really *is* about holiness. Is it the eradication of all hereditary sin-bias in human nature? Can we ever become 'dead to sin'? What is the truth about being 'filled with the Spirit'? Does it have to show itself by our 'speaking in tongues'?" That professor and his wife represent thousands of holiness-hungry hearts. To some of those, at least, may the pages of this little book be as "a light from heaven" (Acts 9: 3).

J. S. B.

SOME PRELIMINARY THOUGHTS

Shall my criterion of the holy life
  Be what mere men may think or write or say?
Does guidance come by clash of wordy strife,
  Or following man-made slogans of the day?

One standard only : the inerrant Word,
  Must guide me into true heart-holiness ;
Then let me follow, prayerful, undeterred,
  For Canaan waits ! Why hug a wilderness?

Oh, precious Word, which truly sanctifies !
  Which brings me inwrought holy joy and rest !
No more shall earthly lures divert my eyes,
  Nor shall the better keep me from the *best*.

                    J.S.B.

SOME PRELIMINARY THOUGHTS

DURING the past fifty years or so the "swing of the pendulum" has brought more vivid and varied changes to the face of human society than in any preceding half-century. Science, discovery, invention, new industrial mechanizations, two world wars, the splitting of the atom, nuclear energy, international Communism, being major contributories. Thought-forms and behaviour-patterns, customs and methods, which had persisted for centuries have suddenly become otiose or irrelevant. Exteriorily, at least, the changes are almost dramatic.

Yet whatever may be the outward changes, this still remains unaffectedly true, that for every Christian believer the most up-to-date concern (whether this is sufficiently realized or not) is *holiness of heart and life*, by which I mean a condition of inward and outward holiness effected in and through the Christian believer by the Holy Spirit.

Today human affairs move on an immense scale never known before. This is the age of collectivisms which make the individual seem (and feel) humiliatingly small against the huge "mass man". Yet we are wrong to let the big voice of collectivist philosophy sweep us off our feet. If the Bible is the Word of God, then this still remains inviolately true, that each individual human is unique, each is just as meaningful to God, just as unspeakably *dear* to God as ever. Despite all our present-day conglomerations, and over against the clamorous new emphasis on ecumenicity, the first message of the Gospel is still to the *individual*. Besides John 3: 16, with its "God so loved the world", is Galatians 2: 20, with its, "The Son of God loved *me*, and gave Himself for *me*". The first approach of the Evangel is the singular, "Believe on the Lord Jesus Christ, and *thou* shalt be saved". It is perilous unwisdom for the Church ever to overlook or obscure this individualistic emphasis of Holy Writ. According to the New Testament, there is no such thing as a "*social* Gospel". The only social salvation is the salvation of the *individual* multiplied.

In no connection is this emphasis on the individual more needed today than in the matter of Christian *holiness*. Indeed, not only is this as up-to-date a concern as ever, it is perhaps more peculiarly so now than at any time before. Not only has the organized Church in Protestant Christendom been fearfully lamed by Liberalism and other latter-day apostasies from "the faith once-for-all delivered to the saints", it has been simultaneously staggered by big-scale problems which the new collectivist age has brought. As an offset to this we are needing a new reminder that the Church's most unanswerable apologetic is always the miracle of trans-figured human character: not brilliant new schemes, mergers, or more ecclesiastical machinery, but saved, sanctified, Spirit-filled men and women; real flesh-and-blood saints who transmit the "*beauty* of holiness" amid the scramble and. congestion of our times. Without such the Church is spiritually limp; for the organized Church is but the aggregate of its individual members. Plato never said a more realistic thing than "The State is but the individual writ large". Nor is anything sounder than this, that the Church as a whole never rises above the moral and spiritual level of its individual member.

I believe that in these days God is wanting to say something new through the churches to our age; but as a prior necessity He is trying to say something *to* them. "He that hath an ear, let him hear what the Spirit saith to the churches." Somehow, with my ear to the Book, I seem to hear a new call to *holiness*. I seem to catch a new insistence in the voice from heaven that without "HOLINESS TO THE LORD" written large across the Church's banners, organized Christianity will not rise from its present spiritual break-down to do mighty spiritual "exploits" again.

It is this most sacred matter of holiness which we are to re-explore in these pages. There will be nothing academic or technical about our terminology; but we may as well say plainly at the outset that this is no book for the superficial or the skimmers. For such, no thought-demanding book can "come alive"; but those who "hunger and thirst" after the fulness of the Spirit, after purity of heart, after inward sanctification, after "reigning in life" through our Lord Jesus, will find herein (so we hope) truth which God can bless to their eternal profit.

The Scriptural teaching as to inwardly imparted holiness is indeed straightforward enough in itself, when rightly interpreted, but, alas, it has been made to seem strangely complicated by conflicting schools and watchwords. For far too long, certain erroneous theories of Christian holiness have been in vogue by which many believers have been beguiled and then brought into bondage. We shall need to refer to these *en route* in order to set off the really true against that which is only *seemingly* true.

Maybe some who chance on these pages will expect me to relate the present-day emphasis on "speaking in tongues" to the Holy Spirit's deeper work of sanctification. After prayerful reflection, however, I purposely exclude any special consideration of "tongues" here. For although that peculiarly sensory manifestation is included (albeit as the least important) in the *pneumatika* of I Corinthians 12-14, it is not vitally connected with inwrought *holiness*. If it were, the New Testament would certainly have said so, which it does not.

Let me speak with appreciative respect toward all those fervent brethren who are spokesmen or enthusiasts of the "tongues" movement. Perhaps they have recaptured for us a missing accent. If so, I would be humbly and truly open-minded about it. I, too, deeply long for all that the Holy Spirit would fain give me. Let me not lag behind with sceptical indifference or turn away in uninformed prejudice. I have had warm, glowing fellowship with not a few who know the "tongues" gift. I have listened absorbingly to their testimony, and have often found my own heart ringing an answering bell. So, if I speak frankly here, in passing, it is with abundant goodwill, without a fleck of captious prejudice.

As all sincere believers will concur, including those who "speak in tongues", inwrought holiness of heart and life is far more important than *any* of the Spirit's "gifts". What is more, character-transfiguring *holiness* is the greatest and loveliest of *all* the miracles which the Holy Spirit ever effects in human lives. Even as Paul says, the love which "suffers long, and is kind" is "more excellent" than even the greatest of the gifts, i.e. "prophecy". Christlikeness is far more than the spiritual "gifts". Of course, the "graces" and the "gifts" may go together, and are meant to do so. What I am stressing here is that the former are our *prior* concern. When at last, in the glory, we meet our Saviour, the first question will scarcely be whether we "spoke in tongues" or not while here on earth, but (1) was He so supreme in our love that through our utter yieldedness to Him the Holy Spirit wrought in us Christlike *holiness* of heart and life? (2) Were we faithful *witnesses* for Him with a view to the salvation of others? Let us never forget it: *those* are the two concerns which outrank all others for the Christian.

After careful study of Scripture, my own persuasion is that the present over-emphasis on "tongues" is unhealthy, and will wear away leaving no residuum of solid benefit. Of all the twenty-one New Testament epistles, First Corinthians is the *only one* where speaking in tongues figures; and the Corinthian church has the unhappy distinction of being the only one to which Paul says, "Ye are yet carnal"; "I could not speak unto you as unto spiritual, but as unto babes" (1 Cor. 3: 1–3). So, clearly, "speaking in tongues" can go with a very kindergarten spirituality! Does that disappoint some reader? Let it be acknowledged then that what I say is Scriptural. How clear is Paul's guarding word—"I would rather speak five words with my understanding, that I might instruct others also, than *ten thousand* words in a 'tongue'"! And how pathetic that he must needs immediately subjoin the further appeal—"Brethren, be not children"!

Yes, more intrinsic than "speaking in tongues" is holiness of heart and its resultant transfiguration of character into Christlikeness. *That* is our transcendent, magnetic, all-important subject in these pages. Oh, that the heavenly Spirit may begin to stir us into new yearning to know the reality of it!

We need that same heavenly Tutor, the Holy Spirit to open our eyes to the "*beauty* of holiness" (Ps. 29: 2), because holiness is one of those concepts which have an *ambivalent* effect; that is, it can both attract and repel at the same time. There is a glory in it which can be awe-awaking, as when Simon suddenly saw it in Jesus, and cried, "Depart from me, for I am a sinful man, O Lord". Yet there is a compelling loveliness about it which, when once seen, breaks the magnetism of all else, as when that same Simon Peter later said to that same meek and lowly Jesus, "Lord, to whom shall we go? Thou hast the words of eternal life. And we know that Thou art the *HOLY ONE* of God".

> What has stript the seeming beauty
>   From the idols of the earth?
> Not a sense of right and duty,
>   But the sight of peerless worth.
>
> 'Tis the look that melted Peter,
>   'Tis the face that Stephen saw,
> 'Tis the heart that wept with Mary,
>   Can alone from idols draw.

Draw and win and fill completely,
Till the cup o'erflows the brim ;
What have we to do with idols
Who have companied with Him ?

My fervent hope is that through the following pages, dear reader, you may see holiness in its magnetic reality. My big dread is, that because a part of this book has to be an argumentative cleaving of our way through entanglements of misunderstanding, some readers will give up, not recognizing that we are having to hack our way back through humanly inflicted complexity to the original simplicities of the Word.

THE SHINING CHALLENGE

Holiness, as taught in the New Testament, is no mere negative concept—a being freed merely from the disfigurements of sin. Besides the negative aspect of being rescued from the tyranny of hereditary depravity, there are all those wonderful *positive* traits which accompany the Holy Spirit's deeper renewal of the mind into the image of Christ. According to the New Testament picture of holiness, the garden is not only cleared of ugly weeds, it is filled with fragrant flowers and rich fruits. Christian sanctity is no mere frigid inhibitionism or austere self-repression; it is release from the wretched bondage of egocentricity into the liberty of a Christlike otherism, through a pervading of the soul with the magnanimous love of God. It is a refining of the whole moral being, and a lifting of the whole life to a level on which pure thinking and gracious behaviour are spontaneous.

In other words, the New Testament emphasis is not so much on our being *ridded* of something (though that is necessarily included) but rather on our being *filled* with a spiritual vitality and health which leave the sin-disease no environment in which to thrive. That life of victorious fulness is the shining challenge of the written Word to every Christian believer. It is a fulness of new spiritual life which is positive *holiness*—brought about through an invasion of our being by the Holy Spirit Himself (wonderful mystery!). One has only to glance through the New Testament to know whether many or few Christians today are living according to the divine standard.

Look again at the New Testament photograph of "a man in Christ". He has within him "the peace of God which passeth all understanding" (Phil. 4: 7). He "rejoices with joy unspeakable and full of glory" (1 Pet. 1: 8). He has "the wisdom that is from above" (Jas. 3: 17). He "walks in the light as God is in the light", having continuous "fellowship with the Father and with His Son" (1 John 1: 3, 7). He is "renewed in knowledge after the image of God" (Col. 3: 10), and is renewed into "true holiness" (Eph. 4: 24). He "beholds with unveiled face the glory of the Lord, and is changed into the same image" (2 Cor. 3: 18). In him "perfect love casts out fear" (1 John 4: 18). He "dwelleth in God, and God in him" (1 John 4: 16). He is "filled unto all the fulness of God" (Eph. 3: 19). He lives the "more abundant life" (John 10: 10).

In his prayer-life he "asks and receives", till his "joy is full" (John 16: 24). He finds God "able to do exceedingly abundantly above all he asks or thinks, according to *the power that worketh in him*" (Eph. 3: 20). To his praying heart the risen Lord "manifests Himself" (John 14: 21). In him, "the Spirit beareth *witness* that he is a child of God" (Rom. 8: 16). The "Spirit of life" has "set him free from the law of sin and death" (Rom. 8: 2). He knows by experience that he is "*sealed*" with the Holy Spirit, and that he has the inward "*earnest*" of the Spirit as a foretaste of the heavenly "inheritance" (Eph. 1: 13, 14). He is "endued" by the Spirit with "the power from on high". His character is beautiful with "the *fruit* of the Spirit: love, joy, peace, long-suffering, gentleness, goodness. . . ."

When "troubled on every side" he is not "cast down" but the life of Jesus is "manifested" through him (2 Cor. 4: 8, 10). In "tribulations" he is "more than conqueror through him that loved us" (Rom. 8: 37). In "infirmities" and "reproaches" he sings, "when I am weak then am I strong" (2 Cor. 12: 10). "I can do all things through Christ which strengtheneth me" (Phil. 4: 13). He has "full assurance of hope" (Heb. 6: 11) and "full assurance of faith" (10: 22). In a word, he is "filled continually with the Holy Spirit" (Eph. 5: 18).

How many (or how few) of us are living that "abiding" and "abounding" life in Christ? How many, or how few of us can truthfully testify that the power of sin has been really broken within us?—that all our thought-life has been "renewed" into holiness?—that we "reign" in constant victory over temptation and circumstance?—that we have the abiding "witness" of the Holy Spirit?—that we live in the "fulness" of peace and joy and love and assurance which belong to the Spirit-filled life? Perhaps, if some of us were to confess the truth, we secretly doubt whether such a life is possible. Yet the stimulating fact is, that in New Testament times the ideal and the actual were one in thousands of transformed men and women; and, in every generation since, there have been witnesses to the continuing reality of it.

Does someone say, "If you knew what I am by hereditary nature, you would know that such a life of holiness cannot be for me"? Our Lord replies, as He did to the Sadducees long ago, "Ye do err, not knowing the Scriptures, nor the power of God". Does someone else say, "If you knew my home, my family, my husband, my wife, my children, my parents, my daily occupation, the people among whom I must continually work, you would know how impossible a life of entire sanctification is for me"? Are your circumstances worse than those of the first-century believers to whom the New Testament epistles were originally addressed? Many of them were slaves. Most of them were poor. Others were illiterate. Probably their profession of the Christian faith brought penalties which most of us escape today. Yet, oh, how real was the deeper work of the Holy Spirit to thousands of them! How vivid was their experience of sanctification and victory!

Does someone ask, "Is such a deeper work of inward renewal and spiritual blessing meant for one who lives an insignificant, hum-drum life like mine? Is it not rather meant for preachers, missionaries, evangelists, and other such?" Let me call your attention to Colossians 1: 11. See the amplitude of the power which it promises—"Strengthened with *all* might, according to *His glorious power,* unto . . ." Well, unto what? Unto spectacular exploits? missionary heroism?—evangelistic campaigns? No; but this: "Strengthened with all might, according to His glorious power unto all *patience and longsuffering with joyfulness*"! Talk about transformation of the hum-drum!

Do others ask: "What about the theory that there are two natures in the Christian"—the "new nature" which came at conversion, and the "old nature" which is the evil old self? Is it true, as some teach, that sanctification is the *eradication* of the evil "old nature"? Or are we rather to believe those others who teach that the evil "old nature" can *never* be eradicated or changed during our present life on earth, but it must be "crucified with

Christ" and thus kept out of operation? Which of those teachings is right? Or is neither of them right? What is the authentic teaching of the New Testament? Or does someone else ask: "When holiness teachers speak of sanctification as 'the second blessing', what do they mean?"

Those questions strike right into our subject, and we shall give earnest answers to them in the following pages. My one dread (let me say so again) is, lest the precious, forthright teaching of Scripture concerning holiness should be made to seem complicated (which it is not) by our having to disentangle it from erroneous theories which have inflicted needless complexity upon it.

The subject is rich, inviting, and important beyond exaggeration. Our first big question will be: Does the Bible unmistakably *teach* a deeper, further work of the Holy Spirit in the believer, distinct from and subsequent to conversion? Then we shall ask in more detail: What is the *nature* of inwrought holiness, and how is it effected within us? We shall find ourselves asking: How do we enter the *experience* of inward sanctification? Can there be complete freedom from sin? Other important questions will arise along the way. But let us come to these enquiries with eager longing to know the truth, and with earnest prayer that God may lead us into "the *fulness* of the blessing."

For the very reason that our subject is of such sensitive concern to Christian hearts, as we now prayerfully approach a careful consideration of it I would ask for a reverent open-mindedness. It is hardly likely that unconverted persons will be curious enough to read a book such as this, but among Christian believers who may chance to read it there are four kinds, with four different attitudes, respectively.

First, there are *young* Christians, truly regenerated, rejoicing in forgiveness of sins and in their newly-found Christian fellowship, but as yet scarcely acquainted with those deeper reaches of salvation implied in the word, "holiness". Second, there are *older* believers who are either discouraged from seeking the blessing of holiness because confused by conflicting theories, or else are still eager to "possess their possessions". Third, there are some who hold a particular theory of holiness, and are *suspicious* of any new interpretation, yet are secretly dissatisfied with their present experience, and hopeful of some new slant on the problematical matter. Fourth, there are the fixedly *prejudiced*. Such is their resentment, that any talk about a crisis-work of sanctification wrought in believers subsequent to their conversion is like "smoke to the nostrils", even if we discard all use of the older title, "second blessing".

A Fourfold Appeal

To *young* believers here is my appeal. Now that you know the reality of conversion and justification, seek the further realities of consecration and sanctification. Now that the Holy Spirit has introduced new spiritual impulses into your nature, learn from Scripture how He can deal with the *un*spiritual propensities still in your nature. Now that you have a blood-bought forgiveness for *sins*, find what the Word teaches about a Spirit-wrought deliverance from the oppression of inward *sin*. Come to this subject of holiness with an open mind. Do not be tempted to skip over the first part of this book to the second area, where we *describe* the further blessing and how it is appropriated. Though you know little about past controversies on this subject of holiness, read the first part of this treatise carefully. You may glean much from both the findings and the mistakes of others. This present chapter, and the one next after, you should find simple enough and pleasant; but patiently ponder, also, the succeeding chapters on divergent theories, and test our own reasonings carefully by the Scriptures, all the way through.

To *older* believers who may have become discouraged through discordant theories, I would appeal. Read carefully through the arguments in the first part of this book. Refuse to let it be tedious. There may be new light for you in these pages, and possibly the answer to your wistful quest after real heart-holiness.

To those who already hold some special *theory* of holiness I would appeal. Let your theory be servant, not master. Distinguish between theory, which is tentative, and truth which is absolute. Your theory may seem right but be wrong; it may need modifying or amplifying or recasting. Can you honestly say that it has proved itself true in the acid test of daily experience? If it has not, then may it not be found, after all, a faulty abstract from the written Word? Do not let wedlock to a theory warp your reaction to new evidence which may emerge from further investigation of Scripture.

To the *prejudiced* I would here appeal. Is not prejudice a

self-inflicted blindness? It is especially reprehensible in relation
to such a tender, utterly important concern as that of Scriptural
holiness. Could your diatribes against this so-called "second
work of grace" possibly be grieving the Holy Spirit and uttering
disguised unbelief? Thousands of the choicest saints have borne
humble, patient, loving, sincere testimony to this blest crisis-
transition which formerly was often referred to as "the second
blessing". Tread cautiously at least, lest you be vainly "fighting
against the truth". Try to read these pages with eagerly open
mind, for so it could happen that unexpected blessing might come
your way.

A Fourfold Reason

Such is my preliminary appeal, and here, now, is my fourfold
reason for making it. First, I verily believe that at this critical
yet opportune juncture in the story of the evangelical churches,
the time is full ripe for a restudy and fresh proclamation of the
New Testament ideal. The ebb has reached a far line; a new
tidal insurge is due, as is indicated throughout our churches in
the many sighings for a deeper kind of Christianity again.

Second, a new discovery and revived experiencing of true holiness would mean more than words can express to thousands of
present-day believers who have not heard the deeper message
of Scripture. Many of us would not have progressed into the
grateful, matured, rejoicing believers which we are today
had it not been that after our conversion to Christ we were
pointed to the "grapes of Eschol", to the milk and honey and
corn and wine of Canaan, to that spiritual "land of promise" in
Christ which is sanctification through the refining fire of Pentecost
and the shedding of divine love within us by the Holy Spirit.

Third, it needs no unusual insight to see that holiness *must*
be the basic quality in true Christian character, the imperative
qualification for true Christian witness, and the vital atmosphere
of true Christian fellowship. It is the first-priority concern both of
the individual believer and of the local Christian assembly. Set
our evangelical churches ablaze with a passion to expound and
experience Spirit-filled holiness as taught in the New Testament,
and, as Samson's foxes ran with their firebrands through the
corn, setting the whole field afire, so will they—our evangelical
groups—set the land aflame with spiritual revival. Give God a
holy church, and who shall set a bound to the possibilities? During

the First World War, when hard pressed on the western front, Marshal Foch once wrote this report to General Joffre: "My right is broken, my left is shattered, my centre is in retreat. The situation is excellent; I shall attack." This unexpected swing-round took the enemy by surprise, and became a turning-point in the war. It is time, too, that the evangelical allies took the initiative again in a sound, sane, counter-attack along this holiness line. Apostolic Christianity is not just superior ethics or even sound theology; it is a supernatural, character-transforming *experience* of reconciliation with God and of inwrought holiness! We need to put new emphasis *there* again.

Fourth, we are convinced that the hour calls for a *re-examination* of the subject. In the words of John Robinson, AD. 1620, we believe that there is "yet more light and truth to break from God's Word". To suggest that *we* have suddenly acquired an insight into it which far greater minds than ours did not have would be vain effrontery; yet we would not be writing this treatise at all unless we had, at least, some cogent further contribution to make to the total thinking. For one thing, we hope to prove that the seemingly irreconcilable breach between the Wesley-ites or "eradicationists" on the one hand, and the "counteractionists" or "suppressionists" on the other hand, can be rendered otiose, or, rather, exegetically irrelevant. Whether we shall succeed remains to be seen; but we invite a sympathetically critical examination of our arguments. If our interpretings are wrong, we shall welcome correction. If they are right, we shall be grateful to have helped.

Dear Christian, what can I say to challenge you afresh on this supreme concern of our high calling and destiny? You and I need to see, more alluringly, more impellingly than ever, the utter *importance* of heart-holiness and the promised *possibility* of it in real experience. Without true holiness we can never be fully pleasing to God. The dear Saviour who redeemed us with His precious blood never sees the "travail of His soul" in us so as to be "satisfied" until we are unobstructedly possessed and sanctified by the Holy Spirit.

Can we ever wonder enough at the miracle of our conversion? —at the mystery of our regeneration?—at the solemn, glorious, thrilling truth that each of us "in Christ" is a very "temple of the Holy Spirit"? Oh, the gracious mystery of it! We are not only regenerated; we are *indwelt*! Familiarity with this, instead of dulling our wonder, should ever deepen it. Even our mortal bodies are now His temples (1 Cor. 6: 19). Think what it means. Not only does it give unspeakable sacredness to the physical frame, it hallows individual *personality*. Every Christian is meant to be a living temple; a cleansed, renewed, transformed, Spirit-filled temple of God, expressing in a unique way the life and love of the indwelling Christ! *That* is Christian holiness. To such holiness the New Testament calls us. That is what we are to re-explore in these pages. Let the thought of it enamour us, captivate us, and stir us into new longings to know the reality of it in our own experience.

> Not merely pardon, Lord, alone
>   My heart can satisfy,
> But Thine indwelling deeply known,
>   To cleanse and sanctify.
>
> Not only pardon for my sins,
>   But vict'ry over *sin*,
> The very source where sin begins
>   Renewed and cleansed *within*.
>
> Not weary strugglings to repress,
>   But all my mind *renewed*,
> Refined by inwrought holiness,
>   With Thine own love imbued.
>
> Illume my mind the truth to know,
>   My heart, my will possess,
> Till others see the gentle glow
>   Of Christlike holiness.

OLD TESTAMENT POINTERS

"Theologians who are convinced that men are polluted through and through, and believe with Hooker that the best thing they ever did had something in it to be forgiven, must take account of this: that all through the Word of God exhortations to holiness appear. They are not sporadic, occasional, or tempered by doubt concerning God's ability to do this thing in us. Underlying them all is the confidence that God can do something more with our sins than forgive them."

W. E. Sangster.

OLD TESTAMENT POINTERS

AN outstanding feature common to all the more recent holiness groups has been the teaching of a distinctive sanctification-crisis in the Christian believer, further to and distinct from conversion, in which the soul is brought into the blessing of inwrought holiness. A few representative quotations will suffice to show this.

John Wesley wrote to Miss Jane Hilton in 1774, "It is exceeding certain that God did give you the *second blessing*, properly so called. He delivered you from the root of bitterness, from inbred as well as actual sin." The venerable founder of Methodism was repeatedly insistent that this deep-going sanctification, or blessing of a "clean heart", is practically always a *second* work, subsequent to conversion. In his *Plain Account of Christian Perfection,* he writes, "We do not know a single instance, in any place, of a person's receiving, in one and the same moment, remission of sins, the abiding witness of the Spirit, and a new, a clean heart".

John Wesley's brother, Charles, named the experience, a "second *rest*". More recently, Andrew Murray refers to it as the "second *crisis*". A commoner name has been, "the second work of grace". The common denominator with all such teachers is that the experience is essentially a *"second"* special intervention of God in the soul.

The Rev. C. E. Ruth, in his book, *Entire Sanctification* (1903) says, "Sanctification is the 'second blessing' exactly in the same sense that justification is the *first* blessing. . . . Whereas justification delivers us from sins committed, sanctification delivers us from the sin-nature inherited; justification delivers us from guilt and condemnation, while sanctification delivers us from unholy appetites; the first gives us our birth of the Spirit, the second our baptism with the Spirit. Just as certainly as justification marks a distinct epoch and crisis in the life of those receiving it, so sanctification marks a second epoch, a second crisis, a second experience."

Again and again the prominent spokesmen of this holiness doctrine have reiterated their sharp distinction between initial regeneration and subsequent sanctification. The saintly Dr. A. J. Gordon of Boston expressed it succinctly when he wrote, "To say that in receiving Christ we necessarily receive in the same act the fulness of the Spirit seems to confound what the Scriptures make distinct. For it is as *sinners* that we accept Christ for our justification, but it is as *sons* that we accept the Spirit for our sanctification." The scholarly Dr. Daniel Steele gives it a more theological touch when he defines regeneration as "the instantaneous impartation of the divine life", and sanctification as "the perfect recovery of the moral image of God which sin has effaced". Dr. Steele also adds, "After a man is born of the Spirit, he needs an interval for a heart-knowledge of Christ through the light of the Holy Spirit, as the basis of that supreme later act of faith in Him as the Sanctifier".

Other quotations of like sort might be given, but the foregoing suffice to represent this characteristic insistence of the holiness groups, since Wesley's days, on sanctification as a post-conversion crisis and experience.

Despite differences in definition and description of that further and deeper work, we find common agreement on the need for it and the reality of it. We find also that rightly or wrongly it early came to be called the "second blessing". This provokes our first big question: Is this "second blessing" real, or merely imaginary? Let me make this preliminarily clear: I myself do not care for the term, "second blessing", nor can I accept certain theories linked with it. But I warn myself: dislike of a *name* should not prejudice us against the *experience* it was meant to represent. The issue is: Does Scripture teach inwrought holiness as a further, deeper work of the Holy Spirit in us subsequent (usually) to our regeneration?

We turn first to the Scriptures, and begin with the Old Testament. Of course, we can scarcely expect to find an exclusively Christian doctrine taught in the pre-Christian oracles of the Old Testament; but if this "deeper blessing" really is a New Testament doctrine, we may cautiously expect that, as with other distinctive Christian doctrines, it may be anticipated in Old Testament type.

We well realise that it is never allowable to build a doctrine on types only. Old Testament types are meant to *illustrate* New

Testament doctrine, but never to *formulate* doctrine. Here, however, we are neither building doctrine on Old Testament types nor assuming more than tentatively that the New Testament teaches a "deeper blessing". We are simply remembering that in some instances the best approach to New Testament doctrine is by way of Old Testament preparation. Such subjects, for instance, as the triunity of the Godhead, or the person and work of the Holy Spirit, are best studied right through from Genesis to Revelation, if the full-flowered finalities of the New Testament are to be most discerningly appreciated.

In this matter of "entire sanctification" considered as a "deeper blessing" there are at least four circumstances which together seem to suggest that it is advantageous to begin with the Old Testament: (1) We know that Christian experience certainly *is* forepictured again and again in Old Testament type-teaching. (2) In 1 Corinthians 10: 6, 11, we are plainly told that the old-time Israelites were made into "types" (*tupoi*) for "our admonition". (3) Teachers of the "second blessing" have uniformly *claimed* that it is adumbrated in the Old Testament just as decidedly as it is iterated in the New. (4) If there *are* prefigurings of it in the Old Testament, they will guide and guard our understanding of the New Testament fulfilment.

So, then, to the Old Testament we go: and what do we find? For my own part, I am obliged to testify that this second soul-crisis *seems* to be repeatedly delineated. I say no more than "seems", without prejudice either way.

We know, of course, on plentiful New Testament evidence, that many Old Testament persons and incidents and institutions were divinely adapted types of Christian truths to be revealed centuries later. Among these types, so it seems to me, there certainly are recurrent anticipations of a post-conversion sanctification crisis, in some of which the correspondences are too vividly drawn to be merely accidental. We cannot expect to find this "deeper blessing" typified in *every* typical person or feature of the Old Testament, any more than we expect to find any other one truth typified in every type. For instance, though it may well appear in Abraham, Isaac, and Jacob, who are strongly typical of human experience, we shall not expect to find it in a character like Joseph, who is peculiarly a type of Christ, first as the son supreme in the father's love, then as the rejected of his brethren, and then as the world's bread-supplier exalted to the throne. However, let us dip into the Old Testament a little, and see what we find.

Abraham

To begin with, take the case of Abraham, the progenitor of the covenant people. The two decisive points are recorded in suchwise as to emphasize them for ever. The first is in chapter 12:

"Now Jehovah had said unto Abram, Get thee out of thy country, and from thy kindred, and from thy father's house, unto a land that I will show thee; and I will make of thee a great nation, and I will bless thee, and make thy name great; and thou shalt be a blessing; and I will bless them that bless thee, and curse him that curseth thee; and in thee shall all families of the earth be blessed. So Abram departed . . . into the land of Canaan . . . and there he builded an altar unto Jehovah."

Here, typically, we have the elements corresponding to what we Christians call conversion. There is the coming out from the worldly Babel, Ur of the Chaldees; the divine call to pilgrimage and fellowship as a believer, or follower of Jehovah; the promise of guidance to a desired inheritance, and of sovereign blessing; there is also the obedient beginning by Abram, and the raising of that significant "altar unto Jehovah".

But now, turn to chapter 17: 1–19.

"And when Abram was ninety years old and nine, Jehovah appeared to Abram, and said unto him, I am the Almighty God; walk before me and be thou perfect. And I will make my covenant between me and thee and will multiply thee exceedingly. And Abram fell on his face; and God talked with him, saying, As for me, behold, my covenant is with thee, and thou shalt be a father of many nations. Neither shall they name any more be called Abram, but thy name shall be Abraham; for a father of many nations I have made thee. . . . And God said, Sarah thy wife shall bear thee a son indeed; and thou shalt call his name Isaac; and I will establish my covenant with him for an everlasting covenant, and with his seed after him."

Mark the special features here. First there is the divine call, "Walk before Me, and be thou perfect". The Hebrew word here translated as "perfect" properly means *complete*, in this instance complete adjustment to the divine will. In present-day converse, it was a call to full consecration. Second, there is the accompanying pledge, "I am Almighty God"; *El Shaddai*, literally, "God all-sufficient". So the God who now called Abram to sanctification would Himself be the enabling. Third, there is the significant change of the patriarch's name from Abram to Abra-*h*am; for equally in the Hebrew as in the English it is the aspirate-letter, the breath, suggesting a new breathing of the Spirit. Fourth, there is the new promise of fruitfulness—"And I will make thee exceeding fruitful. . . ." Fifth, there is the crowning promise that what had so long been withheld should now be given, even the miracle-baby, Isaac. The most wistful prayer and longing of the yielded heart should now be granted. Later, when the acutest of all tests came to Abraham, and when without demur he yielded up even his beloved Isaac, he thereby showed to all generations that he had *indeed* become entirely sanctified—that God was supreme in the love and devotion of his heart.

Jacob

A striking further instance of this second-crisis experience is seen in Jacob. The *first* big soul-impact which came to him at *Bethel* corresponded to what we now call "conversion". Until then, according to Scripture data, he had not known his father's God directly. See again Genesis 28.

"And he dreamed, and behold a ladder set up on the earth, and the top of it reached to heaven; and behold the angels of God ascending and descending on it. And, behold, JEHOVAH stood above it, and said, I am Jehovah, God of Abraham thy father, and the God of Isaac: the land whereon thou liest, to thee will I give it, and to thy seed. . . . And, behold, I am with thee, and will keep thee in all places whither thou goest, and will bring thee again to this land; for I will not leave thee, until I have done that which I have spoken to thee of . . . And [Jacob said] this stone, which I have set for a pillar, shall be God's house; and of all that Thou shalt give me I will surely give a tenth unto Thee."

A big thing happened to Jacob, there on the moors. He met his father's God, Jehovah. He took Jehovah as his own God, and raised a pillar to memorialise it. He swore a vow of faithful response to God, and pledged the tithe as an outward sign of it. That was the *first* big blessing.

The verse after this Bethel paragraph says, "Then Jacob went on his journey" (19: 1), but maybe it is noteworthy that the Hebrew, literally translated, is, "Then Jacob *lifted up his feet*". Up to that point there had been the sagging tread of a conscience-condemned fugitive, but now there was spring in the heel again. A new assurance in the heart gave a new alacrity to the step.

Now travel on to Chapter 32, and see what happens to Jacob a score of years later. He has not forgotten the God of Bethel through the years; but what a lot of self-willed, scheming Jacob has been mixed up with his Jehovah-religion! At last he is returning to the covenant land, but the man himself needs somehow lifting out of his meretricious selfism into a bigger and higher experience of God. Peer through the solemn night-shades as Jacob lingers alone by the ford of Jabbok.

"And Jacob was left alone; and there wrestled a man with him until the breaking of the day. And when he saw that he prevailed not against Jacob, he touched the hollow of his thigh; and the hollow of Jacob's thigh was out of joint as he wrestled with him. And he said, Let me go for the day breaketh; but Jacob said, I will not let thee go, except thou bless me. And he said unto him, What is thy name? And he said, Jacob. And he said, Thy name shall be called no more Jacob, but Israel; for as a prince hast thou power with God and with men, and hast prevailed. And Jacob asked him, and said, Tell me, I pray thee, thy name. And he said, Wherefore is it that thou dost ask after my name? And he blessed him there. And Jacob called the name of the place Peniel: for, I have seen God face to face, and my life is preserved. And as he passed over Penuel the sun rose upon him, and he halted upon his thigh."

Neo-orthodoxy popularized the phrase, "divine encounters". What happened at lonely Jabbok was a critical "divine encounter" to save a man from himself. It was the second of two such encounters in the life of Jacob; but the second was markedly different from the first. Away back amid the sunrise at Bethel, Jacob had resumed his trek with leaping heart and lilting tread, but when dawn drew back the night-curtains from Jabbok, a strangely wondering but wiser Jacob crossed over the brook with a halting thigh and a limping gait into the land of promise again. In the first "divine encounter" at Bethel he had made a life-determining new discovery of *God*. In this second encounter he was given a humiliating new discovery of *himself*. The Bethel encounter had to do with a new Godward *relation*. The Jabbok encounter had to do with a wrong inward *condition*. The Bethel blessing meant to put in Jacob's heart something which had *never been* there before. The Jabbok wrestle meant to crush a wriggling something which always *had* been in his nature heretofore. Jacob the supplanter needed himself to be supplanted. Yet the wrestle which crippled him crowned him, as is indicated in the God-given change of name; for when the out-wrestled "supplanter" became the desperately clinging suppliant, and cried, "I will not let Thee go except Thou bless me!" Jacob became "Israel"—a *"prince with God"*!

Egypt to Canaan

If we move on, now, through Exodus, Leviticus, Numbers, Deuteronomy, Joshua, we find this same twofold pattern pictorially objectified to us on a much bigger canvas in the bringing of the covenant people out from Egypt and into Canaan. It takes all four books to give us this fuller picture, largely because of what intervened between the coming *out* and the going *in*. Who can fail to see. that the "so great salvation" which was then wrought for the chosen nation was in two major parts, contingent on two major crises? There was an *exodus* from Egypt, and an *eisodus* into Canaan. They were both parts of the one big salvation, yet they were distinct from each other in feature, and separated from each other in occurrence. The first was incomplete without the second; and the second was impossible without the first. There were various incidental stages and experiences leading up to each, just as today there may be various incidental stages and experiences leading up to conversion, and then later to inward sanctification; but all such predisposing incidents must be sharply distinguished from the two great crises themselves— first the "exodus" from Egypt, paralleling with our experience of conversion; and second, the "eisodus" into Canaan, corresponding to "entire sanctification".

Yes, they were the two major components in that great salvation of long ago, even as Moses the leader himself said, in Deuteronomy 6: 23—"He brought us *out* from thence, that He might bring us *in*, to give us the land which He sware unto our fathers". It is noteworthy, too, that between the first and the second a stretch of forty years intervened. Someone may well object: "There need not have been the forty years intervening. The people could have gone right out from Egypt and right over into Canaan without any such delay—all in one undivided transaction." That is exactly what we ourselves believe; yet it only emphasizes that in point of actual fact the gap *did* occur; and, remember, *that* is the very juncture of which Paul says in 1 Corinthians 10: 11, "Now all these things happened unto them as types (*tupoi*) and they are written for *our* admonition".

So, we are here in the midst of Old Testament *types*; truths are being typified which pertain to *us*. It is one thing to cross the Red Sea out of Egypt as the redeemed of the Lord; it is a very different thing to cross that river Jordan into the land of promise, and possess that covenanted inheritance with its "milk and honey", its "corn and wine", its peace and joy and rest and "fulness of blessing".

Moses

The venerable Moses himself is another illustration of the same truth—a first crisis corresponding to conversion, then a further and later crisis leading to wonderful new power and usefulness. First, when Moses was "full forty years old" (Acts 7: 23) he made the big and costly choice of identifying himself with his oppressed and despised kinsmen, not only believing in Jehovah as the one true God, but already persuaded "that God by his hand would deliver them" (Acts 7: 25). He now refused any longer "to be called the son of Pharaoh's daughter", but chose rather "to suffer affliction with the people of God than to enjoy the pleasures of sin for a season; esteeming the reproach of Christ greater riches than the treasures of Egypt" (Heb. 11: 24–26). Certainly, in a typical sense, Moses was now a truly converted man, and a well-intending servant of the Lord.

As yet, however, he was far from ready to be the leader of the Exodus. A further and deeper experience of God was necessary; and it came another "forty years" later, away at Horeb (Acts 7: 30). From the flaming bush came a new revelation of God, and a new call to Moses, with a new assurance of the divine all-sufficiency, and a new enduement of "power from on high", symbolised in the now strangely miraculous shepherd's "rod" (Ex. 3: 2–5, 17). We all know the sequel to this; it is one of the classic epics of Hebrew history. Without that second "encounter", Moses would never have led the Lord's host out from mighty Egypt.

Gideon

Scarcely are we through the Book of Joshua and under the regime of the Judges before we find another example of the same thing, though it is very different in its outward details. In Judges 6 the spotlight is suddenly turned on young man Gideon, son of Joash. Verse 11 says, "And there came an angel of Jehovah, and sat under an oak which was in Ophrah, that pertained unto Joash the Abi-ezrite; and his son Gideon threshed wheat by the wine-press, to hide it from the Midianites". Like the other young men of his day, Gideon was sick with a fear of the mighty Midianites who had now oppressed and exploited apostate Israel for seven dragging years. Nervous and furtive-eyed, Gideon was flailing grain in the winepress—away from the proper threshing floor, lest some marauding Midianite should come prying round. Suddenly "the angel of the Lord appeared to him", as verse 12 tells us, and said unto him, "Jehovah is with thee, thou mighty man of valour". At least, that is how our English version gives it; but surely we should follow the Septuagint version, "Jehovah is with thee, the [not 'thou'] Mighty One of Valour". It is Jehovah, not Gideon, who is the "Mighty One of Valour", as the context makes only too clear.

Gideon himself cuts a sorry figure of unbelief. He gasps out, "Oh, my Lord, if Jehovah be with us, why then is all this befallen us? and where be all His miracles which our fathers told us of?" When Jehovah says, "Go, and thou shalt save Israel from the hand of the Midianites", Gideon can only stammer, "Oh, my Lord, wherewith shall I save Israel?" And when Jehovah further adds, "Surely I will be with thee", Gideon can only beg, "Show me a sign. . . ." To be sure, in this quick succession of "oh" and "if" and "why?" and "where?" and "but" and "wherewith?" and "show me a sign", we have a most enlightening sample of the vocabulary of unbelief!

But Gideon became transformed through a vital, twofold experience of God. First he became (as we should say today) truly *converted*. I use that word deliberately, for it really describes what happened. See verse 24: "Then Gideon built an altar there unto Jehovah, and called it *JEHOVAH-SHALLOM*. The altar is ever the place where God and men meet. It is the outward symbol of an inward transaction between the human soul and God. When Gideon built that altar to Jehovah, he made a clean break from false gods, and became a committed worshipper of the one true God. Moreover, for the first time in his life he now found real peace. That is why he called his altar, "Jehovah *Shallom*"— "Jehovah my *peace*"!

Yes, Gideon was now truly converted; but his faith had to be tested (see verses 25 to 33), and he needed also a "second experience" of God, before he could deliver Israel from Midian. That "second" crisis is reported in verse 34: "But the Spirit of Jehovah came upon Gideon. . . ." The Hebrew used here is remarkable. A near translation would be that the Spirit of Jehovah *"clothed Himself with Gideon"*—as with a garment. It reminds us of our Lord's words to the disciples, in Luke 24: 49, "Tarry ye . . . until ye be endued with power from on high"—which, as in some later translations, may well be rendered, "Tarry ye . . . until ye be *clothed* with power from on high". Thus we see that Gideon's transformation was in two distinct parts—first converted to God, at which time he found *peace*; second clothed by the Spirit, at which time weakness was changed to *power*.

Elisha

We travel on now to the Books of the Kings, to the prophet Elisha. In a special way, Elisha is the Old Testament forepicturing of what it means to live the life of resurrection power in Christ. He stands out uniquely as the continual miracle-worker. He wrought far more miracles than his fiery predecessor, Elijah; and even more, so it would seem, than the mighty Moses (2 Kings 8: 4). Moreover, running all through Elisha's miracles the dominating characteristic is that of *resurrection-energy* overcoming the blight and down-drag of death. His first miracle heals the death-spreading waters of Jericho. Next, by miraculous water-supply, he saves an army from death by drought in the desert. Next comes the all-conquering cruse of oil; then the raising of the Shunamite's dead boy; then the healing of the poisoned pottage, so that "death in the pot" becomes life-giving food; then the miraculous multiplication of the barley loaves to save the dearth-plagued people; then the cleansing of Naaman from his deadly leprosy; then the miracle in which the restored axe-head floats on the water, overcoming the down-pull of gravitation, while the astonished beholders exclaim, "The iron doth swim!"

Even after Elisha is buried we are given an eerie, post-mortem corroboration, to make sure that we do not miss seeing in Elisha this typical significance of living in resurrection-power; for later, when the corpse of a certain newly-deceased Israelite happened to contact the bones of the predeceased Elisha, it suddenly came to life again!

If we are asked for yet more conclusive evidence of this significance in Elisha, we only need to see how it *began*. It began at Jordan. Elisha's great master, Elijah, went through the Jordan, then visibly ascended to heaven, and in ascending sent down his prophet's mantle upon Elisha. Even so, *our* great Master, the Lord Jesus, went through the Jordan of His Calvary death, then visibly ascended to heaven, and thereupon sent down upon His disciples the enduing mantle of the Holy Spirit at Pentecost. The parallel is surely too clear to miss.

Elisha, then, is a highly meaningful type, and well claims our thoughtful reflection. He is all the more observable because once again, and in accentuated form, we see the occurrence of *two* determinative crises, the *first* one corresponding to conversion and regeneration, the *second* corresponding to consecration and the enduement of "power from on high". Who can fail to be impressed by *the two castings of the mantle*, first in I Kings 19, then (about ten years later) in 2 Kings 2? Here is the *first* episode, in I Kings 19: 19–21:

"So he [Elijah] departed thence, and found Elisha the son of Shaphat, who was ploughing with twelve yoke of oxen before him, and he with the twelfth: and Elijah passed by him, and cast his mantle upon him. And he left the oxen, and ran after Elijah, and said, Let me, I pray thee, kiss my father and my mother, and then I will follow thee. And Elijah said unto him, Go back again; for what have I done to thee? And he returned back from him, and took a yoke of oxen, and slew them, and boiled their flesh with the instruments of the oxen, and gave unto the people, and they did eat. Then he arose, and went after Elijah, and ministered unto him."

Three things stand out, the first of which is Elijah's *casting of his mantle* upon Elisha. The young ploughman knew at once what it meant, hence his reply, "Let me, I pray thee, kiss my father and my mother, and then *I will follow thee*". That casting of the mantle was the understood call to discipleship and the prophetic office. Elisha's response signifies, in type, that he was what we should nowadays call *"a converted man"*; for his public discipleship of Elijah meant that in face of the national apostasy he now openly avowed himself a believer in Jehovah as the one true God, and a witness for Him in the Protestant reform movement of Elijah. Besides this, Elisha now became a *separated* believer; for according to the Biblical data, he never went back to the old life. Still further, he became an *active* believer: "He arose, and went after Elijah, and *ministered* unto him". Mark it well—converted, separated, active, yet he still needed a *"second"* major crisis and experience if he was to live and serve and witness in resurrection-power.

That second crisis is recorded in 2 Kings, chapter two. By this time, as the narrative implies, Elisha is exercising faith for the blessing; but it seems as though both his master and his fellow-believers are trying to throw him off. Elijah says, "Tarry here, I pray thee; for Jehovah hath sent me to Beth-el;" then at Beth-el, "Tarry here, I pray thee; for Jehovah hath sent me to Jericho;" then at Jericho, "Tarry here, I pray thee; for Jehovah hath sent me to Jordan". Each time, however, Elisha doggedly hangs on: "As Jehovah liveth, and as thy soul liveth, I will not leave thee". Both at Beth-el and at Jericho the sons of the prophets moan to Elisha, "Knowest thou that Jehovah will take away thy master from thy head today?" But both times Elisha rejoins, "Yea, I know it; hold ye your peace". Elisha is really determined to "hang on" and to go "all the way" for the big, vital, further blessing.

At last Elisha accompanies his master through the Jordan: "They two went over". It is there, on the further side of Jordan that the big thing happens. Why? Because of what Jordan typifies. In many of our hymns the ancient river is likened to death of the body; but in Old Testament type-teaching that is never the meaning. Jordan typifies our union with Christ in His utter surrender to the Father's will—"obedient unto death, even the death of the Cross". As soon as Jordan is crossed, Elijah says to Elisha, *"Ask what I shall do for thee. . . ."* What it was not possible to give on the other side, it is possible to give on this side. The startling type-implication is that as soon as we believers are through that Jordan with our Lord, a greater than Elijah says, *"Ask what ye will, and it shall be done unto you".* Christians often wonder why their prayers are not answered, when all the time it may be because they are praying on the wrong side of Jordan!

Suddenly, now, Elisha receives the "double portion" of the Spirit for which he had asked. With lightning swiftness a whirl-wind chariot of fire swoops down, and sweeps Elijah skyward. Elisha gasps, "My father! my father! the chariot of Israel, and the horsemen thereof!" A few electric seconds, and the terrific spectacle vanishes. But, fluttering down through the air . . . the mantle of Elijah!—and it now becomes Elisha's! Yes, and with it Elisha *has the blessing*! Clothed with new power Elisha now returns. The sons of the prophets exclaim, "The Spirit of Elijah doth rest on Elisha!"—and they "bowed themselves to the ground before him", recognising in him a new and divinely empowered spiritual leader. Read the account again (2 Kings 2: 1–15). It is a vivid passage; but its most permanent value seems to lie in its latent type-teaching as to the need and reality of that afore-mentioned second crisis-experience which leads to full enduement by the Holy Spirit, and service for Christ in "the power of His resurrection" (Phil. 3: 10).

Isaiah

Isaiah is the greatest of the writing prophets. The guild of Hezekiah never produced a defter pen-artist. We do not exaggerate in saying that nowhere else in all literature is there such a superb union of exalted prophecy and exquisite poetry; of supernatural inspiration and literary genius. Unfortunately our dear old Authorised Version does not distinguish for us the fascinating use and play of Hebrew poetic parallelism, with its expedients of completive and contrastive and constructive parallels; its strophes and counter-strophes, and so on. It is even more regrettable that the dissective mania of some modern scholars has reduced the "Book of Isaiah" to a patchwork-quilt of various fragments and figments (supposedly so) from numerous anonymous contributors, so that nowadays many people are under the mistaken impression that "modern scholarship" has disproved the unity of this book. If we are sufficiently open-eyed to the orderly internal development and threefold total structure of the work, we see that it *must* be from one author. It runs in three main parts (not two, as is generally supposed):

Part 1	Prophetical:	progressive predictions (1–35)
Part 2	Historical:	re Assyria and Babylon (36–39)
Part 3	Prophetical:	a triform Messianic poem (40–66)

For our present purpose we need only consult part one (1–35). Observe the movement of expansion. In the first six chapters the prophecies are all restricted to Judah. In the next six chapters they overflow to the ten-tribed northern kingdom of Israel. In the next group of chapters (13–23) they broaden out to include the greatest ten powers of the period—Babylon, Moab, Egypt, etc. In the next group (24–27) they encircle the whole world and sweep right on through the coming centuries to the consummation of history. In the next group (28–33) they admonish Ariel ("Lion of God"), i.e. Jerusalem, as the centre of Jehovah's controversy with this world. Finally, in chapters 34 and 35 where this first series ends, the prophecies plunge on through the "great tribulation" at the end of the present age, and emerge in the compensating terminus of the "millennium". In chapter 34, "the indignation of Jehovah is upon all nations", but in chapter 35, "the ransomed of Jehovah return and come to Zion with songs and everlasting joy upon their heads; they obtain joy and gladness; and sorrow and sighing flee away"! (For fuller comment on this I refer the reader to volume 3 in my work, *Explore the Book*.) Who can see this methodical development, crowned and completed in an obviously pre-envisaged literary and historical finale, without recognising in it the product of *one* author?—of one, and *only* one Isaiah?

Yes, it is the product of *one* divinely controlled, prophet-genius, which factor makes Isaiah one of the most transcendent figures in world annals; God-appointed preacher to the nations, with a globe-girdling message, not only to the peoples of his own day, but to the end of the centuries.

What was it, then, that made Isaiah the passionate, powerful, pleading, sorrowing, sighing, singing, soaring prophet of Jehovah which he became? Was it supernormal intellect?—or unsurpassed literary versatility?—or a philosopher's grasp of present enigmas and final harmonies? No; it was a revolutionising spiritual crisis —not at his conversion nor at his induction to the prophetic office, but at a *later* point. That this was indeed a later crisis, most commentators are agreed (see *Pulpit Commentary*, Introduction to Isaiah, also Isaiah 1: 1, which clearly indicates that Isaiah had already been prophesying "in the days of Uzziah" for some time. Isaiah himself describes it in chapter 6.

"In the year that king Uzziah died I saw also the Lord sitting upon a throne, high and lifted up, and his train filled the temple. Above it stood the seraphim: each one had six wings; with twain he covered his face, and with twain he covered his feet, and with twain he did fly. And one cried unto another, and said, Holy, holy, holy, is Jehovah of hosts: the whole earth is full of his glory. And the posts of the door moved at the voice of him that cried, and the house was filled with smoke. Then said I, Woe is me! for I am undone; because I am a man of unclean lips, and I dwell in the midst of a people of un-clean lips: for mine eyes have seen the King, Jehovah of hosts. Then flew one of the seraphim unto me, having a live coal in his hand, which he had taken with the tongs from off the altar: and he laid it upon my mouth, and said, Lo, this hath touched thy lips; and thine iniquity is taken away, and thy sin is purged. Also I heard the voice of the Lord, saying, Whom shall I send, and who will go for us? Then said I, Here am I; send me. And he said, Go. . . ."

This overpowering apocalypse assumes an even more eloquent splendour from the New Testament comment upon it in John 12: 41: "These things said Esaias when he saw His [i.e. *Christ's*] glory, and spake of *Him*" (see John 8: 56 for a similar comment on Abraham). When young Isaiah saw "the Lord" (Hebrew: *Adonay*) He was beholding the preincarnate "Son of Man"!

The two flaming impressions which prostrated Isaiah were those of all-transcendent sovereignty and sin-exposing holiness. There was the glory-flashing "throne, high and lifted up", and the royal "train" filling the heavenly "temple", and "the King" —even *"JEHOVAH OF HOSTS"*, Creator and Controller of the universe. There were the fire-like "seraphs" (or "burning ones") crying, "Holy, holy, holy, is Jehovah of Hosts"—at which cry the very "foundations" (not door posts as in A.V.) "moved", as though the very building was awed into trembling, and "the house became filled with smoke", as though even the heavenly temple sought to veil itself, like the six-winged seraphs, who used *four* wings to veil themselves in worship, and only *two* to expedite service!

But that to which everything leads is the *purpose* of the vision in relation to *Isaiah*. What that purpose was is shown by the impact and outcome. Isaiah sinks down under a dismaying new sense of his own innate depravity. In the exquisite rays from that throne he sees as never before the intolerable ugliness of sin. "Woe is me!" he cries out. "I am undone; for I am a man of unclean lips!" Instantly thereupon, however, one of the seraphs flies down with a "live coal" from the altar, saying, "Lo, this hath touched thy lips; thine iniquity is taken away, and thy sin purged". Then comes the voice of the Lord (*Adonay*; Christ): "Whom shall I send, and who will go for us?" And the wonder-ing, worshipping, overwhelmed Isaiah cries back in new and fuller consecration than ever before, *"Here am I; send me"*.

We do not wish to over-analyse, but it is instructive to distinguish the three components in Isaiah's first reaction to the vision. All in one outcry of astonishment there is (1) a new *conviction of sin*: "Woe is me! for I am undone!" (2) a new *confession of fault*: "I am a man of unclean lips"—the very organs of service are disqualified! (3) a *new conception of God*: "Mine eyes have seen the King, *JEHOVAH OF HOSTS*!" What had been merely religious theory before now became electrified reality. Supreme over the histories and destinies of all nations and peoples, Isaiah saw that flaming super-throne and the all-controlling, sovereign purpose of Jehovah. That was the centre-point of the vision. All the globe-circling, history-spanning prophecies which later flowed from Isaiah's pen were implicit in that one terrific sight of the universe's KING.

The total *impact* of this new conviction, confession, and conception upon Isaiah was utter self-abasement. He had always known that as a member of Adam's fallen race he was a sinner; but *now* the heart-rending contrast between that flame-white throne and his own corruptness abased him with a sense of vileness never experienced before. He had been a very godly and devout young man, but now his very sincerity only made the torture of that exposure the more acute. There was the discovery of sin scarcely detected before. Light always reveals. The light from that heavenly throne always exposes sin. The reason why so many Christians tolerate unworthy things in their life is that they are not "walking in the light as HE is in the light" (1 John 1: 7). How many of us, if we spent an honest hour or two before God, would find ourselves exclaiming with Isaiah, "Woe is me, for I am undone!"

The *outcome* of Isaiah's vision was a new cleansing and a new commission. See that heavenly seraph winging with the "live coal" to Isaiah. "Lo, this hath touched thy lips; thine iniquity is taken away, and thy sin purged." This can mean only one thing: *the unclean may be cleansed*. There is a divine fire which burns away human sin! The unclean *must* be cleansed before it can be used of God. The Lord's servant must have a purified heart and purified lips. Thank God, if there *must* be this inner and outer cleansing, there *may* be. This was the sanctifying experience which now came to Isaiah; and with it came the new challenge and commission: "Whom shall I send, and who will go for us?" "Here am I; send me." "And he said *GO*. . . ."

Such, then, was Isaiah's transforming new vision and experience. It was indeed a "second" crisis-work of divine grace and power in his life; and from it he went forth to become a prophet to the royal house and the covenant people; the greatest voice of God to his own times, a preacher to nations and centuries, and an evangelist whose sermons go on converting souls even to this very day. It was through Isaiah that William Carey caught his inspiration to evangelise India, thereby becoming the father of the modern world-mission era. It was through Isaiah, as quoted by an obscure local preacher, that young Charles Haddon Spurgeon was converted, afterward becoming the most far-reaching Gospel preacher London ever knew. "And what more shall we say . . . ?"

Patterns and Pointers

We have now submitted seven Old Testament type-figures which at least *seem* to portray, in an intendedly significant way, what we may generalise as a "second blessing" crisis and experience: Abraham, Jacob, the Egypt-to-Canaan episode, Moses, Gideon, Elisha, Isaiah. We have picked these seven, not because they are the *only* such available, but because of their prominence and obviousness. We might easily have added Sarai who became Sarah, Isaac, Jeremiah, Ezekiel, or have deciphered recondite intimations in certain Old Testament narratives and institutions.

What of those which we have supplied? They do not establish a doctrine; but do they not seem to indicate a *pattern*? Further, when taken with other Old Testament types and prophecies (Ezekiel 2: 2, 3; 36: 25–27, etc. for instance), they may well be divinely adapted *pointers* to an experience of salvation and sanctification which was yet to be made available to *all* Christian believers under the Gospel dispensation.

We well realise, of course, that for every such Old Testament figure in which this "second-crisis" mode of sanctification seems pre-adapted, other cases might be cited where it does *not* appear; yet that would in no wise invalidate the instances where it *does* occur. It is often claimed that in the Old Testament there are latent pre-intimations of *triunity* in the Godhead, and that the Old Testament thus prepares us for the fuller revelation of the New. Yet for every place in the Old Testament where such triunity might seem covertly suggested, one could give a hundred others where no suggestion exists. Do the latter, then, destroy the significance of the former? Not at all. Nor are those Old Testament types of this "second-crisis" experience nullified by other Old Testament figures which do *not* typify it. To reject those which *do*, because of those which do *not*, is tantamount to insisting that *each* type must typify *all* truth, which is absurd.

Let us not try to see in Old Testament type-teaching anything which is not really there; but, on the other hand, let us be open-minded and alert to appreciate what really *is* there, for it can enrich us with much that is exceedingly precious. To my own mind, the Old Testament instances of a second crisis-point, bringing a deeper work of God in the soul, seem not only impressive but prophetic: and in the fuller light of the New Testament I should scarcely hesitate to call them divinely-intended *types*.

DEDUCTION

These Old Testament pointers may not be over-pressed but they should be impartially appreciated. They seem at least to indicate a usual procedure of the Holy Spirit when He would bring the soul into some further, major, transforming experience of God. In the light of the New Testament they seem like advance types of Christian experience: yet they must not be forced into typifying that entire sanctification always *begins with some outstanding post-conversion crisis. They truly adumbrate the usual, but not the rigidly necessary.*

We claim no more than that.
At least they *seem* to be pointers.

NEW TESTAMENT PATTERNS

"In a very fundamental way these records [of religious experience in the Bible] constitute the norms of genuine religious experience. Spiritual experiences which are diverse in kind from and opposed in nature to Biblical religious experiences are not true experiences with God. The Bible is the source book, not only of true teachings concerning religious experience, but also of genuine religious experience itself."

Chester K. Lehman.

NEW TESTAMENT PATTERNS

THE decisive question is: Does the New Testament teach sanctification as being frequently a "*further*" blessing? Our findings in the Old Testament may have predisposed us somewhat to expect so, but they must not be allowed to influence our thinking *beyond* that.

Someone is sure to say: Give us chapter and verse where such a "second blessing" is directly taught in the New Testament. But what if we cannot? Does that disqualify it? Is there any one verse in the New Testament which directly states the personality and deity of the Holy Spirit, or the threefold personal reciprocity of the Godhead? There is not; yet the implications are so cumulative that we accept the personality of the Holy Spirit and the triunity of God as basic doctrines in our Christian faith.

Is there one single verse which straightly teaches a secret or "pre-tribulation" rapture of the Church? Not one. At the time of my writing these lines, the latest book on the side of the *pre*-tribulation "Rapture" is one issued by the excellent Dr. John F. Walvoord, president of Dallas Theological Seminary. Yet Dr. Walvoord himself agrees, "The fact is that neither post-tribulationism nor pre-tribulationism is an explicit teaching of Scripture. The Bible does not in so many words state either".

Just here, I am neither agreeing nor disagreeing with either the pre-tribulation or the post-tribulation theory; I simply point out that many thousands of evangelical Christians believe in, and sincerely hope for, a *pre*-tribulation translation of believers, even though, on the admission of gifted and scholarly proponents, the New Testament does not actually "state" it.

Perhaps, therefore, those who would impatiently "shoot at sight" the idea of a "second blessing" because it is not specifically *stated* in Scripture, would be kindly advised to "hold their fire" a while, lest they shoot down a friend mistaken as an enemy!

Of course, there are some who unhesitatingly claim that sanctification as a "second blessing" *is* directly taught in the New Testament. On looking up their supposed proof-texts, however, we cannot allow that even the best of them come anywhere near stating such a "second blessing". Matthew 5: 6 is cited: "Blessed are they that hunger and thirst after righteousness, for they shall be filled". It is claimed that the persons denoted in this beatitude are "born again", since only "alive" persons hunger and thirst. They are already "blessed", but they need now the *"second blessing"* taught in the words, "they shall be *filled*", i.e. filled with "righteousness" in the sense of inward *holiness*. Perhaps to some I may seem spiritually unseeing, yet I must frankly confess that I can see no such teaching of a "second blessing" *there*. I freely grant that the beatitude may be given an accommodated *application* to a "second blessing", once the doctrine of a "second blessing" is *proved*; but to say that such a text in itself proves the doctrine is, to my own mind, mistaking a straw for a beam. I cannot believe for a moment that our dear Lord had any such doctrine in mind when He addressed that promiscuous crowd on the Galilean hillside, in those days before ever the first syllable of post-Calvary evangelical truth had been enunciated.

It is claimed that John 10: 10 teaches sanctification as a distinctively second blessing: "I am come that they might have life, and that they might have it more abundantly". The words, "that they might have life" refer to *regeneration* (so the claim goes) while the further words, "more abundantly", refer to *sanctification*. Well, again, while we would not deny that there may be allowable accommodating of those words to *illustrate* the difference between regeneration and sanctification, we flatly deny that the words actually teach it as specific doctrine. If, by comparison with other Scriptures, the words, "more abundantly", can be proved to mean sanctification, well and good; but *apart* from that, John 10: 10, is no proof of sanctification as a "second blessing".

Again, Acts 19: 2 has often been used eagerly and confidently as teaching the "second blessing". According to the Authorized Version, Paul asks the twelve Ephesian believers, "Have ye received the Holy Spirit since ye believed?" Much is made of the word "since", as indicating a second work of the Spirit, subsequent to conversion. But to see the "second blessing" in that word "since" is to run after a mirage. The Authorized rendering is misleading. The truer translation, as in more recent versions, is, "Did ye receive the Holy Spirit *when* ye believed?" Paul's question has nothing to do with a *second* experience.

Other supposed proof-texts need not detain us. Some of them surely have no connection with the doctrine except in the claimant's flamboyant credulity. There is such a thing as "seeing" a truth in the Bible, and then imaginatively seeing it *everywhere* in the Bible; but when we marshal "proofs" which are mere seemings, we weaken the foundation of our superstructure. In the present instance, so I myself believe, it is better to agree that sanctification as a distinctive "second" blessing, is *not* taught in direct New Testament statement. If I may reverently say so, I believe that the Holy Spirit had His own reasons for leaving the reality deducible rather than didactic. Maybe one such reason was that He will not rigidify His sanctifying activity in any one stereotyped form. In sanctification, just as much as elsewhere, "the selfsame Spirit divideth to every man severally as He will" (1 Cor. 12: 11). However, with those cautionary reflections in mind, let us now see what we *do* find in the New Testament.

Our Lord Himself

The late G. Campbell Morgan wrote a great book, *The Crises of the Christ,* which concerned itself with the seven peak events in our Lord's earthly life, i.e. His birth, His baptism, His temptation, His transfiguration, His crucifixion, His resurrection, His ascension. Possibly some of us may hesitate at the using of that word, "crises", in referring to the Eternal Word incarnate. Yet it is well to reflect that our Lord was also truly human. There was no theatrical artificiality about His human experiences. Certainly His temptation, after that exhausting forty days, was in some momentous sense a crisis-encounter. Gethsemane, with its agony of sweat and blood, and Calvary with its awful cry, "My God, why hast Thou forsaken Me?" were in some mysterious and baffling way "crises", even though their outcome was foreknown and certain. If, then, we may devoutly use that word, "crisis", of our divine Lord, it is true to say that even in *His* sinless life there was a special experience which suggests or maybe even sets the *pattern* of an intended "second" crisis-transition in the experience of His people. Moreover, in *His* case it is exhibited in a public way which makes it the more arresting. I refer to His baptism in the Jordan.

The sinless Jesus needed no "baptism unto repentance", as John the Baptist intuitively perceived, and as the voice from heaven soon afterward confirmed; yet Jesus *was* baptised, thereby identifying Himself with those whom He had come to redeem, and at the same moment indicating His transition from private life to public ministry as the promised Messiah.

Of course, in the holy being of our Lord there was no "first" crisis corresponding to *our* being "born again"; nor therefore could there be a "second" crisis in any sense of an operating upon "inbred sin" in the heart. Yet notwithstanding this, there still remains in our Lord's baptismal experience that which seems to make it an intended *proto*type of a post-conversion sanctification-crisis in the hearts of His followers. It has been pointedly observed that "we must accept the historical fact of our Lord's baptism by the Holy Spirit as being a preparation for His ministry". Yes, and we must also accept the accompanying fact that not *until* then do the Gospel writers speak of Him as being "full of the Holy Spirit", and "led by the Spirit", and "in the power of the Spirit".

We readily concede that in some aspects our Lord *cannot* be a prototype of His people; for He is divine whereas we are human; and He is the unique *procurer* of redemption, whereas we are the *receivers* of redemption. Yet in every other respect, that is, in everything *not* exclusively peculiar to His divine and redemptive messiahship, He is our Exemplar, "leaving us an example, that we should follow His steps" (1 Pet. 2: 21).

Equally clearly do we recognise that it was our Lord's *humanity* which was endued in the Jordan baptism; but that only makes what then happened the more meaningful for ourselves. If *His* humanity needed this special enduing with "the Spirit and power" for service, does not ours? A. M. Hills, addressing Christian ministers of fifty years ago, said: "Dear brothers, did it never occur to you that even the holy Jesus was not prepared to preach until He was baptized with the Spirit? He opened His first sermon by saying, 'The Spirit of the Lord is upon Me, because He hath anointed Me to preach the Gospel'. Alas, that so many of us, with amazing presumption, have ventured to enter the ministry and preach so many times without this divine anointing!"

Again, we must accept it as a noteworthy circumstance that before His Jordan baptism our Lord worked no miracles; no, not even one—unless we swallow the spurious gibberish of certain apocryphal pseudepigrapha. But *could* He not have worked miracles before His baptism? Or had He no *desire* to work miracles before His baptism? Were there no lepers to cleanse then? Were there no palsied to heal? Were there no demons to cast out? Were there no blind beggars sitting by the roadsides? Had no compassion begun to stir Messiah's heart before that Jordan anointing? In asking such questions we are thinking not of His boyhood so much as of the years, let us say, from His eighteenth to His thirtieth birthday, when He would look out upon the pathos of human suffering from His human development. But whatever may be our answer, the fact remains that until His Jordan baptism He did no miracles. He tarried until *then*; and thus He fulfilled in advance the counsel He later left with His disciples, to "tarry . . . until ye be endued with power from on high" (Luke 24: 49).

Finally, we cannot but observe that our Lord's baptism drew a *dividing line* between all that had preceded, and the "mighty works" which now followed. Hitherto, He had "increased in wisdom and stature, and in favour with God and man" (Luke 2: 52). There had been real human life and growth; yet even so, He was not ready for the supreme purpose and ministry. There had to be that Jordan baptism. It was a "must". In some deep way it was a dividing *crisis*-point. There was a deliberate publicity about it which makes it the more commanding, and *seems* at least to make it representative of a similarly dividing crisis-point which is intended to take place in the spiritual experience of our Lord's followers. *Before* that crisis there is within us "life" and "growth", as there was with our Lord Jesus; but if there is to be a future of power for victory and service there must be that Jordan crisis of utter self-yielding to God, and a special enduement by the Holy Spirit.

If we look at our Lord's baptism somewhat analytically it seems to become even more clearly, perhaps, the pattern of an intended similar crisis-point in our own experience. Take Mark's concentrated account, in chapter one of his Gospel. It emphasizes three indispensable prerequisites for powerful usefulness in the service of God.

1. *A preliminary twofold separation (verse 9).*
Our Lord's baptism was His initial, deliberate separation of Himself to His public Messianic ministry. This separation was twofold. There was (1) a separation *from* His former kind of life; (2) a separation *to* His new ministry of teaching and healing: an utter separation to God. That is also the first prerequisite for *us*.

There is meant to be the crisis-point of what the Scripture calls, "entire sanctification" or set-apartness.

2. A preliminary twofold anointing (verse 10).

Our Lord (1) *saw* something, i.e. "the heavens opened"; (2) and *felt* something—"the Spirit descending upon Him". That also is the second prerequisite for *us*. We must know the heavens "opened" to our praying, and the enduement with that "power from on high".

3. A preliminary twofold assuring (verse 11).

Our Lord at Jordan received a preliminary assuring (a) as to *sonship*—"Thou art My beloved Son"; (b) as to *character*—"in whom I am well pleased". That is the third prerequisite for *us*. We need the inwrought assurance of the Holy Spirit, and motives well-pleasing to God.

We will not stress our Lord's baptism as being *necessarily* a prototype experience, but at any rate, there it is, right at the beginning of the New Testament. When taken with all the other pointers it seems at least *probable* that it is intendedly representative of an "entire sanctification" meant to take place in ourselves—an experience in which heaven becomes "opened" to us in a new way, and the Holy Spirit suffuses us, bringing a new realisation of heavenly sonship, and an inward cleansing from sin which makes the gracious Father "well pleased" with us.

Calvary and Pentecost

Another feature which meets us with contributory significance in the New Testament is the correlatedness yet *separateness* of Calvary and Pentecost. It is conceivable that they *might* have been separated either more or less than they were; but we are concerned here solely with the fact that they *were* separated by those seven weeks. As we think of Calvary and Pentecost, and what they each mean, we can scarcely help being reminded again of those other two crisis-points, the *exodus* and the *eisodus*, in the salvation of old-time Israel from Egypt to Canaan. There was the *"out of"*, and there was the *"in to"*; and they were forever signalised in two miraculous *"crossings"*, i.e. the crossing of the Red Sea out of Egypt, and the crossing of the River Jordan into Canaan. As the older generation of holiness preachers used to be fond of saying, "It takes the two crossings to get inside Canaan".

Is it not true to say that Calvary and Pentecost *seem* to be the New Testament counterpart or fulfilment of that twofold Old Testament pointer? Is not Calvary the "out of", and Pentecost the "in to"? Calvary speaks of "precious blood" which redeems. Pentecost speaks of heavenly "fire" which endues. Calvary brings us pardon. Pentecost brings us power. Calvary cleanses away legal *guilt*. Pentecost deals with inward *sin*. Calvary does something *for* us. Pentecost does something *in* us. Calvary brings us out from the dark Egypt of "condemnation". Pentecost brings us into the sunlit Canaan of "sanctification". Calvary saves the *soul* from eternal damnation. Pentecost refines the *nature* from internal corruption.

I do not say that Calvary and Pentecost must *always* have a time-break between them in the Christian life, but I do emphasize that they represent two major parts or *experiences* of salvation. In the case of the apostles they were distinguished not only by a time-gap but in their *nature*. I remember how startled I was as a young Christian to hear a Methodist holiness preacher exclaim, "Thousands who have been to Calvary have never gone on to Pentecost". I know now what he meant, and would endorse it as "rightly dividing" the Word.

The Twelve Apostles

Surely, too, the twelve apostles are an object lesson exhibiting the same distinction. In the evening of that immortal day on which our Lord rose from the grave, He suddenly appeared in the room where His bereaved and dismayed apostles had furtively gathered. See the paragraph in John 20: 19–23. When He had first allayed their sudden terror, and then calmed their transport of joy at recognising Him, He said to them, "As the Father hath sent Me, even so send I you". Thereupon, as John tells us, "He breathed on them, and saith unto them, *Receive ye the Holy Spirit*".

But were not those men already believers? Were they not already His disciples? They were. Moreover, besides being believers and disciples, they were His carefully chosen and solemnly commissioned "apostles". He had already told them that their names were "written in heaven". He had made them participants in His own power, the power of the Holy Spirit, so that they had healed the sick and expelled demons (Matt. 10: 1; Luke 10: 17). He had said unto them, "Already ye are clean through the word

which I have spoken unto you" (John 15: 3). In His praying to
the Father, He had said of them, "They are not of the world,
even as I am not of the world" (John 17: 16).

So then, were not those apostles regenerate men? Surely they
were. In that sense they already *had* the Spirit. Yet those were the
men for whom Jesus had afterward prayed "that they also might
be *sanctified* through the truth" (John 17: 19), and on whom He
now "breathed", saying "Receive ye the Holy Spirit".

We all know, of course, that in an historical sense *Pentecost*
was the impletion of that symbolic breathing. What we call attention to here is, that Pentecost was most decidedly a "second blessing" *experientially* in the life of those first believers. Again, we
readily concede that the apostles, viewed dispensationally, were
a group all by themselves, in a suspense-period (the period of the
Acts) which has forever gone. We can countenance no such figment as "apostolic succession". We do not believe that the
apostles were ever *meant* to have "successors", or that they ever
had "successors". None the less, as we see them away back
yonder, silhouetted against the morning sky of our Christian era,
do they not seem to objectify in advance a twofold spiritual experience which was intended to become *characteristically* Christian
from then onwards?[1]

Remember, even before Pentecost those apostles possessed both
the *message* and the *experience* of forgiveness through the saving
death and resurrection of Christ. Luke 24: 45-48 says, "Then
opened He their understanding, that they might understand the
Scriptures, and He said unto them: Thus it is written, and thus
it behoved Christ to suffer, and to rise from the dead the third
day; and that repentance and *remission of sins* should be preached
in His name among all nations, beginning at Jersualem. And ye
are witnesses of these things". Yet those men needed a further,
deeper, bigger thing to happen within them; and our Lord there-

[1] It is surprising what ingenuity most of us display when we want to turn
evidence to our own advantage or in favour of some theory. Only recently I
came across an instance of this in connection with that long-ago Pentecost. A
quite scholarly opponent of "the second blessing idea" argued that inasmuch
as Pentecost effected the *conversion* of 3,000 souls, it surely represents the
"*first*" blessing, i.e. of conversion, not a "second" blessing. But no; that is a
confusing of the historical with the symbolical (the meaningful how and why).
Those 3,000 converts were the *effect* of that "second" big experience which had
come to the Apostles and their companions. Whatever Pentecost may have
been *historically* does not alter the fact that ever since then it has monu-
mentalized what happens when the Holy Spirit falls in sanctifying and em-
powering fulness on those who are *already* born-again believers.

fore added (see verse 49) "But tarry ye in the city of Jerusalem until ye be *endued with power from on high*". That enduement came soon afterward, on the historic day of Pentecost which introduced the dispensation of the Spirit; and it brought not only an accession of power for witness-bearing, but an inward purification and an expansion of spiritual life. Peter attests this in Acts 15: 8, where he alludes to a similar coming of the Holy Spirit on the household of Cornelius: "And God, who knoweth the hearts, bare them witness, giving them the Holy Spirit, even as unto us . . . *purifying their hearts by faith*".

We need not add more; but need we infer *less* than that those Apostles were presumably an intended pattern for ourselves? If they *were* an intended pattern, then certainly nothing stands out more definitely than that we ourselves, as Christian believers today, are meant to experience a post-conversion enduement and transformation corresponding to the wonderful "second blessing" which came to them on that long-ago "day of Pentecost". We dare not say dogmatically that the experience of those apostles was an intended *norm*; yet neither should anyone dogmatically declare that it was not. It *could* have happened differently; but by divine intention it occurred in a manner and sequence evidently meant to be significant. Is there not at least a likelihood, therefore, that it may indicate a pattern?

The Ministry of the Spirit

Again, does not the very nature of the Spirit's ministry in believers seem to intend this further, or "second" major blessing, subsequent to conversion? Can we not all subscribe to the following comments of the late Dr. A. J. Gordon? "It seems clear from the Scripture that it is still the duty and privilege of believers [i.e. of those already regenerated] to receive the Holy Spirit [i.e. as the infilling Sanctifier] by a conscious, definite act of appropriating faith, just as they received Jesus Christ." "To say that in receiving Christ we necessarily receive in the same act the fulness of the Spirit seems to confound what the Scriptures make distinct." "The Scriptures show that we are required to appropriate the Spirit as *sons*, in the same way that we appropriated Christ as *sinners*. Let the believer receive the infilling Holy Spirit by a definite act of faith for his sanctification, as he received Christ by faith for his justification; and may he not be sure that he is in a safe and Scriptural way of acting?" "It is a fact that Christ has made atonement for sin; in conversion faith appropriates this fact in order to our *justification*. It is a fact that the Holy Spirit has been given; in consecration faith appropriates this fact for our *sanctification*."

We hold it as a cardinal evangelical truth that every heart-believer (Rom. 10: 9) on our Lord Jesus Christ is already "*born of the Spirit*" (John 3: 6, 8) into "newness of *life*" (Rom. 6: 4); for "if any man have not the Spirit of Christ, he is none of His" (Rom. 8: 9). Before our saving union with God's dear Son, it was the Holy Spirit who wrought in us to *convict* us of our sin, and *convince* us of the truth, and *convert* us to the Saviour. It would seem that just as really as the Spirit strives in us *before* conversion, to bring about our *regenerating* appropriation of Christ, so He strives in us *after* conversion, to bring about our *sanctifying* appropriation of Christ. Both regeneration and sanctification are parts of the one provided salvation, and both are effected by the Holy Spirit; yet Scripture and experience alike seem to indicate that they are neither identical in nature nor usually synchronous in occurrence.

To any thoughtful reader, the New Testament epistles must surely give the impression that the early Christians lived in a vivid experience of the Holy Spirit which is little in evidence today. Almost at random we recall such references as the following. "The love of God is *shed abroad* in our hearts by the Holy Spirit which is given unto us" (Rom. 5: 5). "The Spirit himself *beareth witness* with our spirit that we are the children of God" (Rom. 8: 16). "The kingdom of God is not in meat and drink but righteousness and peace and *joy in the Holy Spirit*" (Rom. 14: 17). "Who [God] hath also sealed us, and given us the *earnest* of the Spirit *in our hearts*" (2 Cor. 1: 22). "Received ye the Spirit by the works of the law, or by the hearing of faith?" (Gal. 3: 2). "Ye received the Word in much affliction, with *joy of the Holy Spirit*" (1 Thess. 1: 6). "*Quench not* the Spirit" (1 Thess. 5: 19). "Hereby we know that he [Christ] abideth in us, by the Spirit which he hath given us" (1 John 3: 24). "*Praying in the Holy Spirit*" (Jude 20).

These, and other such references to the Holy Spirit's activities in the redeemed, are often quoted with glib familiarity nowadays, and with an accepted superficiality of meaning far removed from their original import. Such phraseology in the New Testament is never the facile overstatement of fervid religious emotionalism, but the honestly worded testimony of glowing Christian hearts to dynamic realities. Over and over, the New Testament writers use the pronoun, "*Ye*", referring to what was indubitable reality in the lives of their first readers. When it was first written, the language really meant what it said.

How, then, did those believers of the early decades enter into their rapturous experience of sanctification by the infilling Spirit? Did they grasp it all at their conversion? I can hardly think so, especially when I remember the background of heathenism and ignorance and immorality from which many of them came. At their conversion they would be solely occupied with the two great leader-truths of the Evangel: remission of sins through the precious blood of Christ, and new life in Christ by being "born again" of the Spirit. The persisting problem of innate depravity, and the possibility of inwrought sanctification through the subduing, renewing, refining ministry of the infilling Spirit would claim concern later. Thus their new life in Christ would become stamped by *two* main crises of causation: (1) new birth by the Spirit as the originating crisis of *regeneration*; (2) infilling by the Spirit as the originating crisis of experiential *sanctification*. They would always associate the first of these with their *conversion* to Christ, and the second with their *consecration* to Christ. Presumably they would always thereafter distinguish between being "*born*" of the Spirit, and being "*filled*" by the Spirit.

This may be illustrated from Acts 8. "Philip went down to the city of Samaria, and preached Christ unto them." "The people with one accord gave heed." "There was great joy in that city." "They believed Philip, preaching the things concerning the kingdom of God and the name of Jesus Christ", and they "were baptized, both men and women". So they were now baptized and rejoicing believers. There had been a wonderful moving of the Spirit among them. Yet verse 16 tells us that "as yet" the Holy Spirit was "fallen on none of them". Even though they were born of the Spirit they were not endued by Him. The Holy Spirit, however, *did* come "on" them later, through the visit of Peter and John (17). I do not cite the incident as proving, but only as illustrating the seemingly twofold activity by the Spirit. He is both the "life" and the "power"; both the "breath" and the "flame"; both the Renewer and the Enduer. To my own mind, at least, it seems as though we are meant to demarcate between His special operation in regeneration and His subsequent operation in sanctification. So distinct, indeed, do the two operations seem, that I, for one, see no exegetical criminality in refer-ring to the latter as being distinctively a *"further* blessing".[1]

Implications in Epistles

To mention only one more aspect of the subject, it seems to me that sanctification, in the sense of an experience distinct from, or further to, conversion is repeatedly *implied in the epistles*. Especially pertinent is the testimony of the Christian Church Epistles (Romans to 2 Thessalonians) because in them the Holy Spirit has deposited that body of evangelical truth which belongs exclusively to the Christian Church throughout the present dis-pensation.

Allow me, then, to alight here and there on just a few repre-sentative references. There is no need to expound them. All we need is to appreciate their self-evident meaning, remembering that they were all written to born-again believers; to persons who had *already* been spiritually "enlightened", and had "tasted the heavenly gift", and had been made "partakers of the Holy Spirit".

Take Romans 12: 2, "Be ye *transformed* by the *renewing* of your mind". That word, "transformed", here, is arresting. It is used by a divinely inspired apostle, and it is used in relation to human character. Its meaning cannot be thinned down; the Greek word is that from which comes our own word, "meta-morphosis". In Romans 12: 2, therefore, the word "trans-formed", must not be denied its maximum meaning; so it indicates nothing less than a radical renovation. Moreover, it is no mere theoretical transformation, or something which the believer has to "reckon" as having taken place, whether the evidences are

[1] Let me re-emphasize that I do *not* cite the Acts 8 incident as *proving* a "second blessing", necessarily separated in point of *time* from conversion. I agree with those who object that the few days or weeks which elapsed between the "believing" of those Samaritans, under Philip's preaching, and then their "receiving" the Holy Spirit, through John and Peter's laying on of hands, is a mere incidence which establishes nothing so far as intervening time is con-cerned. Yet it does seem to underline again a characteristically *twofold activity* of the Spirit. Unless we say that the "believing" of those Samaritans was mere natural credence, we must agree that their believing was a work of the Spirit among them. Philip himself was so convinced of their sincere faith that he baptized them "into the name of the Lord Jesus". Yet they did not experience the *"demonstration* of the Spirit" (as Paul calls it in 1 Corinthians 2: 4) until later, when the two apostles came. We dare not overpress this, as there are the abnormalities of a transition period in the Acts; yet neither should it be discounted. The point here is not that two saving experiences are separated by an intervening *time-lapse*, but the repeated indication of a *twofold activity* by the Holy Spirit in believers.

apparent or not; for, as the text says, it takes place by the actual *"renewing"* of the *"mind"*—something actually effected by divine interference in the deeps of human personality. Well, did all that happen at conversion? Apparently not with those believers in that long-ago metropolis; hence the apostolic admonition in Romans 12: 2. Could they, then, have appropriated and experienced this transformation gradually? Maybe. Somehow, though, I suspect that most of them (like ourselves) would need a crisis of heart-searching prayer, of utter self-yielding, and of appropriating faith, as a Jordan-crossing into that sunlit Canaan.

Turn again to 1 Thessalonians 5: 23: "And the God of peace Himself sanctify you wholly; and may your whole spirit and soul and body be preserved entire, without blame". As with most other transactions between men and God, there are two sides to sanctification: the human and the divine. The human side is stressed in such verses as 2 Corinthians 7: 1, which exhorts us: "Let us cleanse ourselves from all defilement of flesh and spirit, perfecting [i.e. fully completing our] holiness [or sanctification] in the fear of God". But in 1 Thessalonians 5: 23, the emphasis is upon the *divine* side. That is why we have quoted it from the American Standard Version rather than the King James. "The God of peace *Himself* sanctify you wholly. . . ." How, then, is this divinely inwrought condition of sanctification, or holiness, to be entered? Gradually? Well, it is a notable point that the Greek verb translated "sanctify" is here in the aorist tense, denoting a single, completed act, as distinguished from drawn-out gradualness. It does not exclude the thought of sanctification as a process; but it emphasizes that the process begins with an originating *crisis*.

Turn further to Ephesians 1: 17, where Paul prays, "that the God of our Lord Jesus Christ, the Father of glory, may *give unto you the Spirit of wisdom and revelation*. . . ." But did not those Ephesian believers already have the Spirit? They certainly did, for Paul has just said so, in verse 13—"After ye believed ye were sealed with that Holy Spirit of promise which is the earnest of our inheritance. . . ." Why, then, does he now pray that God may *"give"* them the Spirit? Obviously he intends them now to experience the Spirit even more luminously, as the Spirit of "revelation" (*apokalupsis:* unveiling) in the "knowledge" (*epignosis:* special insight) of God. Did Paul mean them

to move *gradually* into this fuller illumination? Without evidence
to the contrary we should assume so; but the fact is that the
grammar of Paul's prayer indicates a *point from which*, rather
than gradual evolution. When he now prays that God may
"*give*" them the Spirit, he puts the verb in the aorist tense, indicating an act complete in itself. Did he use that aorist carefully,
or only casually?

While we are in Ephesians, we may well turn to chapter 3:
17–19, where Paul prays, "That Christ may dwell in your hearts
by faith, that ye being rooted and grounded in love, may be
able to comprehend with all the saints what is the breadth and
length and depth and height, and to know the love of Christ
which passeth knowledge, that ye may be filled with all the
fulness of God".

In those words, Paul climaxes the doctrinal half of his Ephesian
epistle. In so doing he also expresses the top-level possibility of
Christian experience this side of heaven. Three things are peti-
tioned: (1) "That Christ may *dwell* in your hearts"; that is,
by a continually realized indwelling, instead of transitorily or
intermittently. (2) "That ye may be *able to comprehend.* . . ."
A better translation is, "That ye may be fully able to apprehend", or to "grasp with the understanding". (3) "That ye may
be filled unto all the fulness of God." We need not be over-
puzzled here by that expression, "all the fulness of God", as
though Paul were suggesting that a tiny teacup could hold a
million Atlantic and Pacific oceans. *Christ* is the fulness of God,
as is taught by Colossians 1: 19 and 2: 9. To be "filled with
all the fulness of God" is utter suffusion of heart and mind and
soul by Christ.

Now how is all this to be entered into?—this constant consciousness of Christ, this wonderful enlargement of mind to grasp
spiritual reality, this utmost degree of Christ-suffusion? When
once entered into, no doubt, it is meant to be continuous and
ever progressive; but how do we get there? Is it by some gradual
approximation? Or is it by one act or crisis of transposition?
Well, once again, it is observable that in each of his three peti-
tions here, Paul uses that aorist tense, indicating *a point of
ingress* rather than an approximating process.

So we might go on, requisitioning similar incidental indications
from all over the epistles, and filling several more pages; but we
forbear, lest we seem to labour the pleasant argument needlessly.

What shall we say?

So, in the words of Romans 8: 31, "What shall we say to these things?" Is the so-called "second blessing" Scriptural? or is it merely gratuitous theory? We have submitted seven Old Testament examples of a distinctively second crisis-experience which might be reasonably called by that name, and which, when reconsidered retrospectively, in the light of the New Testament, seem to have been intendedly typical. We have also given five items of New Testament data which together seem to show that the antitype, or fulfilment, of those Old Testament types is an intended *further* blessing of sanctification and spiritual enduement in the experience of Christian believers. Let those reject the evidence who will. They have the right to do so if they choose, and we shall respect them still. As for myself, I seem to see with clearer eyes, that a distinctive *further* blessing is no mere elusive mirage of fond imagination, but a reality which is repeatedly prefigured, exemplified, and doctrinally uplifted before us in the written Word.

I do *not* think we are warranted in asserting dogmatically that the higher life of Spirit-filled sanctification can be entered *only* by a single, second crisis; but I *do* think that some such post-conversion crisis, or culminative crisis of a series, is according to an intended usual pattern. I do *not* believe that the so-called "second blessing" is anywhere directly *stated* in the New Testament; but I *do* believe that it is deducible as sound doctrine from a synthesis of *many* Scriptural indications, and that it may perhaps be conveniently generalized in some such designation as "the deeper blessing". My own preference is to call it by the Scriptural phrase, "the *fulness* of the blessing of Christ" (Rom. 15: 29) or, in short, *"THE FULNESS OF THE BLESSING."*

It is always a matter of gratitude with me that in my younger years I came under the influence of fervent but thoughtful preaching on the subject of Scriptural holiness, and that I knew many believers who could testify to the reality of "the blessing". Their faces and voices live on in my memory. I recall their looks and tones as though they conversed with me in my room this minute. As to the genuineness of their "experience" there could be no doubt. Their "second blessing" of inwrought sanctification was *evident* every day and everywhere in transformed disposition and behaviour. It stamped their personalities with a distinctive quality. Some of them were cruelly penalized for their testimony, at home or at work, but they endured (or, rather, reigned *over* it) with the most exemplary patience, kindness, gladness and victorious meekness. In the words of Sam Shoemaker, they had recaptured and reincarnated "the lost radiance of first-century Christianity".

But the feature which I most remember at the moment is, that they *all*, without one exception, said that they had come into this secret of inward holiness by a *post*-conversion crisis. Well, much as I loved and admired them, I dare not let even their *total* testimony convince me—not apart from the written Word of God. But as I now review their testimony against the background of Old Testament pointers and New Testament patterns, it glows with new authenticity; and with united voice they all seem to say, in the words of Scripture, "This is the way; walk ye in it".

DEDUCTION

> *From these New Testament patterns it seems fair to deduce that Scripture does distinguish the soul-saving first "blessing" of the Christian life —forgiveness, justification, regeneration—from the mind-renewing further "blessing" of entire sanctification, or inwrought holiness. Scripture does not statedly separate them, however, nor does it distinguish them in suchwise as to fix a rigid norm. Yet it does seem consistently to indicate an intended usual order of experience.*

POSTSCRIPT

A friendly reviewer of these studies writes: "I am unconvinced that the Bible teaches a second soul-crisis which brings an instantaneous, entire and permanent sanctification. The 'pointers' and 'patterns' appealed to are an inconclusive foundation." That criticism, however, is curiously out of focus, for we, too, reject the idea of an 'instantaneous' and 'permanent' *infixing* of holiness. Surely our volume, A NEW CALL TO HOLINESS, made that clear—and it will be said again in these pages. The one issue in these Scriptural pointers and patterns is, that they at least indicate a seemingly usual post-conversion crisis leading to a fuller experience of God and salvation. As to the specific *content* of that resulting fuller experience, further Scripture must decide.

REAL, OR IMAGINARY?

AN "ADVANCE GUARD"

In the ensuing chapter we requisition evidence from the testimony of outstanding Christians. Let us here and now put it beyond all misunderstanding (if possible!) that we would no more base a theory of sanctification upon subjective human experience apart from clear Scripture teaching than we would formulate a Christian doctrine upon Old Testament "types" without New Testament statement. The clear teaching of the written Word must ever be our decisive court of appeal.

On the other hand, it is just as wrong to ignore or belittle Christian *testimony;* for, reflect, true Christian experience is the Holy Spirit at work. And, while His work in the believer often clarifies or vivifies His teaching in the Scripture, it never contradicts it. Let us learn, then, certainly with due caution but also with reverence, from devout Christian experience and testimony. What we submit in this chapter is no mere buttressing of doubtful theory by appeal to a handful of witnesses regardless of stature or qualification—as our pages will show.

J.S.B.

REAL, OR IMAGINARY?

IF A doctrine is genuinely Scriptural, it will find endorsement in Christian experience. Therefore, if this teaching of "entire sanctification" as (in general) a second, radical crisis-work of God in the regenerated is "according to the Scriptures", there should be ample attestation of it in the life and testimony of consecrated believers.

Is there, then, any such body of witness? If so, are the witnesses trustworthy? Are they first-hand? Are they independent of each other, yet unanimous as to the main issue? Are they sufficiently varied to show that the teaching and experience are not peculiar to only one school or denomination? Are they as mentally discerning as they are religiously zealous? Are there those who lived long enough ago to prove that the experience is no mere present-day novelty? Are there others recent enough to prove that it is no mere story of the past? Is the testimony of the witnesses corroborated by their character, behaviour, and service?

Well, it seems to me (not yet committing myself unreservedly) that the multitude of witnesses to the so-called "deeper blessing" *seem* to measure up collectively to all such requirements. To quote them in plenty and at desired length would need a copious volume, not one short chapter such as this; but we can at least submit here several outstanding yet truly representative testimonies which, we think, should carry considerable conviction to the open-minded.

In submitting this argument from recorded Christian experience, however, let me make this once-for-all plain, especially to my brethren in the ministry; I am not in any subtle sympathy with the modern trend, in some quarters, to make experience a secondary norm of truth along with Scripture (after the manner of Schleirmacherian liberalism) any more than I can mentally tolerate making Scripture and tradition two equal norms. The one safe guide and final authority is the divine Word itself. But as a subordinate partner to Holy Writ, Christian experience can be highly illuminating.

Let me also make clear at the outset that in calling these witnesses I do not necessarily agree with all their doctrinal views on sanctification, nor even with some of the explanations which they give of their own experience. It is their experience itself with which we are here concerned, and their faithful attestation of it.

In requisitioning such as Dr. Asa Mahan, for instance, and Mrs. Hannah Whitall Smith, I am keenly aware of the penetrating hermeneutical criticisms levelled at both by theologian Benjamin B. Warfield in his monumental work, *Perfectionism*. I agree with him (though not without some reservations) as to Pelagian curves in the Oberlin teaching on sanctification, and the Quietist bent in Mrs. Smith's later "Higher Life" teachings: but the deciding factor about all those whose testimony we are here appropriating is that they were truly consecrated Christian men and women, of long-proven integrity, transparent motive, good judgment, and trustworthy as witness-bearers.

Dr. Asa Mahan

We begin by calling on Dr. Asa Mahan, first president of Oberlin College, Ohio, U.S.A. How well I remember poring over writings of his which came my way years ago, when I was a young disciple wanting to know for myself whether there was reality or not in "this second blessing idea". I call on Dr. Mahan first because he was a scholar and a well-known public figure who, having lived a sanctified life before many observers for over half a century, wrote a reminiscent explication of it as a radiant octogenarian. The following are selections.

"On Sabbath, November 9, 1884, I completed the eighty-fifth year of my life. The first seventeen years of this period were spent in the darkness of impenitency and sin, a state rightly represented by the words, 'having no hope, and without God in the world'. The following eighteen years I lived and walked in the dim twilight of that semi-faith which knows Christ in the sphere of 'justification by faith', but knows almost nothing of Him in the sphere of *sanctification* by faith'. During the subsequent fifty years I have found grace to 'walk with God' in that sphere of cloudless sunlight in which we are 'complete in Christ', and know Him as our 'wisdom, righteousness, sanctification and redemption'—know Him not only as 'the Lamb of God who taketh away the sin of the world', but as 'He that baptizeth with the Holy Spirit'.

"Here permit me to say, in general, that while I was in public regard an unexceptionably moral youth, no individual ever did or ever can lead a more godless life than I did. I never in a single instance, excepting at my mother's knee, offered a prayer to God in any form. I never entertained or expressed a sentiment of thanksgiving for a blessing received, or confessed a sin to my God; nor did I ever do or avoid doing a single act from regard to His will, favour or displeasure.

"Of my conversion, I may say of a truth that it was, in the judgment of all who knew me, of a very marked and decisive character, being followed by a visible change in character and life such as was seldom witnessed. During the first five years of my Christian life I was directly instrumental in originating four important revivals of religion—three of these occurring in the schools which I taught, and these where no work of grace existed within hearing distance around. Nor was my ministry of eight years' continuance, during this period, a fruitless one: no less, I suppose, than 2000 souls being added to the churches through my instrumentality.

"There was at length, notwithstanding all my prayers and efforts to the contrary, a gradual fading out of that joy. I found, to my great sorrow and regret, that those sinful propensities which had held absolute control over me during the era of my impenitency still existed, and when temptation arose 'warred in my members' with seeming undiminished strength, and were frequently 'bringing me into captivity to the law of sin which was in my members'. No believer, as it seems to me, ever did or ever could strive more resolutely and untiringly than I did to subdue and hold in subjection such evil propensities, or made less progress to effect his purpose than I did. During those eighteen years, after the fading of my primal joys, I was from time to time troubled and not infrequently agonised with painful doubts— doubts about my standing as a believer, about the truth of the Gospel, and a future state as revealed in the same. I seemed to myself to be among the number who feared the Lord, obeyed the voice of His servants, yet walked in darkness and had no light.

"I saw there was an essential defect in my experience and character as a Christian. I read and prayerfully pondered such passages as the following: 'The water that I shall give him shall be in him a well of water springing up into everlasting life'. 'Thou wilt keep him in perfect peace whose mind is stayed on Thee, because he trusteth in Thee'. 'Whom having not seen, ye love; in whom, though now ye see Him not, yet believing, ye rejoice with joy unspeakable and full of glory'. 'In all these things we are more than conquerors through Him that loved us,' etc. As I read such passages I said to myself, 'My experience hardly approaches that which is here revealed as the common privilege of all the saints'. In the secret of my own spirit I said, 'I will never cease enquiry and prayer until God shall 'open the eyes of my understanding', that I may know 'the things which are freely given us of God'. After some years of most diligent enquiry and prayer my eyes were opened, and 'I beheld with open face, as in a glass, the glory of the Lord', and 'knew the love of Christ which passeth knowledge', and emerged 'out of darkness into God's marvellous light'. In that light I have lived and walked for the past fifty years.

"And here permit me to remark that there has been during this entire period a total disappearance of all those painful experiences which threw such a 'disastrous twilight' over the preceding eighteen years of my Christian life. The peace and joy which, as an unfailing and unfading light, have filled and occupied these past fifty years have so far surpassed and eclipsed the 'peaceful hours enjoyed' during the ardency of my 'first love' that the latter is seldom 'remembered or comes into mind'. During these fifty years I have almost, and might say quite, ceased to be conscious of the existence and action of those evil propensities which, during the preceding eighteen years, 'warred in my members' and so often rendered me a groaning captive 'under the law of sin and death'; for 'the law of the Spirit of life in Christ Jesus' has made me 'free' from that old law. Immediately after my entrance into 'the brightness of the divine rising' I became blissfully conscious that all my propensities were, by divine grace, put under my absolute control; that I was no longer a groaning captive, but the Lord's free man—free and divinely empowered to employ all faculties and propensities, physical and mental, as 'instruments of righteousness' in the divine service.

"As a result of fifty years' experience and careful self-watchfulness I present myself as a witness for Christ, that 'our old man may be crucified with Him', and 'the body of sin destroyed, that henceforth we should not serve sin'. Were those old propensities against which I so long and vainly fought, and whose existence and action within I so long and deeply lamented, now warring at all in the inner man, should I not be, sometimes at least, conscious of the fact?

"My entrance into the higher life was attended by a vast increase of effective power in preaching Christ to the impenitent; and 'the edification of the body of Christ' (believers) became the leading characteristic and luxury of my ministry. Religious conversation became as easy and spontaneous as the outflow of water from a living fountain. Should I designate what I regard as one of the leading characteristics of my experience during these fifty years, I should refer to such Scriptures as, 'Thou wilt keep him in perfect peace whose mind is stayed on Thee'. At intervals my joy in God becomes so full and overflowing that it seems as if 'the great deep' of the mind is being broken up. But my peace, quietness, and assurance know no interruption.

"Should I be asked, 'Have you not sinned during these many years?' my reply would be: I set up no such pretension as that. This I do profess, however, that I find grace to 'serve Christ with a pure conscience'. But while 'I know nothing against myself, yet am I not hereby justified, but He that judgeth me is God'. I do 'have confidence toward God', because 'my heart condemns me not'. I have this evidence, also, that the love which I have does cast out all 'fear that hath torment'.

"This promise . . . has lived in my heart as the light of my life: 'The sun shall be no more thy light by day; neither for brightness shall the moon give light unto thee; but the Lord shall be unto thee an everlasting light, and thy God thy glory. Thy sun shall no more go down; neither shall thy moon withdraw itself; for the Lord shall be thine everlasting light, and the days of thy mourning shall be ended'."

Frances Ridley Havergal

We strike a sharp contrast in passing now from the venerable Dr. Mahan to the gentle, cultured, deft-penned genius whose hymns are now sung all over Christendom, Miss Frances Ridley Havergal. The famous C. H. Spurgeon spoke of her, in his day, as "the last and sweetest of England's religious poets". Much of the spiritual depth and richness of her hymns we owe to a sudden, luminous mind-opening and heart-cleansing crisis which she herself called a "second experience". The approach to this was gradual; but the actual occurrence was that of a sudden sun-burst through cloudy doubts and uncertainties. Although for many years she had loved the Lord and delighted in His service, there was "not so much of a holy walk and conversation or uniform brightness and continuous enjoyment in the divine life". She wrote, "I do so long for a deeper and fuller teaching in my own heart". What she longed for came soon afterwards, and she joyously wrote, "I see it all, and I have the blessing". Here are extracts from her testimony.

"It was on Advent Sunday, December 2nd, 1873, I first saw clearly the blessedness of true consecration. I saw it as a flash of electric light; and what you see you can never *unsee*. There must be full surrender before there can be full blessedness. God admits you by the one into the other. He Himself showed me all this most clearly. You know how singularly I have been withheld from attending all conventions and conferences; man's teaching has consequently had but little to do with it. First, I was shown that 'the blood of Jesus Christ His Son cleanseth from all sin', and then it was made plain to me that He who had thus cleansed me had power to keep me clean; so I just utterly yielded myself to Him and utterly trusted Him to keep me. . . . He brought me into the 'highway of holiness', up which I trust every day to progress, continually pressing forward, led by the Spirit of God. And I do indeed find that with it comes a happy trusting, not only in all great matters, but in all the little things also, so that I cannot say 'so and so worries me'.

"It was that one word 'cleanseth' which opened the door of a very glory of hope and joy to me. I had never seen the force of the tense before, a continual present, always a present tense, not a present which the next moment becomes a past. It goes on cleansing; and I have no words to tell how my heart rejoices in it. Not a coming to be cleansed in the fountain only, but a remaining in the fountain, so that it may and does go on cleansing.

"One of the intensest moments of my life was when I saw the force of that word 'cleanseth'. The utterly unexpected and altogether unimagined sense of its fulfilment to me, on simply believing in its fulness, was just indescribable. I expected nothing like it short of heaven. I am so thankful that, in the whole matter, there was as little human instrumentality as well could be. . . .

I am so conscious of His direct teaching and guidance through His Word and Spirit in the matter that I cannot think I can ever unsee it again. I have waited many months before writing this, so it is no new and untested theory to me; in fact, experience came before theory, and is more to me than any theory."

Dr. Daniel Steele

I doubt whether there ever was a more lucid or penetrating writer on this subject of sanctification than the late Dr. Daniel Steele, formerly a professor in the University of Boston. There is a verve and wit, an originality and directness, which always betoken that what he writes comes fresh and genuine from the living experience of his own heart. If we cannot always "amen" his conclusions, we are always blessed by godly provocation to search the Word further, to see "whether those things be so". Here, in substance, is his impressive contribution.

"I was born into this world in Windham, N.Y., October 5, 1824; into the kingdom of God in Wilbraham, Mass., in the spring of 1842. I could never write the day of my spiritual birth, so gradual did the light dawn upon me, and so lightly was the seal of my justification impressed upon my consciousness. This was a source of great trial and seasons of doubt in the first years of my Christian life. I coveted a conversion of the Pauline type.

"The personality of the Holy Spirit was rather an article of faith than a joyous realisation. He had breathed into me life, but not the more abundant life. In a sense I was free, but not 'free indeed'; free from the guilt and dominion of sin, but not from strong inward tendencies thereto, which seemed to be a part of my nature. In my early ministry, being hereditarily a Methodist in doctrine, I believed in the possibility of entire sanctification in this life, instantaneously wrought. How could I doubt it in the light of my mother's exemplification of its reality? I sought quite earnestly, at times, but failed to find anything more than transient uplifts from the dead level. But when I embraced the theory that this work is gradual, and not instantaneous, these blessed uplifts ceased. For, seeing no definite line to be crossed, my faith ceased to put forth its strongest energies. In this condition, a period of fifteen years, I became exceedingly dissatisfied and hungry.

"I was led by the study of the promised Paraclete to see that He signified far more than I had realised in the new birth, and that *a personal pentecost* was awaiting me. I sought in downright earnestness. Then the Spirit uncovered to my gaze the evil still lurking in my nature; the mixed motives with which I had preached, often preferring the honour which comes from men to that which comes from God.

"I submitted to every test presented by the Holy Spirit and publicly confessed what He had revealed, and determined to walk alone with God rather than with the multitude in the world or in the Church. I immediately began to feel a strange freedom, daily increasing, the cause of which I did not distinctly apprehend. I was then led to seek the conscious and joyful presence of the Comforter in my heart. Having settled the question that this was not merely an apostolic blessing, but for all ages— 'He shall abide with you forever'—I took the promise, 'Verily, verily, I say unto you, whatsoever ye shall ask the Father in My name, He will give it you'. The 'verily' had to me all the strength of an oath. I found that my faith had three points to master—*the Comforter, for me, now*. Upon the promise I ventured with an act of appropriating faith, claiming the Comforter as my right in the name of Jesus. For several hours I clung by naked faith, praying and repeating Charles Wesley's hymn—

> Jesus, Thine all-victorious love
> Shed in my heart abroad.

"I then ran over in my mind the great facts in Christ's life, especially dwelling upon Gethsemane and Calvary, His ascension, priesthood, and all-atoning sacrifice. Suddenly I became conscious of a mysterious power exerting itself upon my sensibilities. My physical sensations, though I am not of a nervous temperament, and was in good health, alone, and calm, were indescribable, as if an electric current were passing through my body with painless shocks, melting my whole being into a fiery stream of love. The Son of God stood before my spiritual eye in all His loveliness. This was November 17, 1870, the day most memorable to me. I now for the first time realised 'the unsearchable riches of Christ'. Reputation, friends, family, property, everything disappeared, eclipsed by the brightness of His manifestation. He seemed to say 'I have come to stay'. Yet there was no uttered word, no phantasm or image. It was not a trance or vision. The affections were the sphere of this wonderful phenomenon, best described as 'the love of God shed abroad in the heart by the Holy Spirit'. I was more certain that God loved me than I was of the existence of the solid earth and the shining sun. I intuitively apprehended Christ. This certainty has lost none of its strength and sweetness after the lapse of more than seventeen years. Yea, it has become more real and blissful.

"I did not at first realise that this was entire sanctification. The positive part of my experience had eclipsed the *negative,* the elimination of the sin-principle by the cleansing power of the Paraclete. But it [i.e. this deliverance] was verily so. Yet it has always seemed to me that this was the inferior part of the great blessing of the incoming and abiding of the whole Trinity (John 14: 23).

"After seventeen years of life's varied experiences, on seas sometimes very tempestuous, in sickness and in health, in tests of exceeding severity, there has not come up out of the depths of either my conscious or my unconscious being any thing bearing the ugly features of sin, the wilful transgression of the known law of God. All this time Satan's fiery darts have been thickly flying, but they have fallen harmless upon the invisible shield of faith in Jesus Christ. The rule of life, I find, must be sufficiently delicate to exclude those acts which bring the least blur over the spiritual eye (Heb. 5: 14). If any act brings a veil of the thinnest gauze between me and the face of Christ, I henceforth and forever wholly refrain therefrom.

"As another indispensable to establishment in that perfect love which casts out all fear, I have found the disposition to confess Christ in His utmost salvation. As no man could long keep in his house sensitive guests of whom he was ashamed before his neighbours, so no man can long have the company of the Father, Son and Holy Spirit in the temple of his heart while ashamed of their presence or their purifying work.

"In this respect I follow no man's formula. The words which the Spirit of inspiration teaches in the Holy Scriptures, though beclouded with misunderstandings and beslimed with fanaticisms, are, after all, the most appropriate vehicle for the expression of the wonderful work of God in perfecting holiness in the human spirit, soul and body.

"I testify that it is possible for believers to be so filled with the Holy Spirit that they can live many years on the earth conscious every day of a meetness for the inheritance of the saints in light, and of no shrinking back through a felt need of further cleansing, from an instant translation into the society of the holy angels and into the presence of the holy God. This has been my daily experience since 1870 [i.e. for the past seventeen years]."

Rev. C. W. Ruth

Only a year or two ago, when casually browsing among the bookshelves of a brother minister, I came across a little book bearing the title, *Entire Sanctification*. Until then I had never heard of its author, the Rev. C. W. Ruth, yet he was one of the most widely travelled holiness preachers at the beginning of our twentieth century; and his little treatise, issued in 1903, is a trenchant testimony. From its introductory "Life Sketch" we cull the following.

"The writer was born September 1st, 1865, in Hilltown township, Bucks county, Pennsylvania. Both my father and mother were devoted and consistent Christians, and members of the Evangelical Association, before I was born; hence I grew up in a home-atmosphere of real spirituality and godliness. For this I am devoutly thankful. I do not think there was ever a day, from my earliest childhood to the time of my conversion, that the Spirit of God did not strive with me, and bring to my heart conviction for sin and my need of a Saviour. Oftentimes I was 'almost persuaded' to become a Christian, and always cherished the purpose to do so at some time; and yet, withal, I procrastinated, and so became more and more hardened and corrupted by sin.

"Living in a country village or on the farm, I never had the privilege of attending even a grade school, and for the most part attended a country school; and even there circumstances compelled an irregular attendance. When I was the age of sixteen it was decided that I should learn some trade, and so arrangements were made for me to go to a neighbouring town (Quakertown, Pennsylvania) to serve an apprenticeship in a printing office. Here again I found myself surrounded with religious influences, as the proprietor of the printing office was a Christian gentleman."

(Mr. Ruth then narrates how, at the age of seventeen, he was truly converted. What happened thereafter, is described in our further quotations.)

"During the following year I lived a most earnest and devoted

Christian life, attending faithfully all the means of grace. I carried two Testaments—one German and one English—in my pockets, and used my spare time in studying the same. Thus I maintained a clear experience of justification. But I had only gone a very short time in my Christian experience until I discovered, much to my amazement, that there still remained a 'something' in my heart which hindered me, and at times even defeated me. The principal manifestations of that 'something' were, a man-fearing spirit, the uprising of an unholy temper, difficulty in forgiving and loving an enemy, etc. I learned that Jesus could remove the root of those difficulties out of the heart. Just one year after I had been so gloriously converted, while yet in my first love, I definitely sought the experience of *entire sanctification*. After seeking earnestly for some days, one Sunday night while walking down the side-walk toward the church, conscious that I had consecrated my all for time and eternity, I was enabled to look up into heaven, and say, 'I believe that the blood of Jesus cleanseth my heart from all sin now; He sanctifies me now.' Suddenly and consciously the Holy Spirit fell upon me, and I knew just as positively and as assuredly that God had sanctified me through and through, as I had known a year before that He had pardoned my sins. I rushed into the church, and before the pastor had time to announce the opening hymn, I told the congregation what had occurred on the side-walk, and that God had sanctified me wholly. Billows of glory swept over me until my joy seemed to be utterly inexpressible and uncontainable. Oh, the blessedness of that hour! Surely heaven could be no better. And from that day to the present—now almost twenty years—Satan has never had the audacity to tempt me to doubt even for one minute that God did then and there sanctify me wholly.

"Since that time I have never had a vacation of three weeks, and have averaged more than one sermon a day each year. I have preached and testified the gospel of holiness everywhere, and have never had services continuing one week or more without there being seekers. I regard it as a conservative statement when I say that in my meetings I have witnessed more than thirty thousand souls kneel seeking pardon or heart-purity. Four times I was elected as Presiding Elder—each time over my protest, but with it continued the work of holiness evangelism. I have travelled more than one hundred and fifty thousand miles in filling my engagements, and have laboured in thirty-three States and Canada, among twenty-five different denominations."

Dr. Edgar M. Levy

In Mr. Olin Garrison's compilation, *Forty Witnesses*, the longest contribution is by the Rev. Edgar M. Levy, D.D. It is too long for full inclusion here, but our excerpts reproduce coherently his testimony concerning entire sanctification.

After describing his conversion at the early age of thirteen, Dr. Levy resumes: "In my twenty-first year I was ordained pastor of the First Baptist Church, West Philadelphia, then just organised. Here God greatly blessed my labours. I was proud of my success. After a pastorate of fourteen years I accepted a call to Newark, New Jersey. Here, also, God wonderfully blessed my labours, and hundreds were added to the Church. But oh, how were all my services, even the best, mixed with selfishness, ambition, and pride! A consciousness of this often filled me with shame and sorrow. Then I would make a new effort to improve my life by more watchfulness, zeal, and prayer; and although failure was sure to follow, yet, not knowing of any better method, I would tread the same weary road over and over again.

"Severe afflictions visited me. The sweetest voice of the household group was hushed; the brightest eyes were darkened in death; health failed; many friends proved unreliable; hopes withered; the way grew rough and thorny. My unsanctified soul, instead of learning submission, became impatient of restraint, would sometimes murmur against the dealings of God with me, question His wisdom, and doubt His love.

"After a residence of ten years in Newark I returned, in the autumn of 1868, to the scene of my early labours, and became pastor of the Berean Baptist Church, Philadelphia. In February, 1871, Mr. Purdy, an evangelist, was holding meetings in the Methodist church adjacent to mine. Many Christians from different churches were also in attendance. Day after day, with meekness and gentleness, and yet with unwavering confidence, they told the story of long years of conflict, and of ultimate and complete triumph through simple faith in the blood that cleanses from all sin, of their soul-rest and abiding peace, of their power with God and man, and the fulness of their joy.

"At first I became deeply interested, and then my heart began to melt. I said: These Christians are certainly in possession of a secret of wonderful power and sweetness. What can it be? Is it justification? No; it cannot be that. I have experienced the blessing of justification; by it I have been absolved from all my past sins; by it I stand in the righteousness of Christ; every privilege of a child of God, and every grace of the blessed Holy Spirit, has been secured to me; but I do *not* find that it has destroyed the power of inbred sin, or brought to me complete rest of soul. I have peace; but it is often broken by 'fear which has torment'. I am conscious of loving God, but it is like some sickly, flickering flame which I am expecting every moment to expire altogether. I have joy, but it is like a shallow brook; the drought exhausts it. I have faith, but it is such a poor, weak thing that I am in doubt sometimes whether it is faith at all. I 'hate vain thoughts'; yet they continue to come, and seem at home in my mind. I believe that Jesus saves from sin; and yet I sin from day to day, and the dark stains are everywhere visible.

"I commenced a careful examination of the doctrine of sanctification. I reviewed my theological studies. I conversed with intimate friends of my own and other denominations. Nearly all of them pronounced the views advanced as nothing else than unscriptural and pernicious errors. They admitted the existence and universality of the disease, but could tell of no adequate remedy this side the grave. They allowed that the malady might be molified; but in this life, they affirmed, it could never be perfectly healed."

Dr. Levy then describes a later meeting in his own church, and continues: "After the sermon a number of persons bore testimony to the fulness and completeness of their present salvation. They represented several evangelical denominations—the Methodist, the Episcopalian, the Presbyterian, the Friends, the Baptists; and there was a beautiful harmony in all they said. I had no reason to doubt the truthfulness of their statements. I might question their logic, and find fault with their theories, and reject their phraseology, but how could I dispose of their *experience*? My judgment was assailed as it had never been before. After the meeting I returned to my study, fell upon the floor, and poured out my soul before God. I did not pray for pardon, but for purity. I did not seek clearer evidence of my acceptance, but to be 'made free from sin', not in a judicial or theological sense, but by a real, conscious *inwrought holiness*.

"That night I was unable to sleep. I was completely broken

down in heart before God. The vision of Isaiah seemed reproduced. 'I saw also the Lord sitting upon a throne, high and lifted
up.' 'Then said I, Woe is me! for I am undone; because I am
a man of unclean lips, and I dwell in the midst of a people of
unclean lips; for mine eyes have seen the King, the Lord of
hosts.'

"The morning at length dawned, and on every ray I could
read, 'Walk in the light, as He is in the light.' 'Holy, holy, holy,
is the Lord of hosts', as chanted by the seraphim, seemed floating
through all the air. As I thought of God, it was not so much His
power or wisdom or justice or love that attracted my attention,
as His infinite holiness.

"That day, Friday, March 9, 1871, was observed by the
church as a special season of fasting, humiliation, and prayer.
My soul was in great agony. I can compare my experience on
that memorable day to nothing else than crucifixion. It seemed
to me that I had gone up with Christ to Calvary and was trans-
fixed to the cruel and shameful cross. A sense of loneliness and
abandonment stole over my mind. 'An horror of great darkness
fell upon me', and all the powers of hell assaulted my soul. The
enemy brought before me with tremendous force my life-long
prejudices, my theological training, my professional standing, my
denominational pride. It was suggested that I must leave everything behind me should I go a step further in this direction. The
dread of being misunderstood, of having my motives questioned,
of being called 'unsound in doctrine', of being slighted by my
ministerial brethren, and of being treated with suspicion and
coldness, filled my heart with unspeakable anguish. Everything
appeared to be sliding from under my feet.

"This mental conflict, however, soon subsided. The storm-
clouds passed away, and light began to stream in. I was now
done with theorising, with philosophical doubts and vain specula-
tions. I cared no longer for the opinions of men. I was willing to
be a fool for Christ and to suffer the loss of all things. I cried
out, 'Teach me *Thy way*, O Lord! and lead me in a plain
path'.

"When the meeting ended I repaired immediately to the par-
sonage. I threw myself into a chair, and at once the wondrous
baptism came. I seemed 'filled with all the fulness of God'. I
wept for joy. At once I had a new and wonderful sense of the
presence of Christ. Those words of Jesus were made real to me:

'Abide in Me, and I in you'. The sovereign will of God seemed at once so sweet and blessed that I felt lost in the thought that God ruled over me and in me. I found myself praising Him for every trial, sorrow, disappointment, and loss. My sense of unworthiness was greatly quickened. I felt a sweet spirit of forgiveness in my heart. My love for the brethren was much enlarged. Denominational distinctions disappeared.

"Answers to prayer now began continually occurring. The personality and work of the blessed Holy Spirit were revealed to my spiritual perceptions as never before. Indeed, all the doctrines of the Gospel at once became luminous in the presence of the Sanctifier. What was formerly a speculative conviction became now a wondrous reality. Life has become marvellously simplified and natural. I no longer work for liberty, but as having liberty. I do not find this life—what in my ignorance I once regarded it—one of mysticism, indolence, and self-congratulation, but a life of ceaseless activity amid undisturbed repose.

"I have not found that this experience exempts us from trial, persecution, or disappointment. For me the way has frequently been strewn with thorns rather than roses. Unkindness has often wounded my heart. Friends have turned away, sometimes with pity, and sometimes with blame. At times I have been in heaviness through manifold temptation, and faith has almost yielded to the outward pressure; but, blessed be God, for sixteen years I have been preserved from all murmuring, disquietude, or fear."

Dwight L. Moody

It may be useful now to draw this chapter to a close by giving a couple of rather briefer testimonials. Was there ever a greater evangelist than D. L. Moody? The impact of Moody and Sankey in Britain, America, and other countries was such that even yet we have not taken its full measure. As to personal character and temperament, Moody was eminently the forthright, practical sort, impatient toward any kind of lazy religious professionalism or sanctimonious bluff. He was the embodiment of downright reality; energetic, blunt, and big in human sympathies. To him, praying without doing was just as wrong as doing without praying. Yes, that was Moody; and his testimony which we here reproduce bears the characteristic impress of the man. After a considerable period of seeking into the blessing of real sanctification and the enduement of power for service, the blessing "came"; and this is how he describes it:

"This blessing came upon me suddenly, like a flash of lightning. For months I had been hungering and thirsting for power in service. I had come to that point where I think I would have died if I had not got it. I remember that I was walking the streets of New York. I had no more heart in the business I was about than if I had not belonged to this world at all. Right there, on the street, the power of God seemed to come upon me so wonderfully that I had to ask God to stay His hand. I was filled with a sense of God's goodness, and felt as though I could take the whole world to my heart. I preached the old sermons that I had preached before without any power; it was the same old truth, but there was a new power. Many were impressed and converted. This happened years after I was converted.

"It was the fall of 1871. I had been very anxious to have a large Sunday School and a large congregation, but there were few conversions. I remember, I used to take a pride in having the largest congregation in Chicago on a Sunday night. Two godly women used to come and hear me. One of them came to me one night after I had preached very satisfactorily, as I thought. I fancied she was going to congratulate me on my success, but she said, 'We are praying for you'. I wondered if I had made some blunder, that they talked in that way.

"Next Sunday night they were there again, evidently in prayer while I was preaching. One of them said, 'We are still praying for you.' I could not understand it, and said, 'Praying for me! Why don't you pray for the people? I am all right.' 'Ah,' they said, 'You are not all right; you have not got power; there is something lacking, but God can qualify you.' I did not like it at first, but I got to thinking it over, and after a little time I began to feel a desire to have what they were praying for.

"They continued to pray for me, and the result was that at the end of three months God sent this blessing on me. I want to tell you this: I would not for the whole world go back to where I was before 1871. Since then I have never lost the assurance that I am walking in communion with God, and I have a joy in His service that sustains me and makes it easy work. I believe I was an older man then than I am now; I have been growing younger ever since. I used to be very tired when preaching three times a week; now I can preach five times a day and never get tired at all. I have done three times the work I did before, and it gets better and better every year. It is so easy to do a thing when love prompts you. It would be better, it seems to me, to go and break stone than to take to preaching in a professional spirit."

Hannah Whitall Smith

Few popular religious books have had such wide and continual sale as Hannah Whitall Smith's judicious little book, *The Christian's Secret of a Happy Life*. All of us who are fond of reconnoitering among the shelves of evangelical bookstores have seen its pleasant title there again and again. Many of us will thank God for what it meant to us in our earlier years as Christian disciples. How, then, did its author come into her "secret"? She herself shall tell.

"I was converted in Philadelphia in 1856, in my twenty-sixth year. As time passed on the Lord graciously led me into the knowledge of much truth. But my heart was ill at ease. At the end of eight years of my Christian life I was forced to make the sorrowful admission that I had not even as much power over sin as when I was first converted.

"I began to long after holiness. I began to groan under the bondage to sin in which I was still held. But so thoroughly convinced was I that no efforts or resolutions or prayers of my own would be of any avail, and so ignorant was I of any other way, that I was almost ready to give up in despair.

"In this time of sore need (1863) God drew into my company some whose experience seemed to be very different from mine. They declared that they had discovered a 'way of holiness' wherein the redeemed soul might live and walk in abiding peace, and might be made 'more than conqueror' through the Lord Jesus Christ.

"I asked them their secret, and they replied, 'It is simply ceasing from all efforts of our own and trusting in the Lord to make us holy'.

"Never shall I forget the astonishment this answer gave me. 'What!' I said, 'do you really mean that you have ceased from your own efforts altogether in your daily living, and that you do *nothing* but trust the Lord? And does He actually and truly make you conquerors?'

"Like a revelation the glorious possibilities of a life such as this flashed upon me, but the idea was too new and wonderful for me to grasp. I was altogether legal in my thoughts as regarded daily living. I had never dreamed of trusting the Lord for that, and I did not know how to do it. I lay awake whole nights to wrestle in prayer that God would grant me the blessing He had granted these other Christians. Then I began anew to search the Scriptures. I found that the salvation He had died to procure was declared to be a perfect salvation, and that He was able to save to the very uttermost. I found that He offered Himself to me as my life, and that He wanted to come into my heart and take full possession there and subdue all things to Himself. He showed Himself to me as a perfect and complete and present Saviour, and I abandoned my whole self to His care; I cast myself, as it were, headlong into the ocean of His love, to have all these things accomplished in me by His almighty working. I believed the truth that He was my practical sanctification as well as my justification, and my soul found rest at last, such a rest that no words can describe it—rest from all its legal strivings, rest from all its weary conflicts, rest from all its bitter failures. The secret of holiness was revealed to me, and that secret was Christ. My soul has entered into that interior rest or 'keeping of sabbath' which the apostle Paul, in Hebrews 4: 9, declares 'remaineth for the people of God'. Not that there are no conflicts; the battle, however, is no longer mine, but Christ's.

"All the former period of my Christian course seems comparatively wasted. I was a child of God, it's true, but my growth was stunted, and my stature feeble. When this secret of faith was revealed to me, I began to grow; and the dedication which was before impossible to me became the very joy of my heart.

"Believing, resting, abiding, obeying—these are my part; He does all the rest. What heights and depths of love, what infinite tenderness of care, what wise lovingness of discipline, what grandeur of keeping, what wonders of revealing, what strength in weakness; what comfort in sorrow, what light in darkness, what easing of burdens I have found; what a God, and what a Saviour, no words can tell!"

"What more . . . ?"

We have now heard these several witnesses. In the words of Hebrews 11: 32, "What more shall we say?"—for the foregoing witnesses are but several out of a host. A. M. Hills concludes one of his chapters in *Holiness and Power* with a shining galaxy of their honoured names. "Why is it," he asks, "that those who oppose this second blessing, this baptism with the Holy Spirit, or holiness, or entire sanctification, or Christian perfection, no matter by what name called, always pick out the cranks and fanatics? Why cannot they be honourable enough to think of and name some whose lives and work are the glory of the Church of God during the last two centuries? Let me name just a few of the mighty host who have received this baptism with the Spirit, and have exhibited its effects to the world, however they may have differed in philosophy and theology: John Wesley, Charles Wesley, George Whitefield, Jonathan Edwards, Mrs. Jonathan Edwards, Adam Clark, John Fletcher, William Carvosso, Hester Ann Rogers, David Brainerd, James Brainerd Taylor, William Tennent; and these bishops of the Methodist Church—Whatcoat, Asbury, McKendree, Hamline, Simpson, Foster, Newman, Ninde, Thoburn, Foss, Mallalieu, Taylor of Africa, Bowman, Goodsell, Pierce; and in other denominations, President Asa Mahan, President Charles G. Finney, evangelists D. L. Moody, C. J. Fowler, R. A. Torrey, Wilbur Chapman, A. B. Earle, Harriet Beecher Stowe, Phoebe Palmer, Frances Ridley Havergal, Mrs. Van Cott, Frances Willard, Hannah Whitall Smith, Dr. A. B. Simpson, Professors Dugan Clark, and David B. Upregraff, Dr. Daniel Steele of Boston University, Rev. J. A. Wood, Drs. Levy, Inskip, McDonald, Lowrey, Gordon, Dunham, Keen, Andrew Murray, J. O. Peck, J. A. Smith, F. B. Meyer, Alfred Cookman, General Booth and his holy wife Catherine, who mothered the most efficient family in the kingdom and service of Christ the century has seen. These are a few godly souls, representatives of the great army of saints who are called 'holiness cranks' by people scarcely worthy to touch their shoe-latchets."

"What then . . . ?"

In the words of Romans 8: 31, we ask again, "What shall we then say to these things?" Were all these eminent witnesses self-deceived? Could all such godly persons be exaggerating to the point of untruth? Was all their experience of this radical and enduring sanctification an abnormal prolongation of delusive auto-suggestion? It may be objected that even the saintliest and most scholarly persons have frequently been mistaken in their theological reasonings, explanations, and conclusions. The validity of that objection we fully admit. We admit much *more* than that: for we take leave to think that some of those whose testimonies we have here reproduced were at least partly wrong in *their* theory of sanctification, and even in their explanation of it in their own experience! Yet that in no way invalidates their witness; for here we are not concerned either with their interpretations of Scripture or even with their explanations of their own experience, but solely with their witness to *the experience itself.*

Can we doubt, then, the factual honesty of the experience reported by witnesses whose lives and words are stamped by such evident integrity? The several whom we have quoted, remember, represent tens of thousands. Must we not accept this body of testimony? Even though we may heartily disagree with some of the contributors in their interpretations or *theories* of sanctification, must we not believe in the reality of the *experience*? In view of the evidence, I, for one, am persuaded that "entire sanctification", in the sense of a further major divine intervention in the already regenerated soul, is not only soundly inferable from Scripture, but amply attested by Christian experience.

I underscore: the foregoing testimonies are *not* a buttressing of mere theory by extra-Scriptural appeal to *experience*. They are adduced as showing a common correspondence with what we find in *Scripture*. Nor are we trying to account theologically for what can be explained temperamentally. Those witnesses record a transformation *beyond* explanation in terms of natural psychology. That experience did *not* bring a once-for-all, indefectible sanctification. It depended on *continuous* yieldedness to God. But it was real—and wonderful.

DEDUCTION

> As complemental to Old Testament pointers and New Testament patterns the foregoing testimonies represent a large body of Christian experience which surely confirms that the conscious realization of entire sanctification often or even usually comes by way of a post-conversion crisis. All the foregoing witnesses and the many others whom they represent sought the blessing in that way on the basis of what they understood Scripture to teach; and the Holy Spirit answered them on that basis. This parallel between what Scripture seems to teach and what the divine Spirit seems to endorse in experience should not be lightly dismissed.

INSTANTANEOUS OR GRADUAL?

"Theology has been taken captive by the modern spirit. The theory of evolution has relegated everything sudden and supernatural to the limbo of superstition. . . . We can understand culture, but distrust conversion. Growth appeals to our sense of reason, but a sudden elimination of inherited tendencies is not in harmony with the processes of Nature. That is why so much modern preaching is vague and ineffective. It is of the sheet-lightning sort; it shines but does not strike. Glittering generalities may dazzle, but they accomplish nothing."

Samuel Chadwick.

INSTANTANEOUS OR GRADUAL?

As we have seen, Scripture teaches an inward holiness and spiritual fulness far above the average Christian experience of today. We have lingered over Old Testament pointers to it, and New Testament patterns of it, and well-known witnesses to it. Before we examine more closely the *nature* of it, there is a further aspect which claims consideration, namely, the teaching that this inward liberation and expansion is wrought *instantaneously* in the consecrated believer.

This insistence, that "entire sanctification" is wrought *instantaneously*, has been a prominent feature of nearly all holiness teaching in its more recent and specialised forms. In the life of full deliverance from "inbred sin", and full enduement by the Spirit, and full fellowship with God (so the teaching runs) there are two major crises: (1) regeneration, (2) entire sanctification; and the second is as instantaneous as the first.

All will agree that *regeneration* is instantaneous. There is a moment up to which an unconverted man is spiritually dead, and from which he is spiritually alive. In an instant the divine Spirit creates life where there has been death. There may be a long process leading to it, but regeneration itself is necessarily instantaneous.

Just as decidedly, all who have followed the Wesley teaching, and certainly all who have advocated the "eradication" theory, have emphasized that the causative crisis of entire *sanctification* is instantaneous.

John Wesley

John Wesley, in his *Plain Account of Christian Perfection*, clearly teaches that while there may be a gradual process both to and from entire sanctification, the transition-point itself necessarily occurs in an instant. With some persons, that instant is pronounced and memorable; with others it is reached so gradually as to be scarcely distinguishable; but in either case the becoming *entirely* sanctified is strictly instantaneous.

87

Most of Wesley's treatise is in the form of question and answer. In reply to the query, "Is this death to sin, and renewal in love, gradual or instantaneous?" He says, "A man may be dying for some time; yet he does not, properly speaking, die till the soul is separated from the body; and in that instant, he lives the life of eternity. In like manner, he may be dying to *sin* for some time; yet he is not dead to sin till sin is separated from his soul; *and in that instant* he lives the full life of love".

Making himself once-for-all clear, he commits himself to this manifesto: "(1) That Christian perfection is that love of God and our neighbour which implies deliverance from all sin. (2) That this is received solely by faith. (3) That it is given *instantaneously*, in one moment. (4) That we are to expect it, not at death, but every moment".

Most forcibly of all (see *Journal of Hester Ann Rogers,* p. 174) he writes, "You may obtain a growing victory over sin from the moment you are justified. But this is not enough. The body of sin, the carnal mind, must be destroyed; the old man must be slain, or we cannot put on the new man, which is created after God (or which is the image of God) in righteousness and true holiness; and this is *done in a moment.* To talk of this work as being gradual, would be nonsense, as much as if we talked of gradual justification."

Tyerman says (*Life and Times of Wesley,* see vol. 2, pp. 346, 416, 444), "The doctrine of Christian perfection, attainable in an instant by a simple act of faith, was made prominent in Methodist congregations in 1762, and ever after it was one of the chief topics of Mr. Wesley's ministry and that of his itinerant preachers".

Representative Others

Since Wesley's time this insistence on the instantaneousness of entire sanctification has remained emphatic among his successors in holiness teaching.

The Rev C. W. Ruth, in his *Entire Sanctification,* says: "The human side of sanctification . . . may be gradual. That is, the individual may be some time in completing a 'dedication' of his all to God. But the moment this is completed, with faith really touching the promise, then the divine side of sanctification, which is 'to make holy or pure' . . . is instantaneously and divinely inwrought through the power of the Holy Spirit" (p. 29).

The Rev. A. M. Hills is equally incisive when he writes, "This idea of growing into holiness is contrary to sound theology. Growth is a gradual process. The Bible always represents sanctification as an *act*. Growth is the work of man, life-long. The sanctifying 'baptism with the Holy Spirit and with fire' is an *act* of God, given as suddenly today as on the morning of Pentecost. The cleansing, purifying work of the Holy Spirit was wrought instantaneously in every case recorded in Scripture. There is no such command or thought in the Bible as 'Become holy by degrees'." (*Holiness and Power,* p. 322).

The Rev. Isaiah Reid, in his trenchant little work, *How They Grow,* says, "The people who have this grace, and who confess it, are not those who have come into possession of the experience by the method of gradualism. On the other hand, their universal testimony is that the work was instantaneous, and by grace, through consecration and faith. . . . Testimony proving that we are correct comes from people in all ages and in all denominations. We have tested it again and again in large meetings, and have never yet found one in possession of the grace of entire sanctification who reached the experience by growth. All gradualists are in a state of growth, and hence they are growing and groaning after it, but do not have it. The people who have the experience are qualified to tell how they received it. The get-it-by-growth people never know how to tell anyone how to obtain a holy heart so as to have it. They cannot, till they have it themselves; and as they are still in a state of growing into it, they are not yet in a state of entire sanctification. They have *some* [sanctification] they say, but how much they cannot tell; nor how long the growing may yet continue they have no idea. Many of the 'growth' advocates honestly say, while they claim a growth of forty years or more, that they are no better in this respect than when they first began."

Experiential Counterpart

The foregoing quotations are representative enough to make further cullings superfluous; yet it may well be added that this *doctrine* of instantaneous sanctification seems attested by a "great cloud of witnesses" as being correspondingly instantaneous in *experience.* (For Wesley's testimony to this see appendix on *Instantaneous Sanctification,* p. 248).

I remember reading, in my youth, the life of the Rev. William

Bramwell, a lusty earlier Methodist. His testimony runs: "The Lord, for whom I had waited, came suddenly to the temple of my heart, and I had an immediate evidence that this was the blessing I had for some time been seeking. My soul was all wonder, love and praise."

Dr. Daniel Steele's testimony is of like sort: "Six months ago I made the discovery that I was living in the pre-pentecostal state of religious experience—admiring Christ's character, obeying his law, and in a degree loving his person, but without the conscious blessing of the Comforter. I had settled the question of privilege by a study of St. John's Gospel and St. Paul's Epistles, and earnestly sought for the Comforter. I prayed, consecrated, confessed my state, and believed Christ's word. Very suddenly, after about three weeks' diligent search, the Comforter came with power and great joy into my heart. He took my feet out of the realm of doubt and weakness, and planted them forever on the Rock of assurance and strength."

Dr. Carradine is certainly forceful: "Cannot God witness to purity of heart as he does to pardon of sin? Are not his blessings self-interpreting? He who impresses a man to preach, who testifies to a man that he is converted, can he not let a man know when he is sanctified? I knew I was sanctified, just as I had known fifteen years earlier that I was converted. I knew it not only because of the work itself in my soul, but through the Worker. He, the Holy Spirit, bore witness clearly, unmistakably and powerfully to his own work; and, although months have passed away since that blessed morning, yet the witness of the Holy Spirit to the work has never left me for a moment" (*Sanctification*, p. 22).

President Asa Mahan says, "Forty-seven years ago, when my desire for the open vision had become almost insupportably intense, in a moment, in the twinkling of an eye, I stood face to face with the Sun of Righteousness, feeling his divine healings through every department of my being" (*Autobiography*, p. 6).

Dr. Asbury Lowrey thus describes his entrance into the blessing: "About three months after this date, God, in his love, gave me the evidence of full salvation. Observe, I did not approach it *gradually* by any sensible increase of joy or power. My soul did not flower up into it by successive blessings. I remained as far from the actual grasp of the great salvation an hour before it came as I had been for nine years. And I suppose it would have continued so but for one mighty resolve, and that was to bring on a

crisis. I found I must fix a time and limit my faith to it! Therefore
under the conviction that it must be now or never I dismissed
every other subject, suspended every pursuit, and retired into a
room, bowed all alone before God, and pleaded for *immediate*
redemption, *immediate* deliverance, *immediate* cleansing from all
sin, the fulness of the Spirit and perfection in love. I soon
realised the unfailing truth of these words: 'Faithful is He that
calleth you, who also will do it'. Somehow I was moved and
inspired to *trust*. . . . In conjunction with this trusting and praying, a joyous impression, a divine conviction amounting to an
evidence, came upon my mind to the effect that God had graciously
granted my request—that I was healed of all sin; that I had
entered into rest from sin; that its corrodings had ceased. I was
happy but not ecstatic. The prevailing feeling seemed to be that
of rest, satisfaction, great peace, and a consciousness of cleansing
and sanctity. My joy was more solemn and sacred than ever
before. My soul seemed hushed into silence before the Lord on
account of his nearness and realised indwelling, and the over-
shadowing of the Holy Spirit" (*Possibilities of Grace,* pp. 436–
465).

We recall, too, a sentence from D. L. Moody's testimony,
already quoted: "This blessing came upon me suddenly, like a
flash of lightning". The mighty revivalist, Charles G. Finney,
had a similarly sudden, whelming experience of the Holy Spirit.
So had the globe-circling evangelist, R. A. Torrey. And the same
has been true of many others, whose names are not so widely
known.

Feminine Witnesses

Among the foregoing witnesses no feminine volunteers are included. That, however, can easily be remedied. Here are several
brief but telling extracts all together.

Mrs. Anna M. Hammer, a former Episcopalian preacher of
New Jersey writes: "My sanctification was a second actual
experience; and from that time my life has been changed; is
deeper, stronger, steadier, sweeter, richer."

We recall, too, Miss Frances Ridley Havergal's words that *her*
"second experience" was a clearly-dated crisis on "Advent Sunday, December 2nd, 1873". It was an inward renewal, an "utterly
unexpected and altogether unimagined fulfilment" of which she
wrote, "I expected nothing like it short of heaven"!

Mrs. Phoebe Palmer, evangelist, says, "While I was thus exulting, the voice of the Spirit again appealingly applied to my understanding: 'Is not this sanctification?' I could no longer hesitate; reason as well as grace forbade; but I rejoice in the assurance that I was wholly sanctified—body, soul, and spirit. Oh, into what a region of light, glory and purity was my soul at this moment ushered! I felt that I was but as a drop in the ocean of infinite love, and Christ was all in all."

Mrs. Sarah L. Palmer, a Methodist, wrote at the age of 81, "The baptism of the Holy Spirit came in its glorious fulness; it seemed as a baptism of love almost to the overwhelming of the physical frame, accompanied with an inexpressible consciousness of purity, a consciousness only understood by those who have received it. Since that blessed day, May 21, 1835, I think there has not been one hour in which my soul has not been sweetly resting in the precious Atonement. . . . After more than seventy-six years of conscious adoption, and fifty-two of dwelling in the peaceful land of perfect love, my heart is singing, 'Blessed be the Lord, who hath given rest to his people Israel, according to all that he promised; there hath not failed one word of all his good promise'."

Is the evidence conclusive?

Such, then, has been both the teaching and the testifying: entire sanctification begins at a crisis-point which is *instantaneous*. A. M. Hills seems to bring it to a final focus when he claims: "This gift of the divine fulness must be *instantaneous* because it is conditioned on a definite act of faith. . . . In all ages of the Church the experience of the holiest men and women attests this doctrine of the fulness of the Holy Spirit as a work distinct from regeneration. Let the fulness of the Holy Spirit be the experience of the preacher, and he will no longer feebly enunciate Gospel truth. Our pulpits will no longer be afflicted with impotency, but be girded with strength."

The question, here, is: Does the evidence warrant our saying that inward sanctification *always* comes in this instantaneous way? The quotations which we have submitted, though necessarily restricted, are sufficiently representative. Do the premises, then, warrant the conclusion that inward sanctification is necessarily instantaneous, as is argued? Perhaps most who read these lines will expect my reply to be "Yes"; but although it may come as a surprise, my own view is otherwise. The foregoing testimonies are valid as far as they go, but they are not conclusive. An experience of inward sanctification may indeed begin quite suddenly; but despite the insistence of many holiness teachers that it *always* comes so, I believe that it not infrequently comes as the crowning point of a *gradual* process; and I believe that this can be supported both by Scripture and by Christian experience. Moreover, it is my opinion that the holiness cause has suffered much through the sincere but hard and fast insistence that experiential sanctification *must* come instantaneously.

Years ago, I used to wonder *why* holiness preachers and writers were so emphatic that entire sanctification must come instantaneously. I now marvel that I could have been so slow in seeing the obvious. If by entire sanctification is meant the utter eradication of inbred sin, then it can *only* happen instantaneously. Healing therapy, whether in body or soul, may be gradual; but *surgery*, whether it be to cut cancer out of the body, or inbred sin out of the soul, *must* be instantaneous. Surgery is *never* gradual.

Let it be clearly grasped: the teaching that entire sanctification necessarily comes instantaneously is a twin of the theory that such sanctification effects the total *destruction* of the sin-bias in our human nature. Many quotations might be given making this crystal clear, but the following comment by Professor Dougan Clark will suffice: "Growth in grace is a most blessed thing in its right place . . . but it can never bring us *to the death of the old man* [i.e. of the evil nature within us] nor therefore to the experience of entire sanctification" (*Theology of Holiness*, pp. 5, 9).

Yes, the theory that sanctification is necessarily instantaneous is a travelling companion of the idea that hereditary depravity may be utterly eradicated. Therefore, if the theory of "eradication" be found erroneous, then also the theory of necessary instantaneousness collapses along with it. But *is* the "eradication" theory wrong? I believe that it is; and one of my earnest purposes in this book is to *prove* it wrong. Those beloved brethren who have taught "eradication", have thought that others who differed from them did not "go all the way" with the written Word of God; but it will be our endeavour to show exegetically that perhaps this has been unsuspectedly true of themselves, and that there is something better even than eradication! After all, as any doctor will tell you, eradicative surgery, however brilliant, is a form of defeat, an admission of failure to heal without resort to the knife! Would not any doctor prefer to defeat cancer by *cure*, rather than by surgically removing it and leaving the body prone to further recurrence of the deadly malignancy?

Eradicationist contradiction

Eradicationists, from saintly John Wesley downwards, seem to contradict themselves as to this instantaneousness, which fact itself may well arouse our suspicions that their doctrine is fallacious. Wesley admits, "As in the natural birth a man is born at once, and then grows larger and stronger by degrees, so in the spiritual birth, a man is born at once, and then gradually increases in spiritual stature and strength. The new birth, therefore, is the first point in sanctification, which may increase more and more unto the perfect day" (*Sermons*, vol. 2, p. 390). So after all there *may* be gradual increase in sanctification!

A. M. Hills tells us that "the great growth of the soul into Christian maturity comes *after* the sanctifying gift of the Holy Spirit, but does not precede it". Yet Hills agrees that "the new birth begins with the love of God shed abroad in the heart by the Holy Spirit"; and that "*any* grace already in possession may be *increased*" (*Holiness and Power*, pp. 320–22, 128). So we have the strange mix-up that this "growth in grace" comes only *after* sanctification; yet "any grace already in possession may be increased" *before* sanctification! The able exponent admits what he denies, namely, that there can be *gradual* sanctification. If we ask *why* there is this discrepancy in holiness writings, especially in those of the so-called "eradication" school, I think the answer is not far to seek.

A Needful Distinction

To begin with, there has not been enough care always to distinguish between sanctification and "*entire* sanctification". Obviously there cannot be degrees in *entire* sanctification, for the simple reason that it *is* entire; but prior to that there *can* be degrees of sanctification; there can be degrees of yielding and trusting on the human side, and corresponding degrees of response on the divine side. When Paul would have the Thessalonians "sanctified *wholly*" (1 Thess. 5: 23) does he not imply that they were already sanctified *partly* (see 1 Cor. 1: 2, and 6: 11). Was he envisaging a jump from *no* sanctification to *all* sanctification? And when John would have us "made *perfect* in love" (1 John

4: 18) does he not obviously imply that there are degrees? Or must it be the vast leap from *no* love to *all* love?

Why, even viewing sanctification in the strictly eradicationist way, as a divine destruction of innate sin, cannot there be degrees of such destruction? Not only Scripture, but experience comes to our aid here. A Christian man once described his conversion to me in somewhat the following wording. "For years before my conversion I knew that I needed to get right with my Maker and Judge. For years I knew that in Christ He had become man's Saviour. For years I fought against His interference in my life, and knowingly refused the slightest response to His existence. Then, through a variety of circumstances I fell under a frightening sense of conviction. I knew with a burning torture that I had sinned against special light and peculiar privilege; and I realised that I was more deeply damned than the proudest Pharisee or the blackest felon in jail. Strangely enough, with my midnight of fear there came also a pitiful yearning to know and please God if that were still possible. Then, one night, under the preaching of a simple Gospel sermon, the pent-up flood of my repentance broke loose. The love of Christ utterly conquered me, with no resistance on my part, but only an eager willingness to be conquered. I knew, with an inward relief and certainty, which no words could tell, that my awful guilt was washed away in the atoning blood of Calvary, and that I was truly saved. In that glorious moment, every worldly ambition, every appetite for fleshly pleasure, every hankering after earthly glamour, passed away, and they have never returned; for I became 'a new creature' in Christ, and I wanted nothing henceforth but to live for Him alone."

Well, that transforming earthquake of the soul occurred at *conversion*, not at some later point of sanctification. Our brethren who insist that sanctification necessarily comes *later* than regeneration may truly argue that even after such a radical conversion the saved man would still find the so-called "old nature" within him, yet the fact remains that in the conversion itself, there was a divine work which went to the depths of the human personality, uprooting and renewing. Moreover, what God did in that man's soul at conversion was the same in its *nature*, even though not in its *extent*, as what God does in sanctification. Surely, then, it is wrong to say so sharply that there are no possible *degrees* in the experience of sanctification. What needs to be made plain is that only in *entire* sanctification is the entire blessing realised.

Positive Aspects

We gratefully revel in John Wesley's glorious insistence on "perfect love" as the *essence* of sanctification. He says, "Scriptural perfection is pure love filling the heart, and governing all the words and actions". Our conviction is that he thereby puts the supreme emphasis where Scripture puts it. In its truest and sublimest meaning, sanctification is the all-purifying love of God flooding the heart and mind and soul. But are there not *degrees* in our human experience and possession of that love? And does it not purify or sanctify us just to the degree in which it indwells us? In that sense, at least, may there not be gradualness in sanctification? I know that when the heart is utterly subdued, purified, and *filled* with the divine love, we have reached "*entire* sanctification"; but surely such fulness or entirety is a "maximum" *degree* of what precedes; not a detached "absolute". John Wesley simply could not help admitting this when he wrote: "Love is the sum of Christian sanctification; it is the one kind of holiness which is found in various *degrees* in believers."

It is the same when we regard entire sanctification as a purifying fulness of spiritual *life*. The fulness which sanctifies entirely is a maximum of something already possessed in *degree*. Again and again Wesley is obliged to acknowledge this, despite his usual insistence on the instantaneousness of sanctification.

In Conclusion

What, then, do we conclude? Is sanctification instantaneous or gradual? Well, as we have said, we must distinguish between "sanctification" and "*entire* sanctification". The former may be partial, in different degrees, and progressive. The latter, just because it *is* "entire" is entered at a certain cross-over point, and in that sense *must* be instantaneous.

But (it may be asked) if entire sanctification can thus be the final point of a gradual process, how can it be outstandingly a "*second* blessing"? The answer is ready to hand. The two all-determining crises of the Christian life are regeneration (which brings *newness* of life) and entire sanctification (which brings *fulness* of life). All in-between crises are subsidiary, and are meant to lead from the one to the other. A sharp contrast between the two is, that before regeneration there are *no* degrees—for there are no degrees in death; whereas before entire sanctification there is spiritual life in varying stages of growth. Now while entire sanctification truly *may* come as the comparatively unobtrusive completion of a steady progress, yet with most of us it comes in a critical or momentous form which emphasises its "second-crisis" nature. Our experience usually runs somewhat as follows.

At our conversion, we become "born of the Spirit", and go on our way rejoicing in "newness of life". Later we encounter the problem of the "wretched man" in Romans 7: "sin that dwelleth in me". We learn also, however, that in Christ there is not only forgiveness for sins, but provision against indwelling *sin*; that in Him there is not only positional justification, but practical *sanctification*; that besides being "born of the Spirit", we may be "*filled with the Spirit*"; that besides the impartation of new life at regeneration, there may be a renewal of our very *nature,* with all its inclinations, through entire sanctification. We begin "seeking the blessing". By this time we know that the "way in" is utter consecration and then appropriation by faith alone, both of which are obnoxious and painful to "the flesh". We struggle toward the point of abandonment to Christ. All the higher strata of our being endorse the immediate desirability of this. Intellect says we could not do anything higher. Reason says we could not do anything wiser. Conscience says we could not do anything better. But there is an evil substratum, call it "the flesh" or what we may, which bitterly opposes this to the last inch. So the bosom bleeds with civil war. Some give up and sink back. Those of us who struggle on now find ourselves with Jacob at Peniel. We begin to discern that it is the Holy Spirit who is precipitating the crisis, and that instead of *our* wrestling for the blessing, it is *God* who is wrestling with *us,* to overthrow our stubborn selfism! We recognise Him. We are beaten. We can only cling. He breaks our thigh. But we still cling and cry, "I will not let Thee go except Thou bless me!" The moment of moments comes; we utterly abandon ourselves to Him; somehow faith suddenly becomes easy; we claim the promise; the Holy Spirit sweeps in upon us; the inward witness to entire sanctification flames up within our consciousness! The blessing is ours! Is it any wonder that thereafter some refer to it as the "*second* blessing"?

Yes, entire sanctification *may* come gradually, as earlier explained, but far more often it comes in suchwise as we have just described. The Holy Spirit would fain cut short a needlessly long-drawn process, and bring on the decisive crisis at the earliest point.

Finally, if entire sanctification is wrought *immediately* by the infilling of the Holy Spirit, how can there possibly be gradualness in *that*? Again the answer is clear. We must distinguish the infilling itself from its *manifestations*. Where entire sanctification is the sudden outcome of a dramatic soul-struggle, the fulness of the Spirit may come as a consuming fire, or as a "rushing mighty wind", or as a prostrating subduement, or as an overwhelming immersion, in which case its immediateness is emphasized. On the other hand, where there has been a gradual progress toward entire sanctification, the act of completive consecration and appropriation may *not* be accompanied by such tumultuous emotional experiences ; yet the infilling is just as real and immediate.

But in whichever way entire sanctification is reached, and in whichever way the Holy Spirit infills, if the entirely sanctified believer *abides* in the blessing by faith and love and prayer, there certainly will be inward emotional attestations, from time to time, and probably outward attestations too. Our supreme concern must be the urging of all Christian believers to *seek* the blessing of entire sanctification, not by a gradual process, even though it sometimes comes that way, but at the earliest point, by utter yielding and trusting. We should urge believers to the *crisis*-point of this "second" divine intervention in the soul. Long ago, when the Israelites were to enter Canaan, God brought them to a crisis-point, first at Kadesh-barnea, where they failed and sank back ; second at the Jordan, where they obeyed, trusted, crossed over, and actually entered the inheritance. It could have been gradual, piecemeal, bit by bit ; but why drag out the operation? As soon as ever Israel was ready, God designed the cross-over as one, concentrated act. The whole thing lights up with vivid significance for Christian believers today because of Paul's comment on it in I Corinthians 10: 6, "Now these things happened *as types for us*".

DEDUCTION

> *From regeneration onwards there certainly can be degrees of experiential sanctification, corresponding to degrees of yieldedness: but "entire" sanctification must necessarily begin instantaneously since it begins precisely at the crisis-point of utter hand-over to the divine posession.*

THE FOUR BIG DELIVERANCES

In this chapter we cannot avoid some brief, incidental re-treading of ground more fully covered in our companion volume, *A New Call to Holiness*. Some who read these pages may not have read that volume, and for them this shorter reference to the Romans epistle is necessary here.

J.S.B.

"It is always a marvel to me that the street preacher goes straight to the point in Paul, and finds all his answers where the ninety-and-nine just men find all their difficulties."

Principal James Denney.

"In our study of the Scriptures, etymology or word-study, by itself, may often mislead us; attention to context always safeguards us."

Dr. William Evans.

THE FOUR BIG DELIVERANCES

To UNDERSTAND most easily and clearly what the New Testament teaches us about the Holy Spirit's deeper work of sanctification in us, perhaps the best and safest beginning is to see *the four big deliverances* which are opened up to us in Paul's Epistle to the Romans. Seeing those four deliverances as they successively occur in that epistle not only makes plain God's method of dealing with our innate predisposition to sin, and His way of begetting holiness within us, it guards us from certain errors of interpretation which have tripped all too many into delusion. No verse in the New Testament has been more of a battle-focus between rival theories of holiness than Romans 6: 6.

"Knowing this, that our old man is crucified with Him, that the body of sin might be destroyed, that henceforth we should not serve sin."

This is said by holiness teachers of the Wesley succession to teach a complete *eradication* of the so-called "old nature" or "old man" or "body of sin" in the believer. By others it is limited to teaching that the inbred evil is rendered more or less "powerless" or "inoperative".

Eradicationists on Romans 6: 6

John Wesley comments on Romans 6: 6, "I use the word, 'destroyed', because St. Paul does: 'suspended' I cannot find in the Bible" (*Letters* 4, p. 203). Again he says, "The body of sin, the carnal mind, must be destroyed: the old man must be slain, or we cannot put on the new man" (*Christian Perfection*, pp. 54, 55).

Dr. Daniel Steele writes, "The Greek for 'destroy' is never used by Paul in the sense of rendering inactive, as those assert who insist that the root of sin is not killed till it is plucked up by old Mortality himself" (*Half Hours with Paul*, p. 10).

Dr. Asa Mahan, also, comments on Romans 6: 6, "All admit that the terms, 'sin that dwelleth in us', the 'body of sin', the 'old man', the 'law of sin and death', the 'body of this death', mean the same thing, and constitute what is called 'indwelling sin'. What then do the Scriptures mean by such expressions as these: 'That the body of sin might be destroyed', 'Our old man is crucified with Him'? No dogma can be more obviously unscriptural than is that of the non-destruction of the body of sin in believers" (*Autobiography*, p. 344). Many other such eradicationist comments on Romans 6: 6 might be given, but the foregoing are sufficiently representative.

Counteractionists on Romans 6: 6

Recently I read a booklet by a well-known spokesman of the *counteractionist* theory. Understandably, *he* wants to *weaken* the word, "destroyed", in Romans 6:6. He says: "What does the word, 'destroyed', mean? It is translated seventeen different ways, the general meaning expressing the root of the Greek word, which means 'lazy'. . . . In four of the five times it is rendered 'destroyed' that is the sense in which it is used. Thus, in Hebrews 2: 14, 'that He might *destroy* . . . the devil', that great being is not made non-existent, but inoperative, for he is finally cast *alive* into the lake of fire. This single word in Romans 6: 6, then, is a very slender and uncertain basis upon which to make the claim 'that the body of sin might be made non-existent', as is taught by some, or, in other words, eradicated. . . . God's process, as expressed here, is to make the sinful nature *inoperative*".

Another able writer, an "undisputed authority" on the counteractionist theory, after somewhat similar comment adds, "The very fact that the 'law of the Spirit of life' (Rom. 8:2) is ever a continual necessity [in the believer] is a proof that the 'law of sin and death' is not extinct [in the believer] but is simply *counteracted*".

Now unbelievable though it may seem to some of us who have long been taught either the eradicationist or the counteractionist idea of Romans 6: 6, that text, when rightly interpreted in keeping with its location in the structure of the Romans epistle, has nothing whatever to do with sin in the believer. Those two phrases, "our old man" and the "body of sin", do *not* refer to a suppositionary sinful "old nature" inside each of us (as we now hope to show). Therefore all the arguing as to whether "crucified" means outright eradication or only counteraction is rendered irrelevant. I have gone into this more fully in my book, *A*

New Call to Holiness, so I need only revert to it abbreviatedly here.

Romans in Perspective

Scan the Romans epistle again. Catch its main movements in perspective. After a brief introduction (1: 1–16) Paul first shows the *need* for the Gospel (1: 17–3: 20). Both Jews and Gentiles need it for the same two reasons: (1) both have "sinned" and are therefore *legally guilty*, (2) both are "in sin" as a condition and are therefore *morally corrupt*. Mark that well: the twofold plight of man is "sins" (plural) and "sin" (singular):

> (1) "SINS"—accumulated *transgressions*
> (2) "SIN" —an hereditary *corruption*

As soon as Paul has shown this twofold need—"sins" and "sin", he proceeds to expound how the Gospel *deals* with it. This runs right on to the end of chapter 8. All through those first eight chapters of Romans the subject is, *how the Gospel saves the sinner*.

THE FOUR BIG DELIVERANCES

The methodical progress of Paul's masterly exposition is fascinating and unmistakable. First he shows how the Gospel deals with *sins* (3: 21–5: 11). Then he shows how the Gospel deals with *sin* (5: 12–8: 39). There is no doubt about the sharp break at chapter 5: 12 from "sins" (plural) to "sin" (singular). Up to that point "sin" (singular) occurs only three times, whereas afterwards it is the main subject.

Judicial versus Experiential

Now it is noticeable that in both those sections Paul follows the same procedure. In both parts he first tells us how the Gospel deals with the problem *judicially*, and then how it deals with the problem *experientially*.

Take the section on *sins* (plural). First Paul explains how the Gospel answers the problem of man's transgressions and guilt *judicially*. Justification is provided through the substitutionary atonement and imputed righteousness of Christ (3: 21–4: 25). After that, Paul shows how this justification by faith is registered in our human *experience*: "Being justified by faith *we have* . . .

and the love of God is shed *in our hearts* by the Holy Spirit"
(5: 1–11).

Take the second section, on *sin* (hereditary). First Paul shows
how the Gospel deals with this in the *judicial reckoning* of God
(5: 12–7: 6). Deliverance from our hereditary involvement in
Adam's sin is provided on the principle of new federal headship,
or transference from being in the "old man", i.e. Adam, to being
in the "new man", i.e. Christ. Finally he shows how hereditary
sin-proclivity ("sin that dwelleth in me") is dealt with *experientially* (7: 7–8: 39). It is by the new "law of the Spirit of life in
Christ Jesus" which operates in the regenerated Christian believer.

See this methodical progress more sharply delineated in the
following flat analysis of the eight chapters, and then ask yourself:
What does the location of chapter 6: 6 tell us about its meaning?

THE FIRST EIGHT CHAPTERS OF ROMANS
SUBJECT: HOW THE GOSPEL SAVES THE SINNER

Introduction 1: 1–15.   Key, 1: 16, 17.
The twofold need: "Sins" and "Sin": 1: 18–3: 20.

THE GOSPEL ANSWER AS TO "SINS" (3: 21–5: 11).

(a) *Judicially* (3: 21–4: 25).
Justification is through the substitutionary work of Christ
appropriated by faith (imputed righteousness).

(b) *Experientially* (5: 1–11).
Justification by faith brings peace with God. His love is
shed in us by the Holy Spirit.

THE GOSPEL ANSWER AS TO "SIN" (5: 12–8: 39).

(a) *Judicially* (5: 12–7: 6).
Deliverance from racial death through racial sin is on
the principle of new federal headship.

(b) *Experientially* (7: 7–8: 39).
"Sin that dwelleth in me" is now so counteracted by
the indwelling Holy Spirit that the "wretched man" is
transformed into "more than conqueror"!

Well, does that sixth chapter, with its controversial sixth verse
about the crucifixion of the "old man", occur in the section which
deals with inward *experience*? No, it does not. It has to do solely
with the objective and judicial aspect of our salvation through the
Cross, not the subjective and experiential. How this can have been
so generally unperceived is a puzzle, except that we know how

wonderfully unseeing many of us can become when held by an hallucinating theory.

As soon as we see that Romans 6 has to do with God's objective and judicial dealing with racial sin (not with interior individual sin-bent—which Paul deals with later) we find confirmations leaping up everywhere around us. To begin with, the original Greek does not say, "Our old man *is* crucified" (as in the King James Version), but "Our old man *was* crucified", indicating a past crucifixion, over and done with. The "old man" is not a suppositionary "old nature" in the believer, but a Paulinism for the whole human race in Adam (more of that later). There is not a fleck of suggestion anywhere in the New Testament that the once-for-all judicial putting away of that "old man" through the cross of Christ is to have a present-tense, subjective counterpart or simulated re-enactment in the inward *experience* of the Christian believer.

Confirming this, in chapters 6 and 7 all the verbs, "died", "baptized", "buried", "crucified", "destroyed", "freed", "made dead", "delivered", in verses 2, 3, 4, 6, 7, 8, 10, 18, 22, 7: 4, 7: 6, are aorists, referring to a past, historical, objective occurrence, not to some present and continuing experience in the believer.

Many a Christian, seeking victory over sin and self, has been exhorted, "Believe that your 'old nature' is crucified with Christ, and then, as Romans 6: 11 says, 'Reckon yourself to be dead indeed unto sin' ". And how many have thus "reckoned" themselves dead indeed unto sin, only to find they were *not* so, despite their most desperate reckoning! How many have similarly struggled to persist in reckoning what they have known to be unreal until they have made themselves ill!

When that eleventh verse says, "*Likewise,* reckon . . ." it connects with the preceding verse, which says that our Lord "died unto sin *epaphax*"—which Greek word means *once for all*. We are to reckon ourselves dead to sin "likewise", in that once-for-all way. How then can it possibly refer to our inward sin-proneness? —for no Christian in history ever had such a once-for-all, absolute inward death to sin. What verse 11 actually *does* mean is, that since in the judicial reckoning of God we died with Christ in His once-for-all penalty-bearing, guilt-removing death on the Cross, we are now to reckon ourselves once-for-all "dead indeed" to Sin and the Law in a *judicial* sense, inasmuch as their death-penalty upon us has been executed, and they can exact no more. Exactly the same is taught in 2 Corinthians 5: 14, "One died for all, therefore *all* died". Thank God, in Christ we *are* "dead once-for-all" to Sin as a guilt-inflicter, and to the Law as a penalty-exactor! We are *legally* freed because we legally died, so that being now *"risen* with Christ" to "newness of life" we should serve God as born-anew persons, with no cloud of guilt between us and Him.

If further corroboration is required that what we are saying about Romans 6: 6 is true, all one has to do is to look up the *terminology* employed throughout the context (5: 12–7: 6). It is all about the "law" (5: 13, 20, 6: 14, 15, 7: 1–6).

Another indication that the whole passage is judicial is the *non-mention of the Holy Spirit* anywhere in it (5: 12–7: 6). If the passage referred to inward sanctification the Holy Spirit assuredly would be mentioned, for everywhere in New Testament teaching He is the effecting Agent in experiential salvation.

A further confirmation is the way Paul himself *applies* the sixth chapter of Romans. What he states in chapter 6 he illustrates and applies in chapter 7: 1–6. This is how he applies it: "Wherefore, my brethren, ye also were made *DEAD TO THE LAW*".

Yes, all the way through, it is a past, once-for-all death in a judicial sense. It has nothing to do with an inward death of some supposed "old nature". See it clearly as one of the four big deliverances which are progressively expounded to us in Romans:

1. Deliverance from SINS (3: 21–4: 25) — *objectively and judicially,* justification through the atonement and imputed righteousness of Christ.

2. Deliverance from SINS (5: 1–11) — *inwardly and experientially,* "peace with God", the "love of God shed" within by the Holy Spirit.

3. Deliverance from SIN (5: 12–7: 6) — *objectively and judicially,* by transference from the headship of the "old man" to that of the "new man".

4. Deliverance from SIN (7: 7–8: 39) — *inwardly and experientially,* through "the law of the Spirit of life in Christ".

The Baptismal Symbol

Another evidence that the death to sin which Romans 6 teaches is *not* a death in present experience, but a non-repeatable *judicial* death, is that Paul connects it back with the baptism of those early believers. It is not a death effected *now*, but a death professed *then*. Read the opening verses of the chapter again (which we here quote from the English Revised Version) because the Authorized Version blurs the aorist tenses.

"What shall we say then? Shall we continue in sin that grace may abound? God forbid. We who *DIED* to sin, how shall we any longer live therein? Or are ye ignorant that all we who *WERE BAPTIZED* into Christ Jesus were baptized into His death? We *WERE BURIED* therefore with Him through baptism into death: that like as Christ was raised from the dead through the glory of the Father, so we also might walk in newness of life."

The verbs in capitals are all aorists, indicating a completed action in the past. Note that the "we who *died* to sin" and the "we were *buried* with Him" evidently synchronise with "were *baptized* into His death". So, as plainly as wording can make it, that death had been symbolized as an already completed act at the public baptism of those long-ago Christians.

Most commentators agree that the reference there *is* to water baptism. There is pretty general agreement, also, that at least the *original* mode of baptism was by immersion—an immersion which, of course, pictorially represented a burial of the old life and a rising into the new. Even the Roman Catholic Bible (Confraternity Edition) has a marginal note to verse 4, "Baptism was ordinarily conferred in the primitive Church by immersion". So far as I know, denominational difference as to baptism is not on the meaning of the Greek word, *baptizo*, which is commonly admitted to mean immersion.

I am glad, also, to find that very few expositors tax their wit to make the baptism in Romans 6: 1–4 a purely *spiritual* baptism. Those dear brethren who *do* try to make it mean a purely spiritual baptism certainly prove themselves masters in the art of verbal circumlocution—as any interested student can verify by looking up their commentaries. The baptism in Romans 6: 1–4 *must* be the rite of water baptism if for no other reason than this, that it was a baptism into *death*, whereas in the New Testament *spiritual* baptism is never a baptism into death, but an immersion into the Holy Spirit, the "Spirit of *life* in Christ Jesus".

We need not debate incidental points. There is sufficient agreement that the death and burial referred to in Romans 6 were *past*, and were symbolized in the rite of water baptism. How decisive, then, are those past tenses! "We who *died* to sin . . . were *baptized* into His *death*. We were *buried* . . . through baptism into *death*." Plainly the death taught in Romans 6 is not a death yet to be effected in the believer's inward condition; much less is it a maintained condition of *dying*. It is a death as completely past and done with as our Lord's own crucifixion. Therefore it *must* be a judicial death, and *cannot* be a present interior death.

New Testament Testimony

Another factor which has a decisive bearing on our interpretation of Romans 6 is, that not once, anywhere in the New Testament, is the believer's death with Christ, or death to sin, spoken of as taking place in the present, or as being a continuous dying. The following are all the references. They should be looked up in a version other than the King James, as the latter does not truly translate the aorist tenses. Romans 6: 2, 4, 7, 8, 10, 11, and 7: 4. 2 Corinthians 5: 14, Galatians 2: 19, 20, Colossians 2: 20, 3: 3, 2 Timothy 2: 11, 1 Peter 2: 24. So far as I know, there we have all the data. Not one of those texts speaks of a present dying or becoming dead. (See our fuller comment on them in Appendix, *New Testament Verb-tenses and the Believer's Death to Sin,* p. 235.) And in line with all this, does not the aorist tense in Romans 6:6 make it similarly clear that it does *not* teach a present, experiential death or dying to sin inside the believer? Is is not equally clear that theories of holiness by a present, inward continuing crucifixion with Christ are mistaken?

That "Wretched Man"

The only other factor we mention here is the "wretched man" at the end of chapter 7. There he is, groaning, "The good that I would do, I do not; but the evil which I would not, that I do." "It is no more I that do it, but sin that dwelleth in me." "Oh, wretched man that I am! Who shall deliver me?" What a problem that "wretched man" is to all those theories which tell us that Romans 6 teaches either the "eradicating" or the "rendering in-operative" of the so-called "old nature"! If Romans 6 teaches *that*, how is it that right after it, in chapter 7, we are back again at, "Oh, wretched man that I am! Who shall deliver me?" Among all the various interpretations which I have come across, not one of them alters this fact, that if Romans 6 teaches the way of inward victory and sanctification, then that "wretched man" of chapter 7 is a strange drop-back, an anti-climax, a sudden denial of all that Paul has just said.

THE TRUE MEANING OF ROMANS 6

What then does Romans 6: 6 really teach? We have seen that the crucifixion of which it speaks is a past, once-for-all, judicial death; but what does Paul mean by our "old man"? The only other two places where the expression occurs are Ephesians 4: 22–24 and Colossians 3: 9, 10, both of which tell us that believers have "put off" the "old man" and have "put on" the "new man". Therefore the "old man" simply cannot be an evil old nature within us, for *we* can no more "put off" our hereditary sin-bent than we can regenerate ourselves.

Let it be emphasized repeatedly: we must fling away that wrong idea of innate sin as a kind of evil *entity* inside us, a so-called "old nature" distinct from the basic human self. It is that idea of "two natures" in the believer—an "old" and a "new", which has fostered the eradicationist error that our hereditary sin-bias can be removed by spiritual surgery as a malignant growth can be removed from the physical body. We must rather think of sin as blight in a tree, or as a disease in the human blood-stream. Our sin-infection is coextensive with our whole mental and moral nature.

We often hear it said that at conversion to Christ we receive a "new nature". That also is unscriptural. At our regeneration we receive, not a new "nature", but a new spiritual *life* which regener-ates *us*—and interpenetrates the one human nature which we really *are*. Just as our hereditary sin-infection is coextensive with our nature, so is the regenerating new spiritual life which has come to us through our union with the risen Saviour.

When Paul says that our "old man" was crucified with Christ he means *THE WHOLE HUMAN RACE IN ADAM*. Chapter 6, remember, is a continuation from chapter 5, where Paul contrasts the "one man", Adam, through whom "the many were made sinners", and the "one Man", Christ, through whom "the many are made righteous". It is all about the "*old* man" and the "*new* Man". Romans 6: 6 completes it by telling us that in the judicial reckoning of God the "*old* man" was once-for-all put away.

Now Paul says that the "old man" was crucified with Christ

"that the *body of sin* might be destroyed". What is the "body of sin"? That, too, is a figurative phrase. It cannot mean our *physical* body (as some have argued because it is the "instrument" or "vehicle" of sin) for the physical body has never been jointly "crucified" or "destroyed" or "done away" in one completed act (aorist)!

Nor can the "body of sin" mean a supposed lump-mass or *aggregate* of sin somewhere inside us (a so-called "old nature"), as though sin were a "foreign body" in the system (as doctors would say). Many of those who hug the error that the "old man" and the "body of sin" both mean the "self-nature", the "carnal" nature, the "Adam nature", "inbred sin", etc., insist on thinning down the words, "that the body of sin might be destroyed", making them mean no more than "that the body of sin might be *rendered inoperative*"—which at once exposes how wrong their crucifixion theory is; for when a person has been crucified, in one completed past act, does it much matter whether we say he has been "destroyed", or "rendered inoperative", or "nullified", or "done away"? The effect is the same any way!

Those who would fain restrict Romans 6: 6 to mean that our so-called "old nature" is pinioned to the Cross, struggling but fastened, not yet dead but "rendered inoperative", are obviously much astray; for when a man has been *"crucified"* (as the text says, in the aorist tense) he is not merely dying, he is *dead*. That is how Romans 6: 6 plainly uses the words, "crucified", and "destroyed", therefore it cannot refer to our so-called "corrupt self", for in no Christian's experience has there been such an absolute death to sin.

By the "body of sin" Paul means figuratively, the whole *physical* part of the old humanity in Adam. Just as the new humanity in Christ is called His "body" (see the "new man" in Ephesians 2: 15 with the "body" in chapter 3: 6), and as the Church is called His "body" (Rom. 12: 5, 1 Cor. 12: 27, Eph. 1: 23, etc.), so all the members of the Adam race, in the aggregate, are figuratively *his* "body".

That the two phrases, "our old man" and "the body of sin" are simply two aspects of the same thing is made clear by the fact that the one is "crucified" that the other might be "destroyed". There is coming a time when the whole physical creation in Adam will be done away *actually*; but even now it is done away judicially. That is why our Lord said, *"Now* is the judgment of this world"

(John 12: 31). Up till then the Adam race, as such, had been
on probation. The Cross marked its final failure. It was judged
and judicially done away. That is why 2 Corinthians 5: 16 says,
"Henceforth we know no man after the flesh" (i.e. in Adam),
for if any man be in Christ, he is (in) a new creation." That is
why, also, in Romans 8: 10, Paul says, "If Christ be in you, the
body is dead, because of sin"—not *physically* dead, of course,
but in a judicial sense, inasmuch as the "old man" (the old Adam
humanity) was judicially put away in the death of Christ (2 Cor.
5: 14). So, then this is the meaning of Romans 6: 6—

"OUR OLD MAN	—all that we were by position and relation in Adam, with all our culpability and condemnation ;
"WAS CRUCIFIED WITH HIM	—was judged and executed in the One-for-all death of Christ ;
"THAT THE BODY OF SIN	—the whole Adam humanity as guilty before God ;
"MIGHT BE DESTROYED	—completely done away in the judicial reckoning of God ;
"THAT WE SHOULD NO LONGER BE IN BONDAGE TO SIN"	—that is, no longer in *legal* bondage through *judicial* guilt.

Once we see that this is the true purport of Romans 6: 6, we
find endorsements of it by parallel with other New Testament pro-
nouncements such as Galatians 2: 20 and 5: 24. We need not
go into that here, however, as it is covered in our companion
volume, *A New Call to Holiness*.

THOSE FOUR BIG DELIVERANCES

Dear Christian believer, as we press on through these chapters
to a new definition and understanding of Scriptural holiness, I
ask you at this point to get clearly in your mind those four big
deliverances which are expounded in the Epistle to the Romans.
This will safeguard you from the several big errors which have
complicated the subject and have erected wrong signposts for
pilgrims seeking "the way of holiness". If our own pages just now
seem to suggest that the subject is complicated, that is solely

because we are trying to remove well-intending but misleading theory based on faulty exegesis of Scripture. Soon now we shall be through to where we can set forth simply enough the deeper message of the Word on inward sanctification.

Meanwhile, take another steady look at those four big deliverances in Romans. As we survey them let us thank God for their wonderful reality. The first three we have now briefly considered:

1. Our *judicial* deliverance from the guilt and condemnation of our *sins*, through the imputed righteousness of Christ who was "delivered up for our offences and was raised again for our justification" (3: 21–4: 25).
2. Our *experiential* deliverance from the inward sense of *sins* and guilt, through a Spirit-wrought inward realization of our justification, and the "love of God shed abroad in our hearts" (5: 1–11).
3. Our *judicial* deliverance from the bondage of hereditary sinnership in the old Adam-humanity (the *"old* man") through a divinely reckoned identification with Christ by whose representative death the old man was put away; and by our union with Him as the *"New* Man" (5: 12–7: 6).

So we have deliverance both legally and inwardly from *sins*; and we have deliverance legally from hereditary sinnership in the "old man" Adam humanity. But there is a *fourth* deliverance which we all need, that is, an inward, vital, experiential deliverance from "*sin that dwelleth in me*". That is the wonderful deliverance which transforms the "wretched man" of chapter 7 into the "more than conqueror" of chapter 8.

Oh, how many Christian believers there are who, although they gratefully rejoice in the first three, are wearily sighing to know the victorious release of the *fourth*! How often they groan in bondage to "sin that dwelleth in me"! How often they secretly sigh, "Oh, wretched man that I am! Who shall deliver me?" In what sackcloth and ashes of exasperating defeat and helpless mourning they travel through their days on earth, always feeling that somehow there must be some secret of deliverance and victory through Christ, yet not knowing how to find it or bring it into operation! Many of them have followed the usual theory of sanctification, yielding themselves in full surrender to Christ, then, believing that the "old nature" (that fictitious bogey) was now "crucified with Christ" they have "reckoned" themselves to be "dead indeed unto sin"—only to find, in agonizing disillusionment, that "sin which dwelleth in me" was no more dead than before! Perhaps some who now read these pages are among the many who have had that experience.

All of us need to understand *truly* what Scripture teaches about the promised deliverance and victory; for error, even the most attractive and spiritually-minded, always ends in some ironic recoil or further bondage. So, with least possible delay, we shall enquire carefully into that *fourth* big deliverance which the Romans epistle sets before us: "The law of the Spirit of life in Christ Jesus hath *set me free* from the law of sin and death" (Rom. 8: 2). Meanwhile, however, if you and I would most transparently understand that spiritual liberation, we need to push out of our thinking two widely taught, much-respected errors which hang like a confusing mist over the subject. Those two are: (1) the "identification theory" and (2) the prevalent fallacy of "two natures" in the Christian believer. We shall "encounter" them in our next two chapters.

THE "IDENTIFICATION" THEORY

"Again, at this point, we would remind the reader that although in these midway chapters we are having to pick our way through thickets of well-meant errors, the subject of Christian holiness itself need never have become so seemingly involved as its human exponents have made it. The fault is not in the Scripture data, but in earth-spun theories. Let it be kept patiently in mind that we are cutting back through present complexity to what we believe is the original reality in its Scriptural simplicity."

J.S.B.

THE "IDENTIFICATION" THEORY

WE ARE now well on the way to fulfilling our special aim in these studies, which is to present lucidly the New Testament teaching on heart purity or practical sanctification. However, lying athwart our path there are two popular errors which we must here disprove if we are to exhibit the truth itself in sharp enough distinction from theoretic subtleties. The first of these is what is known as the *"identification"* way of sanctification.

The teaching is, that through identification with the Cross of Christ the "self-life" or "old nature" in the Christian believer may be put to death, or at least effectively put out of action. It was supposedly nailed there with Christ, in virtue of which I may now "reckon" (and prove) myself "dead indeed unto sin".

It will be our endeavour in the next few pages to show that this theory is wrong. But before we dare to make our first comment on it we pay sincere tribute to the many gifted, earnest brethren who preach it (as I myself used to do). They are such valorous servants of our dear Lord that it is not easy to disagree with them. Let it be understood, therefore, that amid our frankness there is utmost brotherly esteem.

Now as already observed, those New Testament texts which speak of our identification with the Cross nowhere teach a *present* joint-crucifixion of the believer's so-called "old nature" with our Lord. How *could* they teach such a plain impossibility? How *could* this present hereditary condition of yours and mine today have been crucified with Jesus nineteen hundred years ago? Must we not brand such an idea as strange credulity?

Yet for so long now has that idea been one of the main axles on which the wheels of conventional holiness teaching rotate, that many of us evangelical preachers and writers simply *assume* its Scripturalness, and apparently suppose that the holiness message would break down without it. For instance, coincidentally with my writing these lines a magazine comes to hand in which an excellent preacher says,

"I—that old bankrupt, sinful nature with which I was born, as the fallen seed of the fallen Adam—'I am crucified with Christ' (judged, sentenced, executed, and buried); 'nevertheless I live, yet not I, but Christ liveth in me'."

Think of it (for it represents the usual teaching), the "old, bankrupt, sinful nature" in you and me today is *actually* "executed and ·buried" by an experiential identification with our *Lord's* crucifixion centuries ago! To know what well-meaning make-believe the theory is, all you need do is ask that dear brother, "Is your 'old sinful nature', then, *really* dead to sin? Is all unholy thought, desire, motive, irritation, inclination, utterly non-existent now?" Of course he might resort (as many do) to the usual expedient of saying that we must "*reckon* our old nature to be dead despite appearance". Yet to keep on making oneself "reckon" so when it is not true to experience is a self-delusion which usually exacts painful vengeance later on.

This theory of an experiential identification with the crucifixion, death, and burial of our Lord is firmly entrenched in various holiness conventions. Honoured names are associated with it. Simply out of cordial respect for such I leave my next quotations anonymous, so that we may think exclusively of the *subject,* without any reflection whatever on brethren whom I regard as far worthier than I. With rhetorical vigour an eloquent preacher of recent days suggests the following soliloquy:

"Have you ever done this: have you said to your sinful self—that self for which there is no healing medicine except death; have you ever said to that sinful self, 'My sinful self, thou hateful thing, breaking out now in pride, and now in passion, and now in jealousy, and now in indolence, and now in selfishness, breaking out in a thousand hateful forms; my sinful self, I put thee where the sinless Christ put thee, on the Cross; hang there, for God has put thee there. I choose of my own will, that thou shalt hang in the place where God has chosen to put thee—on the Cross of Calvary'?
"Here is the secret of victory! Reckon on this glorious fact; reckon yourself dead in the death of Christ, and dare to say, 'In Him I am dead to sin'."

How impressive it sounds! Yet what pathetic error it expresses! How nobly emotional it is! Yet what a galling illusion it hugs! How confidently it pledges deliverance! Yet what a forlorn hope it proves! If ever a theory was a house of cards, a broken reed, a mirage of mere seemings, this is.

All of us certainly *were* identified with our crucified Representative in the judicial reckoning of God: but to take that long-since, never-to-be-repeated *penal* death of the whole Adam race, and misconstrue it into a present-day co-crucifixion of the individual believer's "sinful self", inwardly and consciously, is a vagary of plastic misadaptation.

The New Testament never once uses the present tense in speaking of our identification with the crucifixion of Christ, but always the aorist or perfect. It never says that we *are* crucified with Him, but that we *were*. It never says that we now *die* with Him, but that we then *died* with Him. It never speaks of a *continuing* crucifixion with Him, but only of a completed identification with Him in a representative, judicial sense, even as in Romans 6: 10, 11:

"For the death that He died [aorist] He died unto sin *once for all*. . . . Likewise [in the same judicial, once-for-all way] reckon yourselves to be dead indeed unto sin."

What tangles our "identification" theory gets us into! Some say one thing, and some another, until, to use an old saying, they make "confusion worse confounded". One of them has me on the Cross. Another has me in the grave. One says I am dying but never quite dead. Another says I am not only dead, but buried. One leading exponent tells me that all in one I am on the Cross, dying but not dead, yet I am also actually dead and buried! Let me quote his own words. First, "Jesus Himself . . . took *me* to the Cross, and nailed up my 'old man' to the accursed tree". Next, "Jesus can keep that 'old man' from *coming down*". Next, I am to "reckon myself . . . dead and buried", for Jesus can "make the reckoning good"! Even to an agile imagination all this is gymnastically awkward!

One after another these dear brethren of well-known holiness platforms aver that it was the "I", the "me", my "sinful self" which was slain on the Cross; yet they say that although the "I" is now dead to sin in me, sin in me is not dead to the "I". In other words, the "sinful self" is not really dead at all! (Incidentally, this is one of the ways in which the simplicities of New Testament teaching about holiness are made to seem complicated or unrealistic by exegetically defective theories.) Let me quote actual words: "Now we too have a nature which in itself is absolutely sinless, a new 'divine nature'[1] (2 Peter 1: 4); but

[1] This, too, is surely an inaccurate over-statement, and not warranted by 2 Peter 1: 4.

although we dare not say, even when in the most glorious enjoyment of full salvation, that *sin is dead* [i.e. in us] yet we can
truthfully say (and we dare not say otherwise) that when abiding
in Christ, and fully believing in Romans 6, *we are dead,* dead
to sin, dead with Christ".

Is not that merely a contrary play on words?—sin is not dead
in me, but I am dead to sin. What irony!—these dear brethren
tell me that it was the "sinful I", the "old self", the "carnal
nature", the "flesh", which, with its inbred sin, was crucified with
Christ; yet although crucifixion plainly means death, and they
therefore exhort me to "reckon" myself as "dead indeed unto
sin", the above-quoted preacher says that "the 'flesh' is to be
incorrigibly bad to the very end"; and another warns me that
"the corrupt thing we call sin" must continually "remain" in us
"to the last"! In other words, the very thing which *needed* to
be "crucified, dead, and buried", and which supposedly *was*
"crucified, dead, and buried", is (they now tell me) not "crucified,
dead, and buried" at all, but lives on within me "to the very
end". So, if the "old nature" is *not* really "crucified, dead, and
buried" after all, which part of me *am* I to "reckon" as "dead
indeed unto sin"? Which part of the human "I" *needed* to be
crucified to death if the "old nature" *cannot* be? We are wriggled
into the tantalising absurdity that the only crucifiable part is the
part *not* needing to be so treated! Surely this is the big contradiction of the current "identification" theory. It tells me to reckon
myself dead indeed unto sin, yet the one part of me which *needs*
to be made dead to sin (so it says) cannot die, and I must never
be deceived into thinking that it can!

As one reads the vivid portrayals of the "old self" as pinioned
on the Cross, undergoing protracted crucifixion, yet never put
out of its misery, one is tempted to feel pity for the Christian
believer, who has to live with such an interior torture perpetually
going on, in order to be sanctified! In my own judgment, it is a
morbid caricature of the true New Testament doctrine.

What strange ideas go with this "identification" theory! It
causes one of the saintliest writers to tell us, "We must live
in the grave of Jesus". Well, if we do, we certainly shall not find
our *Lord* there! Nor is it any such melancholy picture of sanctification which Scripture itself gives us. Nay, our true dwelling is
"heavenly places in Christ Jesus"!

One speaker after another tells me I am to be "sanctified

wholly", yet when it really comes to it, they deny the possibility. For instance, one of them whom I much admire objects: "You *cannot* sanctify the evil nature". In fact, he says of my human nature itself, "The nature remains *unchanged*". So I am to be "sanctified wholly", yet there is a persisting part of me which *cannot* be! How different is the Scripture itself, which tells me that my "whole spirit and soul and body" (does not that include *all* my human "nature"?) may be divinely sanctified!

A Regeneration Error

More serious is the defective view of *regeneration* which clings around this "identification" doctrine. I quote again from an able representative.

"And, therefore, as far as you are a person born again, so far and only so far, that holy nature of yours is a sinless nature."

Mark those words: "as far as . . . only so far". They teach new birth in *degree*, which is error. The New Testament nowhere teaches that we can be *partly* born again. There can no more be degree in birth than there can be in death. Either I am born again or I am still spiritually dead; and there is no in-between condition. I cannot be a bit dead and a bit born again; or partly one and partly the other. Once I am born again there may be degrees in my spiritual *life and growth*, but that is a different matter. Alas, even in *that* aspect, the foregoing quotation is strangely astray. "So far and only so far", it says, "that holy nature of yours is a *sinless* nature". This purports that there can be degrees of *sinlessness*, which is absurd, for sinlessness is a negative absolute. You cannot be *partly* "sinless". If you are sinless, then you have no sin at all.

I know, of course, what lies behind such inconsistencies: it is the idea that at our new birth there was imparted to us an "absolutely sinless, new 'divine nature'" (that is the very phraseology used); but if our quoted preacher meant *that* (as he did) then why does he now say, in our quotation, "That holy nature of *yours* is a sinless nature"? What he *should* have said (according to the theory) is, "That holy nature which is *not* really yours, and is not really *you*, but which came *into* you at conversion, is a sinless nature." He dare not have said that, however, for it would plainly have exposed that according to his theory the new birth is not real regeneration of the human "I" at all, but only an addition of something from without. What the New Testament itself teaches is that *I myself* am regenerated, not merely that a "new nature" is superimposed which is *not* really "I".

Even more disconcerting are the involved *peculiarities* of the theory. For instance, I can have a regenerated "heart" but not a regenerated "nature". Let me quote again the same expositor: "The *heart* may be cleansed, sanctified, and made the dwelling-place of God." "The *nature* remains unchanged." This means part born again, and part *not* born again. Oddly enough, on the heels of that, he adds, "If you are regenerate, you can never become unregenerate, but you can have an evil *heart*". What a back-fire! For if, as he says, the "nature" *cannot* be regenerated, and only the "*heart*" can, then how can the regenerate heart be an "*evil* heart"? Has the regenerated heart itself now become *de*generate? Or are there now *two* "hearts"? He himself says, "The evil heart is not the evil nature". So, if the "evil" heart is neither the new heart nor the old nature, what is it?

According to these carefully quoted brethren, we can be partly born again and partly not!—part sinless and part sinful!— having two hearts, with one of them born again and the other evil, plus a "nature" which can *never* be regenerated. Some of the unwisest aberrations have thus been uttered by holiness teachers who, in being wisely zealous against the eradication theory, have been *un*wisely zealous of this counterfeit "identification" theory.

What self-delusion, bondage, and sickening recoil have been caused by this theory of so-called "death by identification"! Where is it taught in the New Testament? Nowhere, except (as we have shown) in a judicial and racial sense. Where does the New Testament say that there are "two *natures*" in the Christian —an "old", and a "new"? Nowhere! As we have shown, Paul's phrases, "our old man" and "the body of sin", do not mean some entity within the Christian *individual*, but the whole Adam humanity. What the New Testament *does* teach is, that in *all* human beings, whether regenerate or unregenerate, there is a higher and a lower reach of the self (the conflict of which is vividly dramatized in the "wretched man" of Romans 7). The sinful bias within us is not a local growth or "body" which can be "crucified" or surgically "eradicated", but an infection co-extensive with the whole system and all its members. What is required is not surgery, but *renewal*.

Mark it well: the new birth is the introduction of a new moral and spiritual *life* into the system. It is *not* the impartation of a new *"nature"* which exists side by side with a so-called *"old* nature", and which is not strictly *myself,* but only something put *within* myself. All these current but incorrect notions come from the "identification" theory.

Is it not time that we Evangelicals revised our phraseology on this matter? In regeneration it is human nature itself which is regenerated; and in the born-again there still remains just that one nature, the human "I", though it is now a spiritually *renewed* "I". In that one human nature, there still persists the lower as well as the higher; and the lower still pulls the wrong way; but now, all the higher is strengthened, while the lower is resisted, weakened, countered, by the new spiritual life (which Paul calls "the Spirit", for it is indeed the Holy Spirit, communicating Himself). The struggle between the two is depicted in Galatians 5: 16, 17. "Walk in the Spirit, and ye shall not fulfil the desire of the flesh. For the flesh desires against the Spirit, and the Spirit against the flesh, and these are contrary the one to the other; so that you should not do just whatever things you may wish." Note the distinction here between (1) "the flesh", (2) "the Spirit", (3) "so that *you* should not do". The "you", i.e. the human personality, remains one entity. The human *nature* remains just as individually *one.* The "higher" and the "lower" within it are still there; but the personal "I" which thinks, knows, feels, wills, chooses, in and through that nature is changed, is regenerated; and the nature itself is interpenetrated by the life-giving Holy Spirit.

Does the Theory Work?

Coming back, now, to the "identification" theory, i.e. of supposed inward death to sin, or death of the so-called evil self-life, by realistic identification with our Lord's crucifixion, we ask: Does the theory prove itself true in Christian experience?

It does not. One of the most decisive evidences of this came to me, some years ago, from a keenly spiritual and quite scholarly friend of mine. Having secured his M.A. and B.D. degrees in Britain, he went out to the Far East as a missionary-teacher. Some years later, he wrote to me the following paragraphs in a letter which deeply impressed me.

"I have always believed, theoretically, that sanctification, like salvation, is a matter of grace, and is appropriated by faith ; but I did not realise to what an extent 'having begun in the Spirit' I was continuing 'in the flesh'. On coming here I met those whom the Lord was using in an outstanding manner, and who claimed to have met Him in a way that transformed their lives and lifted them on to a new level of Christian living. It all appeared to me to savour of a type of mysticism from which I had long since become alienated, and to be coloured by a doctrine of sanctification which I regarded as unsound and unscriptural. Yet the challenge was such as to make me more conscious than ever of my own spiritual impoverishment, and to send me back to the Word of God for more light. And the light came, slowly as the dawn yet just as surely. First, God brought me to an end of my own resources. Then He made me willing to accept teaching, no matter from what source it might come. Finally, He taught me to lay aside all the theological problems involved, as mere irrelevancies, and to accept His Word as the ground of an unshakeable conviction. With that conviction was born a new experience of God through the Holy Spirit.

"The truth came home to me through a prayerful consideration of Romans 6: 1-14. I saw that in Christ I died, and that all which was required of me was to take that place and count on the life of Christ manifesting itself through me. The Holy Spirit convinced me of two things: first, the facts stated in Romans 6: 6, and then the true nature of the 'reckoning' spoken of in verse 11. I saw that my 'reckoning' did not create the facts ; it followed as a result of *realising* the facts, and of taking my stand upon them by a decisive act of will. 'Reckoning' is now no longer a desperate attempt to convince myself of something which all the facts of experience appear to contradict ; it is an attitude of simple trust in the facts stated in the Word of God. And I find that as one stands on the fact the experience follows.

"As I look back, I see that for years I have been reversing the true order. Consecration *follows* as a consequence of realizing that we have been crucified and raised with Christ. We then yield our members to Him, once and for all. I had heard so much about consecration and surrender, it is little wonder I had come to assume that the way of deliverance from sin, and of fruitful Christian living, lay in my consecration and earnestness. I now see in a vital way that the important thing in sanctification, as in justification, is not what I do, but what God has done in Christ. I rest on *His* work."

Could anything be sincerer, more intelligent, or more devoutly calculating than that? Yet how did it work out? Some years later I met my esteemed friend, and asked him would he care to tell me, for guidance in my own thinking, if this "reckoning" on the basis of "identification" had proved valid in experience. He looked at me gravely, then sadly but frankly replied, "I am afraid it has *not*."

Thousands of others have had to admit the same, and have wondered why. Some have become sceptical of the Scripture through it, but far more have become sceptical of their own sincerity. As one of them said in my own hearing not long since, "It cannot be that God's Word is wrong; the fault must be in myself somewhere, but where, I don't know. I sincerely yielded myself up, believed that my 'old nature' was now crucified by identification with Christ, and then I began to 'reckon' myself to be 'dead indeed unto sin'. Somehow, though, I just was *not* 'dead' to sin, and the 'reckoning' became such a strain that it was affecting my nervous system. I fought intensely to maintain the 'reckoning', until I was weary with pretending what I knew was a contradiction. The conflict between the 'reckoning' and the reality made the reckoning hypocrisy. My faith collapsed, and I flopped into gloomy doubt. I still don't know why the failure, but I do know that it has left me shaken, so that now I doubt my own motives every time I pray."

How many others there are, who *"still don't know why"* the reckoning mocked them! Yet the simple answer is that the theory of inward crucifixion and death to sin by supposed identification with our *Lord's* crucifixion and death is an unscriptural delusion. It can be presented in such a specious way that it really does sound like the true way of relief for weary battlers with inbred sin; yet it is a snare. Take the following, from a valued friend of mine:

"Instead of leaving me to struggle with my sinful nature and its promptings, Christ took that nature with Him to be crucified, 'that the body of sin might be done away'—made inoperative, put out of business—'that so we should no longer be in bondage to sin' (Rom. 6: 6 ERV). Thus Christ made it unnecessary and unreasonable for me to sin. Knowing that the self in me which gets angry died with Christ, was put out of business, I am free not to get angry; and I never do. I used to be subject to the movings of envy and jealousy, but no longer, since I count myself dead to all such. I used to worry, but the 'I' that worries, Christ included in His death. I used to be impatient, but the self in me which would get impatient, died with Christ, and I am free."

But if that evil self was *indeed* "crucified" and "done away", why weaken the force (as above) by preferring to render it, "made inoperative" or "put out of business"? To be "crucified" and "done away" can mean no less than *dead and gone*! But would our "identification" theorists dare to take that outright position? No; for they know that however much victory they may enjoy through Christ, they have to be on guard all the while against subtle uprisings of wrong thought or impulse from within their own nature; they know that if they neglect prayer, for instance, it will not be long before troubles arise from within, proving that the "nature" which produces them is *not* really "dead and gone"!

But what then of my friend's testimony that the "movings" of envy, jealousy, worry, impatience, had subsided? Simply this: they were the result of his "abiding" in Christ and of Christ's abiding in *him*. Oh, for more such experience!—but the experience is one thing, the theory of it is another! Many a choice saint has had a wrong explanation of a right experience!

Experience Versus Theory

Yes (indulge the repetition) many a choice saint has held a wrong explanation of a right experience. What is more, many a sincere believer, through self-surrender and prayerful seeking, has come into the blessing of sanctification on an incorrect theory of it. Our sympathetic heavenly Father does not demand alphabetic exactitude of doctrine before He answers the heart-cry for holiness. The enduing Paraclete does not hold aloof until His stumbling human scholars have mastered the strict grammar of it. God is far more responsive to hunger than to theory. He observes sincerity of heart and tenacity in prayer far more than nicety of formula.

Some while ago I was asked, "If the eradication teaching is wrong, how have so many come into such blessing by it?" The answer is: God has honoured the seeker rather than the theory. The acute abhorrence of inhering sin, the painful hunger for holiness, the intense longing for unclouded fellowship with Christ, the mastering purpose to be completely possessed, set apart, cleansed, filled, and used to the glory of God; the scrutiny of heart, the searching of the Word, the waiting in prayer, the hanging on and crying with Jacob, "I will not let Thee go except Thou bless me!"—all these have brought the soul to the place where God could indeed impart "the fulness of the blessing"; and often, amid the rich wonder of the new experience, the grateful-hearted believer has *named* it according to his own *theory* of it. There are many such who have sanguinely presumed that all sin-tendency was now obliterated, only to find otherwise later (often with sad setback); but their having misnamed the experience has not nullified the *reality* of it; neither has their later discovery that it was not "eradication" negated the sanctifying enduement which had become theirs.

More recently I was asked, "How is it that outstanding Christians who have testified to sanctification as a 'second' work of the Spirit within them, have reached what is substantially the same experience, by seemingly irreconcilable theories, some as 'eradicationists' and some as 'counteractionists', and others with little or no theory at all?" It is because the Holy Spirit overrides mere mechanics in favour of the reality, especially so when a theory clamps error to the truth. (See appendix on *The Identification Theory and Hudson Taylor*.)

The other day I picked up a useful little book on practical Christian living. There too I found this idea of "reckoning" oneself to be dead to sin by reason of a supposed inward identification with the death of Christ.

"What, then, is the practical idea behind this 'reckon'? Does it mean, it is not actually so, but pretend that it is—as you do with your dog, when he lies down and you put a lump of sugar by his nose, and say, 'Dead!' Poor brute. No, no; it means that it is actually so, therefore act on it. Act as if it were true, and you'll soon find that it is true. Dead men have no temptation. A very giddy young lady was converted and felt that everything must now be different. 'If any man be in Christ, he is a new creature: old things are passed away, behold all things are become new' (2 Cor. 5: 17). The very next morning she happened to receive an invitation to one of the usual loose goings-on. Her prospective hostess was staggered to receive the 'R.S.V.P.' in the following terms: 'Miss A regrets that she is unable to accept Mrs. B's invitation because she died last night!' Imagine the consternation. I am not sure that it was very tactful; but it was certainly true. She reckoned herself 'dead indeed unto sin'. And the invitation was now no temptation to her. Try it!"

Along with true appreciation, I recoil from this easy-sounding, "Act *as if* it were true [i.e. that you are dead to sin] and you'll soon find that it *is* true . . . Dead men have no temptation." For the hard reality is that no such acting "as if" can juggle figment into fact. I deny that *anyone* has ever found such acting to beget actuality. To preach that it does, can only foster false hope at first with embittering disenchantment at last. As for "Miss A", who wrote that she had "died last night", we all know what she meant, and rejoice at the change-over which her conversion wrought; but her break-away from those "loose goings-on" is no illustration of Romans 6: 6 and 6: 11, with their supposed crucifixion of the self-life and a resultant inward death to *all* sin.

I, too, knew a young woman in the English midlands who, after her conversion, said the very same thing to her former dance-companions. "No, I'm not coming to dances ever again; I'm dead to all that." She said it and she meant it. So far as will and choice and decision were concerned, she *was* dead to it, and she never once went back to it; yet she told me, with weeping, more than two years later, that sometimes the lure of the old dancing thrill seemed almost more than she could resist.

After my own conversion I made a complete break with the "world". I could truthfully say that I was "dead" to the old way of living; but I could not have truthfully said that every secret relish for certain of my former diversions was dead. For far too long I had to do battle against persisting inclinations. My death to the old way of living, though real enough so far as my deepest longings and purpose went, was certainly not death to all sinful tendencies and appeals such as is supposed to be taught in Romans 6.

This theory of death to sin by a supposed inward crucifixion with Christ, and this exhorting of believers to "reckon" themselves on that basis as inwardly "dead indeed unto sin", is a deviation from sound exegesis, a snare into bondage, and a hindrance to true holiness teaching.

Notwithstanding all we have said, however, there are those who will still persist in the assumption that *somehow* the Cross must have an intended counterpart inside the nature of the Christian believer. So widely and so closely has that idea now become interwoven with Christian holiness teaching that many find themselves scarcely able to disentangle their thinking from it. Yet they must do so, or else alter all Paul's aorists and perfects and contexts pertaining to the subject.

In one guise or another the idea retains its mesmeric hold. Among the more scholarly it reappears today with a new touch of theological subtlety. It asks: "If *God* says that I am dead with Christ to sin, is not that the true fact about me as a Christian, even though not yet fully actualized *within* me? Ought I not therefore to stand by faith *inside* the fact, and claim its realization within me?" The big mistake, of course, is that the whole idea of "if *God* says" is built on a vacuum, for nowhere does God say that I was impaled on that long-ago Cross in an inward, mental, moral, or spiritual sense; nor does God anywhere say that the Cross has any such post-datable *effect* within me as to crucify and slay the moral perversity in my hereditary nature. Let us repeat it with a final emphasis: the teaching of inward death to sin through a subjective, present-experience "identification" with our Lord's crucifixion is unscriptural and therefore delusive. Let the following truths become axiomatic in all our further thinking on sanctification:

1. JUSTIFICATION IS BY IDENTIFICATION WITH OUR LORD IN HIS CALVARY *DEATH*.

2. SANCTIFICATION IS BY IDENTIFICATION WITH OUR LORD IN HIS RISEN *LIFE*.

3. OUR LORD JESUS, THROUGH HIS ATONING DEATH, IS THE *PROCURING CAUSE* OF OUR SANCTIFICATION.

4. THE HOLY SPIRIT, BY WHOM CHRIST INDWELLS US, IS THE *EFFECTING AGENT* IN OUR SANCTIFICATION.

We can never separate our sanctification from that "wondrous Cross", any more than we can separate any other part or aspect of our salvation from it. But sanctification does not come through the Cross by any such imagined interior identification with it as is taught by the so-called "identification" theory. Inwardly experienced sanctification comes through full union with our dear Lord *in His risen life*.

HAVE WE "TWO NATURES"?

"We always try to identify ourselves with our good and Christian self. If at moments we become aware of a different and less attractive self, we tend to treat him as a tramp who has somehow strayed into the back kitchen and is not really a member of the family. This will not do. That self is also ourself; and it is the sad but inescapable fact that we can never in reality rise higher than he rises. . . . That dark other self of instinct, impulse, emotion, whatever it may be, is also a self whom God loves, and who can be redeemed by Christ."

Bishop Stephen Neill.

HAVE WE "TWO NATURES"?

EAGER as we are to expound the positive aspects of the Holy Spirit's deeper work in us, and much as we dislike touching on the controversial, before we reach our final objective in these studies there is one further misunderstanding which we must try to clear away. I refer to the conventional teaching that there are "two natures" in each Christian believer, the "old nature" and the "new".

Many of us have been so thoroughly bred on this "two natures" doctrine that any challenging of it arouses our suspicious surprise. With some of us the indoctrination has been almost a brain-washing. No thought of possible error in it could be entertained for a moment. Yet I believe that the idea is an unscriptural detriment which should be discarded. All too often it has turned holiness expositions into a jig-saw puzzle, as also it has made Christian experience a Jekyll and Hyde mystery for many.

At regeneration, so it goes, the believer received a new nature, but the old nature remained. There are now, therefore, two natures in the Christian, irreconcilably antagonistic to each other. The new nature is "sinless", indeed "divine" (so some say), and therefore cannot sin. When the born-again Christian sins, it is never the new nature, but always the old. Everything that is spiritual and good is from the new nature; everything from the old is unspiritual and evil. The ugly obstacle to holiness is the old nature. The big deliverance which the Gospel provides to make holiness possible is that the old nature may be "crucified with Christ", whereby it is eradicated (according to some) or "rendered inoperative" (according to others).

What hurt has this "two natures" teaching inflicted, especially upon the spiritually sensitive! At one time or another, many have told me of distressing perplexity provoked by it. Again and again I have observed how it engenders unhealthy introspection and a distrust even of one's own sincerest motives. Is it the new nature, or the old, which is thinking, speaking, moving within me at any given instant? How do I discern with certainty which of the two it is? How may I ensure that it is never the old, but always the new? If deliverance from the old comes by its being crucified with Christ and thus either "eradicated" or rendered "inoperative", why is it that although I have wholly yielded all I am to Christ, and have "reckoned" myself "dead" in Him to sin, there still are subtle murmurs and persistent movings of wrong within me?

Among Christian believers of an intellectual but highly-strung type, this "two natures" theory has sometimes had nothing less than a *schizophrenic* effect. The protracted enigma of inward duality, self-contradiction, self-suspicion and chronic uncertainty has gradually weakened the power of decision and resolution, thus disunifying the personality. I recall one person in particular, a likeable middle-aged man, whose nervous breakdown had been psychiatrically traced to an obsession with this "two natures" idea. He told me how a sense of inward cleavage had gradually taken hold on him, until at last he came to the despairing conclusion that he was a split personality. But even where results are far from being so pronounced, the "two natures" theory tends to introversion and bondage.

So far as our practical sanctification is concerned, if this usual teaching of "two natures" in the believer were merely a matter of phraseology it need occupy no space here. But it is far more than that. A short time ago it was my privilege to give a series of addresses on Scriptural holiness at a ministers' conference. In a discussion session one of the brethren raised the "two natures" question very pertinently as follows: "We all agree that there is a duality in our moral nature; that there are in us both an upward reach and a downward pull; but does it much matter whether we call them two 'natures' or not? Does it not amount to the same thing whether we call them two 'natures' or two 'dispositions' or two 'sets of desires' or the 'higher and lower' within us?" The answer is that *it matters very much*. For if there are two "*natures*" in the believer, and the evil "*old* nature" can neither be regenerated nor eradicated but (despite supposed crucifixion) must remain alive within us to our last day on earth (as is usually taught) then entire sanctification in this present life is impossible; there is a whole area which is *un*sanctifiable, and those Scripture texts which teach *entire* inward renewal cannot mean what they say. On the other hand, if the higher and lower in us are both alike inherent in the *one*, inherited, indivisible human nature which may be regenerated, interpenetrated, and *renewed*, then entire sanctification *is* possible.

The Scriptural Evidence

Which are the texts supposed to teach "two natures" in the believer? One is Romans 6: 6, "Our old man was crucified with Him", in which the "old man" is a supposed "old *nature*". We have already shown how wrong that interpretation is.

The "wretched man" paragraph (Rom. 7: 15–25) is another place said to teach the two natures. The Scofield note on it says,

"The apostle personifies the strife of the two natures in the believer, the old or Adamic nature, and the divine nature received through the new birth (1 Pet. 1: 23, 2 Pet. 1: 4, Gal. 2: 20, Col. 1: 27). The 'I' which is Saul of Tarsus, and the 'I' which is Paul the apostle are at strife, and 'Paul' is in defeat."

Excellent indeed are most of the notes and summaries in the Scofield Bible. Many of them are remarkably apt; but in the note here quoted not one of the four texts which it cites says that a new nature is "received through the new birth" (on which see Appendix: *The Supposed "Two Natures" in the Believer*, p. 242). It is surely off focus in its observation (based on Galatians 2: 20) that in the "wretched man" of Romans 7,

"The 'I' which is Saul of Tarsus, and the 'I' which is Paul the apostle, are at strife, and 'Paul' is in defeat."

The Scofield note plainly equates what it calls "the divine nature received through the new birth" with the new "I" which is "Paul the apostle". How then can that "*divine* nature" be "in defeat" to the sinful *old* "I"? (For 1 John 5: 4 says, "Whatsoever is born of God overcometh"!). Even more than that, how can there be a strife between the new Paul and the old Saul when Paul himself says that the old Saul no longer exists?—"I live, yet *not I*."

Where, then, does Paul teach an old "I" and a new "I" in himself or in any other believer? Certainly not in the "wretched man" of Romans 7. The paragraph in question preserves only the one "I" all the way through. What Paul *does* show is that in the

one "I" there are both the good and the evil, the higher and the
lower. This can be verified by drawing a vertical dividing line,
then writing out the passage sentence by sentence, letting each
occurrence of the "I" take the side of the line to which it belongs—
the good or the evil. The alternation reveals the same "I" all
through. Or, another way is to read "I myself" in each case where
the "I" occurs:

"For that which I MYSELF [the lower part] do I MYSELF [the
higher part] do not approve: for what I MYSELF [the higher] *would*
do, that I MYSELF [the lower] do not; but what I MYSELF [the
higher] hate, I MYSELF [the lower] do.
"If then I MYSELF [the lower] do that which I MYSELF [the
higher] would not, then I MYSELF [the higher] consent unto the
law that it is good.
"So then it is no more I [*ego:* the one undivided personality] who
do it, but sin that dwelleth in *me* [singular: not 'us']. For I MYSELF
[the higher and intellectual] *know* that in me, that is, in my 'flesh'
[the lower and animal] good does not reside; for to will is present
with me [the higher] but how to perform the right I MYSELF [the
higher] find not. . . .
"For I MYSELF [the higher] delight in the law of God after the
'inward man' [the higher and spiritual], but I MYSELF [the higher]
see another law in my members, warring against the law of my mind
[the higher and spiritual] and bringing *me* [not 'us'] into captivity
to the law of sin which is in *my* [singular] members."

This expose, in which both the "I" and the "me" are both the
good and the evil alternatingly, surely settles it that Paul here
speaks of one human nature only, having within itself both
higher and lower desires and qualities. This is confirmed by Paul's
own observation that even those lower desires and qualities are *not*
an "old *nature*", separate from the essential "ego", but "*SIN*
that dwelleth in *ME*"—i.e. in the one human being and nature.
Only the arts of a mystagogue could make this passage teach "two
natures", two separate entities, two "I"s in a duplex being.

Another verse which is often appropriated as teaching two
natures in the Christian is Romans 8: 6, which says, "For the
mind of the flesh is death, but the mind of the Spirit is life and
peace" (E.R.V. & A.S.V.). These two "minds" are assumed to
be two "natures" in the believer. That, however, is not what the
verse teaches. The Greek word for "mind" (*nous*) does not occur
in the original. The word is *phronema*, which means inclination
or disposition. Of course, inclination or disposition, although not

the mind itself, expresses *direction* of mind. I think it is near the mark to say that the difference between *nous* (mind) and *phronema* is the difference between "mind" and "mindedness". Therefore, my own preference would be to render the verse: "For flesh-mindedness is death, but Spirit-mindedness is life and peace". Whichever way we phrase it, that is the purport of the text. To make it teach two "*minds*" or two "*natures*" in one person is leagues astray.

Still another verse which is sometimes expounded as teaching two natures in the believer is Romans 13: 14, "Put ye on the Lord Jesus Christ, and make not provision for the flesh". Yet to synonymize our Lord Jesus with the so-called "new nature" is surely an over-bold licence. The very fact that we are here exhorted to "put on" our Lord Jesus (as an old-time warrior would "put on" his armour: see verse 12) indicates that Paul does not mean our putting on a regenerate "nature", for none of us can do that. God alone regenerates.

Galatians 5: 16–17

Perhaps the "ace" passage which is adduced to validate the "two natures" error is Galatians 5: 16, 17,

"This I say then, Walk in the Spirit, and ye shall not fulfil the lust of the flesh. For the flesh lusteth against the Spirit, and the Spirit against the flesh ; and these are contrary the one to the other ; so that ye cannot do the things that ye would."

Expositors usually emphasize, and properly so, the contrast here between "the Spirit" and "the flesh". Then they educe and elaborate that these are the two mutually antagonistic "natures" in the believer. What they do *not* sufficiently observe is Paul's distinguishing of both "the Spirit" and "the flesh" from the "*you*", i.e. from the one personal entity. The "you" is the indivisible human *being* with the human *nature*. Within that being, within that nature, there are the lower and the higher areas or reaches of desire, inclination, activity. Paul names the former "the flesh" because of its continual pull that way, and the latter "the Spirit" because, in the regenerated, it is indeed the self-communicating Holy Spirit who is the new activator of all the higher. Notice especially Paul's final touch—

"These are contrary the one to the other, so that YE [emphasis on the higher] should not do the things which YE [emphasis on the lower] would."

The higher and the lower both inhere in the one nature, and are ingredients of the one human ego. They cannot possibly be two separate entities which are *not identical* with the human person, for the human ego is conscious that both are part of itself. And, as Paul's words show, the two exist, not only *in* the "you", but *are* the "you". The higher and the lower are both still present in the born-again; but the one, indivisible, personal "I" which thinks, knows, feels, wills, chooses, in and through the one complex human nature, is changed, is regenerated; and the nature itself is now interpenetrated by the life-giving Holy Spirit.

Ephesians 4: 22–24

Maybe I ought to mention here yet another passage which is supposed to teach the "two natures". I refer to Ephesians 4: 22–24.

"That ye put off, concerning the former manner of life, the *old man*, which is corrupt according to the deceitful lusts. . . . And that ye put on the *new man* which after God is created in righteousness and true holiness."

Yet, as we have remarked in an earlier reference to these verses, the "old man" and the "new man" simply cannot mean here an old and a new "nature", for none of us can either "put off" our unregeneracy or "put on" regeneration. Only God can do that for us. Moreover, in the Greek, the two verbs, "put off" and "put on" are aorist infinitives, indicating two things already completedly *done* (as in the parallel passage, Colossians 3: 9, 10). This absolutely settles it that "the old man" cannot mean a so-called "old nature", for if *it* had been thus "put off" there would be only the "*new* nature" left in the believer, and the bliss of Paradise would be already ours!

If we would know what that completed act of "putting off" and "putting on" *was*, Galatians 3: 27 and Colossians 2: 11 both synchronize it with the initiating rite of baptism (see Appendix on *The "Two Natures"*, p. 240).

John 3: 5–8

The most famous New Testament passage on the necessity of regeneration is John 3: 5–8. Most of us, since our conversion, and some of us even from childhood, have been given to understand that it teaches the "two natures" in the born again, especially verse 6: "That which is born of the flesh is flesh; and that which is born of the Spirit is spirit." Yet here, again, supposition has been allowed to gloss over the true meaning. Our Lord did not use the word, "flesh", here in one of the later Pauline senses as denoting those lower tendencies within us which some insist on calling "the old nature"; nor did He anywhere else use the word in that way, as a concordance quickly verifies. He simply meant the physical, or humanly natural. Equally definitely, by "the Spirit" He did not mean an imparted "new nature", but the Holy Spirit Himself. Nor did He say that the Holy Spirit *imparted* a "new nature". What He did say was that the human *individual* needed to be "born from above", that is, quickened by the Holy Spirit into new spiritual life. But for the human *person* to be thus spiritually regenerated is a very different thing from a duality of *"natures"* in that one person!

Are there, then, other passages which teach "two natures" in the believer? If so, we are only too willing to be corrected. Our New Testament certainly does make a sharp difference between what we *were* and what we now *are*; between our condition *out* of Christ and our condition *in* Christ; between being spiritually *dead* and being spiritually *alive*; between the degenerate life which came to us from Adam and the regenerate life which is ours in Christ; but where does it teach or imply or assume or in any way recognize two *"natures"* in the believer? Nowhere.

The New Testament Attitude

All the way through the New Testament, Christian believers are addressed as individual *unities*, never as dualities. For instance, in Philippians 1: 9, 10, Paul writes, "That your love may abound yet more and more in knowledge and in all judgment; that ye may approve things that are excellent; that ye may be sincere and without offence till the day of Christ". Now if there are *two* natures in the believer, there is one of them which *cannot* "abound in love", or "approve things that are excellent", or be "sincere and without offence". Is it only the *new* nature, then, which Paul addresses?

Or, again, in chapter 2: 13, Paul writes, "For it is God which worketh in *you*, both to will and to do of His good pleasure". If the "you" is a duality with two uncoördinative natures, neither of which is the actual "you", which of the two is it within which God works "to will and to do of His good pleasure"? It cannot be in the supposed "*old* nature", for that (so we are didactically warned) is so intractable that it can only be crucified. Yet nor can it be the "new", for that *already* "wills to do His good pleasure", and needs no exhorting to do it.

Or again, in chapter 4: 7, where Paul says, "And the peace of God, which passeth all understanding, shall keep *your hearts and minds* through Christ Jesus",—here, surely, the whole interior life is meant, without any thought of two co-existing natures, in one of which the peace of God simply could *not* dwell.

We think of words such as, "To the end He may stablish your *hearts* unblameable in holiness before God" (1 Thess. 3: 13); and "Now the end of the commandment is love out of a pure *heart*, and of a good *conscience*, and of faith unfeigned" (1 Tim. 1: 5); and "Let us cleanse ourselves from all uncleanness of *the flesh and spirit*, completing holiness in the fear of God" (2 Cor. 7: 1). All those texts, representing hundreds more, plainly address the undivided human personality, and they leave no foothold anywhere for the "two natures" phantasy.

Partial Crucifixion Unscriptural

Corroborating all we have said thus far is the fact that never once does the New Testament portray only a certain *part* of us, i.e. an "old nature", as crucified with Christ; neither does it ever speak of such a part *only* as dying or dead or buried with Christ. The crucifixion of the believer with Christ is that of the whole person; so is the dying, the death, the burial. Here are all the references:

Rom. 6: 2   "How shall *WE* [whole not part] who died to sin . . . ?"
 6: 6   (See our next paragraph)
 6: 7   "For *HE* who died is justified. . . ."
 6: 8   "Now if *WE* died with Christ . . ."
 6: 10, 11   "He [Christ] died unto sin *once for all*. . . . Likewise [i.e. once for all] reckon *YOURSELVES* [not just a part] dead indeed to sin."

2 Cor. 5 : 14	"One died for all, therefore *ALL* [persons not parts] died in Him."
Gal. 2 : 19, 20	"For I [the whole person] died to the Law. . . . I [not just an evil 'nature' in me] have been crucified with Christ."
6 : 14	"The cross of our Lord Jesus Christ, through which the world hath been crucified unto *ME*, and *I* [the whole self] unto the world."
Col. 2 : 20	"If then *YE* died with Christ from the elements of the world . . ."
3 : 3	"For *YE* died, and your life has been hid with Christ in God."
2 Tim. 2 : 11	"For if *WE* died together with Him, we shall also live together with Him" (This verse, however, may possibly refer to *physical* death).
1 Pet. 2 : 24	"Who His own self bore our sins . . . that *WE* having died to sins . . ."

The only other such text is Romans 6: 6, which we exempted from the foregoing list for particular mention again here, solely because its misuse has been the centre-point of all the misunderstanding as to the believer's joint-crucifixion with Christ, and the supposed co-existence of two natures in the regenerate. As we have already pointed out, the phrase, "our old man", cannot refer to a supposed "evil *nature*" within us, as a comparison with its recurrence in Ephesians 4: 22 and Colossians, 3: 9, 10 confirms. It is a convenient Pauline synedoche for the whole human race as it is in Adam. His combining of the plural pronoun, "our", with the singular noun, "man", surely betokens that he uses the phrase collectively of all, not distributively of each. If not, then why did he here use the word, "man" at all (*anthropos*) for an individual nature when he elsewhere uses the proper Greek word for "nature" (*phusis*) in referring to individual nature (Gal. 2: 15; 4: 8, Eph. 2: 3, 1 Cor. 11: 14, Rom. 11: 24, etc.)?

Strange Contradictions

Those who hold to this idea of "two natures" in the believer involve themselves in strange contradictions when they preach holiness, whether they are eradicationists or suppressionists or counteractionists. We say this with nothing but esteem and sympathy, having in mind many of the excellent brethren who minister from Christian convention and conference platforms. Yet sometimes these illogicalities are peddled with such bland obliviousness to their wrongness that they could provoke a wry smile were it not that this matter of holiness is such a sacred and serious issue.

For instance, turning again to a volume of convention addresses, I find the speaker thus describing the new "nature" supposedly received at conversion: "That holy nature of yours is a sinless nature. St. John distinctly says, 'Whosoever is born of God sinneth not' (1 John 5: 18), and he also says, 'He cannot sin, because he is born of God'. It is of first importance to understand this." As for the "*old* nature", the speaker assures me that our Lord "nailed up" that old man "to the accursed tree", so that now, "when abiding in Christ and fully believing in Romans 6, *we are dead,* dead to sin, dead with Christ". Well, if the "new" nature *cannot* sin, and the "old" nature is now *dead* to sin, how explain the sins which *still* keep occurring? The speaker's answer is, "the 'flesh' is to be incorrigibly bad, even to the very end". Is then the "flesh" *not* the crucified old nature? Instead of the "two natures", is there now a triangularity—(1) the "old", (2) the "new", (3) the "flesh"?

I turn to another page of the same excellent volume and find this: "We have a new nature which is the life of Christ, and we have an old nature which is the life of sin within us. Saul and Paul dwell together in the same body of the Christian". Now that certainly is not Scriptural, for, as already noted, Paul distinctly says in Galatians 2: 20 that Saul, the old "I", was now no more. His words, "yet not I", mean the total non-existence of the former "I". How then can Saul and Paul still "dwell together"?

A few sentences later, the speaker says of the supposed old nature (Saul), "The only thing is to bring it to be crucified". That again is badly out of focus, for converted Paul says that the old "I" already "*has been*" crucified (Gal. 2: 20, perfect tense).

Even more peculiarly, having thus politely by-passed Paul, our well-intending expositor now proceeds unfortunately to contradict himself still further, for he frankly confides to us that the crucified "old nature" somehow is not really crucified at all; apparently it keeps getting off the cross and indulging its impiousness again! What happens then? The speaker tells us: "Then, swiftly, I say,

Lord, there was that old nature again. It broke out! Wilt Thou crucify it right now, and restore me to the fulness of Thy fellowship?" So, instead of the aorist, once-for-all crucifixion of the "old man" which the New Testament uniformly teaches, there is a continuous on-and-off-and-on-again *repetition* of crucifixions!

Stranger still, the same speaker refers to what he calls "the *good* elements in my old nature"! Has he forgotten Paul's word, "In me, that is, in my flesh dwelleth no good thing" (Rom. 7: 18)? Finally comes the strangest surprise of all (mark the words which we italicise):

"There shall come a time when I stand before God in all the holiness of Jesus Christ, in my condition as well as in my position, with *my old nature gone for ever*, with the root of sin then destroyed for ever, since *it passes from me with the death of this body* or its transformation at the Coming of my Lord."

That surely is a serious aberration. The grand climacteric which supposedly does away with the old nature (says the speaker) is the doing away of the present *body*! That makes the body itself the seat of sin, and we are back again among the Gnostics; matter itself is evil; and the source of human sin is not a perverted moral nature, but a sinful *body*! There is no Scripture anywhere for such a notion.

Other such instances might be given of incongruities arising from the "two natures" theory, but we forbear lest our criticisms should seem even slightly captious. Our esteem for those beloved and gifted brethren from whom we here differ is only equalled by our concern to rescue holiness truth itself from admixture with such well-meant but unallowable error.

Correction and Restatement Needed

Where do all these inconsistencies point? Surely to this: Ought we not at once discard this aberrant concept of "two natures" in the believer? Ought we not correct and restate our doctrine of the believer's identification with what happened on Calvary? Ought we not revise our thinking as to hereditary effects of sin in human nature? My own view is that on the latter two matters we are sadly out of orbit. Much as I revere that epochal figure, John Wesley, I believe with others, including Methodist scholars, that he is a prime contributor to error in our thinking as to inbred sin. To him, sin was as distinguishable a malady in our moral nature as a cancer is in the physical, and, therefore, somewhat similarly removable by spiritual surgery. A recent re-reading of his historic treatise on "Christian Perfection" confirms my so thinking. Nor am I alone in this. Dr. Newton Flew, a Methodist of the Methodists, and correspondingly favourable to Wesley, frankly agrees, in his fine work, *The Idea of Perfection*:

"Inheriting as he did the Augustinian doctrine of original sin, Wesley tends to speak of sin as a *quantum*, or hypostasis; as a substance which might be expelled, or rooted out, or as an external burden which might be taken away. As Dr. Sugden has pointed out, he never quite shook off the fallacious notion 'that sin is a *thing* which has to be taken out of a man, like a cancer or a rotten tooth'. This is not in the least the Biblical idea of sin. Sin is a far more subtle, pervasive and persistent enemy than that. And if we start from a non-biblical idea of sin, it is unlikely that we shall arrive at a truly Biblical idea of holiness."

The Bullinger Thesis

Sometimes, when I have wanted to test my view of a debated theory, I have found help in reading the strongest case written for the opposite. I have done that before discarding this "two natures" error. There could hardly be a more concentrated argument in its favour than Dr. E. W. Bullinger's *The Two Natures in the Child of God*. Dr. Bullinger was a painstaking scholar and a skilful penman. His treatise is a pamphlet of 52 pages. With characteristic forcefulness he says just about all that can be said in support of the theory, but the more he adds, the more does he placard the sophistry of it. Rather than occupy pages here, we have given our animadversions in an appendix: *Dr. E. W. Bullinger on Two Natures in the Believer* (see page 242).

It is a perplexity to me that this "two natures" phantasy has for so long dominated and dislocated evangelical holiness teaching. Exegetically it is a distortion, and in experience it makes sanctification an agony instead of a glad release. It makes the inward condition of the believer even more "wretched" than that of the average unconverted person. Dr. Bullinger himself says practically that in his comment on the *result* of the warfare between the (supposed) two natures:

"The result of this unceasing warfare is the *wretchedness* which leads the ego in the next verse to cry out in broken gasps, 'Oh, wretched-I-man!'"

Is there no mitigation, no relief from this wretchedness? Dr. Bullinger's reply is: "He [God] will deliver all who have this conflict, in the only possible way: by death, or the Rapture, or the Resurrection".

Surely what we have tracked down already is enough to show that the "two natures" theory is unscriptural, self-contradictory, and baneful. My own conviction is that Christian holiness teaching should at long last disown it.

Christian believer, reject the idea of "two natures" within you. At your conversion to Christ, the new birth which came to you was not the adding of a "new nature"; it was the Holy Spirit's imparting of a new spiritual *life* which regenerated the one nature which you *are*. That new life which then came to you as a regenerating *infusion* is now meant to become a sanctifying *suffusion*. Our Lord wants to sanctify all that you are. The figment of an evil "old nature" in you which (as many teach today) is to be "crucified" yet is never actually dead, but must remain an evil, ugly thing inside you to your last day on earth, will prevent you (if you let it) from ever seeing the true, simple, Scriptural doctrine of holiness. You are one, indivisible human entity. In your one nature there is the higher and the lower, the up-reaching and the down-pulling. That one nature which is the real *you* may be "sanctified *wholly*". So says the Scripture (1 Thess. 5: 23). That is what will claim our attention from this point onwards in these studies.

"No man excogitate am I,
But man made up of contrariety".

Conrad Meyer.

"Such polarities are possible only to personality. They are polarities inside one nature, however, and not two personalities. They both exist inside the one personal consciousness. When I do good, I know that it is *I* who do it: and equally when I do wrong, I know that it is *I* who do it. What staggers Paul in Romans 7 is that it is one and the same 'I' all the time".

Anon.

THE "WRETCHED MAN" RESCUED

"You'll never get me out of the seventh of Romans while I'm your minister."

Alexander Whyte
to St. George's West Congregation
Edinburgh, Scotland.

"If we have here [in Romans 7] the normal Christian life, then grace offers us at best nothing more than a spiritual stalemate."

Steven Barabas.

"But why linger in Romans 7 when Romans 8 waits to welcome us? The 'wretched man' who groans at the end of chapter 7, 'Oh, wretched man that I am!' exults at the end of chapter 8, 'We are more than conquerors!'"

J. A. Yoxall.

THE "WRETCHED MAN" RESCUED

IF WE would learn the true way of victory over sin, we see it vividly drawn for us in the rescue of that "wretched man" in Romans 7. We may well take a steady look at him. Who is he? What does he represent? What is the wretchedness in which he groans? What is the deliverance of which he sings?

Already we have found ourselves asking: If chapter 6 teaches (as is generally supposed) a being inwardly "dead indeed unto sin" through co-crucifixion with Christ, how comes it that right afterward, in chapter 7, we are back at "Oh, wretched man that I am! Who shall deliver me?" Many a Bible expositor, assuming that chapter 6 teaches an inward crucifixion and banishment of inbred sin, has been puzzled by the dismaying picture of that "wretched man" who follows in chapter 7, crying, "For the good that I would, I do not; but the evil that I would not, that I do.... When I would do good, evil is present with me . . . sin that dwelleth in me".

What, then, are we to say about him? There seem to be some seven main "explanations" (for comment on which see Supplement: p. 207). Strangely enough, that which most peculiarly slants away from Scripturalness is the interpretation put forward by the regular "two-natures-in-the-believer" theory; but to save appearance of needless criticism we relegate comment on that, also, to the same supplement. However, we are obliged to make just one reference to it here because of its wide vogue, and because it probably obscures the true doctrine of holiness to some who chance on these pages. I quote from a well-loved writer.

The "wretched man" (so he avers) is a "converted man", but "contemplated" as "apart from Christ" (a strangely contradictory contemplation!). Then, being linked to the usual misinterpretation of Romans 6: 6, there is the usual figment of "two natures" in the believer, with the inference that the wretched man's problem is the strife of those "two natures"—of which

(strangely enough) the *old* is "the more powerful of the two"!
It all leads to this final comment on Paul's "I myself" in verse 25—

"The 'I-myself-life' is one thing, but the 'Christ-life' is another.
There are multitudes of Christians who are living the 'I-myself-life'
. . . instead of the 'Christ-life'.

But Paul makes no such contrast between the "I myself" and
the so-called "Christ-life". Nay, on the contrary, he *commends*
the "I myself" as being the *ally* of Christ! His words are, "So,
then, with the mind *I MYSELF SERVE THE LAW OF GOD*",
by which he means that the mind, the intellect, the true human
self, is altogether on the side of the divine law. The *real* contrast
which Paul makes is between the "I myself" and "the *flesh*", for
he says, "With the mind 'I myself' serve the law of God, but with
the flesh the law of sin" (25).

The unallowable contradiction of Scripture by that current
theory is very plain; and the reason why we must get it out of
our way is, that it destroys the very thing which makes sanctification possible, namely, that the "I myself", the basic human
mind, is *on the side* of the divine law: "With the mind '*I MY-
SELF' SERVE THE LAW OF GOD*". True holiness comes
through the liberating and renewing of that "I myself".

A Needless Problem

That "wretched man" of Romans 7 would never have been
an exegetical problem if he had always been interpreted with
due regard to the structure and progress of the apostle's argument.
As we have shown on an earlier page, by the time Paul reaches
our "wretched man" of chapter 7, he has expounded *three* profound Gospel deliverances—

1. From *sins*, judicially, through the imputed righteousness of Christ
   (3: 21–4: 25).
2. From *sins*, experientially, through the shedding of God's love in the
   heart (5: 1–5: 11).
3. From hereditary *sin*, judicially, by inclusion under the new headship of Christ (5: 12–7: 6).

It is wonderful to know those three deliverances. But there is one
more which we need as members of Adam's fallen race. We need

deliverance from this interior evil, "sin that dwelleth in me". *That* is why Paul introduces the "wretched man" *here,* in this completive section of his dissertation on how the Gospel saves the sinner. It is to show that the Gospel has an answer even to *this* sore problem, this hereditary inner perversion. The answer, of course, is chapter 8, with its climactic contribution on deliverance through the indwelling Spirit—"The law of the Spirit of life in Christ Jesus hath set me free from the law of sin and death. . . ."

That "wretched man", therefore, depicts neither an unconverted man nor a believer's imaginary quandary of "two natures" in life-long struggle. He exhibits the experience of any human being at the stage which Paul has now reached in his exposition of how the Gospel saves the sinner. He represents all who know three out of the four big deliverances from sin, but still need to know the fourth: deliverance from hereditary sin-power *experientially*. He must now learn deliverance through the inward operation of the Holy Spirit; a deliverance which Paul calls "the glorious liberty of the children of God" (8: 21). Then, indeed, he can leave the wailing wall and join the victor-throng who sing, "We are more than conquerors through Him that loved us!"

THE FOURTH BIG DELIVERANCE

Only too clearly Paul's "wretched man" lets us know what it was from which he sought release. "Who shall deliver me from *the body of this death*?" So, what is "the body of this death"?[1] It simply cannot be the *physical* body (as some have supposed) for Paul certainly was not begging escape from *that,* as his epistles certify. Nay, even when he was nearing the end, and had a "desire to depart and to be with Christ", he preferred to linger longer in the earthen body for the sake of his beloved children in the faith, and for opportunity of further service on earth. The context makes trebly plain what "the body of this death" is.

[1] That word, "body", occurs 100 times in Paul's letters (including Hebrews); 69 times of the physical body; 16 of the Church as our Lord's mystical body; 8 of bodies terrestrial, animal, vegetable; and 7 times *figuratively*. One instance of its figurative use has already occurred in Romans (6: 6). It is equally obvious that here, in chapter 7: 24, it is again used figuratively in the phrase, "the body of this death".

"It is no more I that do it, but *sin that dwelleth in me*" (17).

"It is no more I that do it, but *sin that dwelleth in me*" (20).

"Captivity under the law of *sin which is in my members*" (23)

"Sin that dwelleth in me." "Sin which is in my members." This is no localised "foreign body" in the system; it is a toxin throughout the blood-stream affecting the whole organism. It is not a malignant growth, like a cancer, which can be removed from man's spiritual nature by divine surgery. It is a disseminated moral schlerosis weakening all the "members". Who shall deliver from *that*?

Well, hear the shout of thanksgiving: "I thank God, *He delivers me*, through Jesus Christ our Lord"! The words, "He delivers me", do not actually occur in the Greek text but they are implied in the grammatical ellipsis. And *how* does the deliverance come? For answer note the emphasized words in the following quotation from chapter 8.

"For what the law could not do in that it was weak through *THE FLESH*, God, sending His own Son in the likeness of sinful flesh, passed judgment on sin in *THE FLESH*; that the righteousness of the law might be fulfilled in us, who walk not after *THE FLESH*, but after *THE SPIRIT*. For they that are after *THE FLESH* do mind the things of *THE FLESH*, but they that are after *THE SPIRIT* mind the things of *THE SPIRIT*. For the mind of *THE FLESH* is death, but the mind of *THE SPIRIT* is life and peace. . . . But ye are not in *THE FLESH*, but in *THE SPIRIT*, if so be that the Spirit of God dwell in you."

How often has that point-by-point contrast between "the flesh" and "the Spirit" riveted the attention of Christian believers! Well it may, for indeed it holds the true secret of transformation from inward defeat and bondage to victory and liberty. Romans 8: 1–13 is the most notable passage on "the flesh" and our rescue from its tyranny. It does not tell us the *whole* secret, any more than any other single passage tells us everything about any given subject; but it opens the door wide. Look carefully at those three new Pauline expressions which we have now come upon:

1. "The flesh" (7: 5, 18, 25; 8: 1–13).
2. "Sin that dwelleth in me" (7: 17, 20, 23).
3. "The body of this death" (7: 24).

They all refer to the same inner problem. They are practical equivalents, and they interpret each other. If we once understand Paul's figurative use of that phrase, "the flesh", we understand the other two, and begin to see how the Holy Spirit effects deliverance.

What, then, is "the flesh". The Greek word so translated is *sarx*. It occurs 91 times in Paul's epistles, and in 27 of those occurrences it is used in a recondite way to mean the sin-proclivity in our human nature. For a detailed treatment of them see our companion volume, *A New Call to Holiness*. Here we simply give the result of our scrutiny. The phrase is used collectively in each case to mean *our animal and selfish urges, inclinations, predisposition*.

"The flesh" is neither the body itself nor the mind itself, but a predisposition which inheres *in* the mind, and behaves *through* the body. It is not a mind within the mind, a self within the self, or a nature within the nature; therefore it cannot be detached like a parasite or an interloper. It is not a *locality* of the mind, but a *condition* of it. In Romans 8: 6 the "mind of the flesh" and the "mind of the Spirit" are not two minds in one person, but two *states* of mind—the one being predominantly set on sensory, earthly gratification, the other on *spiritual* satisfactions. Therefore, although a human mind may be either of these at any given time, it cannot be both simultaneously.

Perhaps that word, "animal" in our definition of "the flesh" may seem strange to someone. Does not the word, "animal", refer only to the *body*? How then can it be a predisposition of *mind*? The answer is, that the term, "animal", refers just as definitely to the mind as it does to the body. Is that dog of yours a dog just because it has a dog *body*? No; it has a dog *mind*. It thinks, reacts, desires, as a dog. There is a similar relatedness between mind and body in our human nature. There can be animal *mindedness*, the mainspring of which is self-gratification of both body and mind through earthly things. That, indeed, is what Paul denotes in Ephesians 2: 3, "The desires of the flesh and of the *mind* [or thoughts]". See also Romans 8: 6 again: "the *mind* of the flesh". Paul could scarcely have used a more photographic phrase for our selfish and animal predisposition than "the flesh".

Once we grasp that "the flesh" (when thus used figuratively) means, not a so-called "old nature", but our inborn selfish and animal proclivities which we have inherited along with all the higher and nobler impulses of our total humanhood—once we grasp that, and then realise that the Holy Spirit can refine our *whole* moral nature in all its propensities, we have taken the first big step toward a truly Scriptural doctrine of holiness.

Dear Christian, the great thing to get hold of firmly is, that *the mind itself* may be renewed, cleansed, renovated, sanctified, so that the "mind of the flesh", i.e. the state in which the selfish and animal predominates, may become a "mind of the Spirit", in which the spiritual and holy reigns victoriously over the whole territory of thought and being. Yes, Christian believer, this is Scripture truth, not error, despite what some may be at first inclined to say. The mind *itself* may be renewed, through and through, without some evil "old man" left forever inside it and continually contaminating it. I will tell you why. Although our hereditary sin-infection inheres throughout it, the mind itself, the basic human being, is on the side of the divine law. As we have seen, that is what the Holy Spirit himself says through Paul:

"WITH THE MIND I MYSELF SERVE THE LAW OF GOD."

Lay hold on it so as never to let it go again: your mind, i.e. the basic human *YOU*, is fundamentally on the side of the good. Think carefully: if your mind, the basic "you", were constitutionally evil, you could never have become regenerated, much less could you ever become sanctified. See how careful Paul is to guard us from error. He makes unmistakably clear that although the disease is "sin that dwelleth in me", sin is not the "me" itself. And although he says, "in my flesh [my animal and selfish propensities] dwelleth no good thing" (18) he makes equally clear that "the flesh" is not identical with the human self. Because a patient *has* a disease we must not say that the patient *is* the disease! Despite all the bad *in* us, it remains true that because of what we basically *are*, as human beings, we are both redeemable and *remediable*. You, dear Christian, have already been regenerated into new spiritual life; and that divinely infused new life may now infill you, interpenetrate you, refine you, transform you, so that from the very springs of your thought-life your mind *thinks* holiness, loves, chooses, produces and expresses holiness.

Some years ago a crowded congregation sang the hymn, "Rescue the perishing." As the last note died away, the minister, a leading evangelical and holiness teacher, said to them, "We shall never sing that hymn again while I am minister here. That third verse is utterly wrong—

> 'Down in the human heart, crushed by the tempter,
> Feelings lie buried which grace can restore ;
> Touched by a loving hand, wakened by kindness,
> Chords that were broken may vibrate once more.'

"It is wrong," he added, "to sing that feelings lie buried which grace can *'restore'*. The grace of God does not merely 'restore' the *old* heart; it gives us a *new* heart." The criticism sounded rather brave and jealous for the truth, but in reality was it quite worthy? Everything depends on what we mean by the "old heart". If we take the "heart" to mean the centre of affection and desire (which it *uniformly* means when used in a figurative sense) then grace *does* design to "restore" it.

I do not forget Ezekiel 36: 26, "A new heart also will I give you . . . and take away the stony heart, and give you a heart of flesh". But it is absurd to press that over-literally. The "stony heart" is not stone in a physical sense, nor is the "new heart" literally a heart of flesh. The words are simply a figurative describing of a gracious change which will yet be wrought in the moral nature of the covenant people when God "sprinkles clean water" (another figure of speech) upon them. What about Zechariah 13: 9, "I will refine *them* as silver is refined"? It cannot be the "new heart" that is refined, for that is what "refines" *them*. It is the people themselves who are to be refined in their own *human nature*.

What about Ephesians 4: 23, "Be *renewed* in the spirit of your mind"? What about Romans 12: 2, "Be ye transformed by the *renewing* of your mind"? Those are exhortations to born-again Christian believers. But if those already regenerated persons were to be still further renewed, in what sense could they be but by some deeper, further, sanctifying work of the Holy Spirit within them? Let the new spiritual life which came to us at our conversion be thought of as a wonderful, fresh, blight-counteracting sap spreading throughout the tree, or as the transfusion of rich, new, health-bringing blood through the entire blood-stream of an ailing body, or better still as being, in actual fact, a vitalizing new *life* from the Holy Spirit, interpenetrating the whole of our mental and moral and spiritual nature. Yes, let us recapture the great and precious truth that our human nature *itself* may be "renewed", even "sanctified wholly" and "blameless" (1 Thess. 5: 23).

HOW DOES IT OPERATE?

How does this liberation through inward renewal operate? Paul's first answer in Romans 8 is, "The law of the Spirit of *life in Christ Jesus* hath set me free from the law of sin and death". So it operates through union with our Lord in His risen life. Instead of the usual idea that release from sin-tyranny begins by an inward identification (supposedly) with our Lord in His *death*, we must learn that it comes through fuller union with Him in His *life*.

It is unmistakable that the Holy Spirit really *does* something to the believer's moral nature, for Paul says that it has "set me *free* from the law of sin and death". In the preceding paragraphs he has told us that formerly when the Law said, "Thou shalt not covet", there was a surreptitious contrariety deep within him which was irritated into opposite activity by the very command, so that the Law (which was the "law of God" to his *mind*) became a "law of sin and death" because of the selfish and animal propensity within him:

"Sinful passions which were [provoked] through the Law [of Moses] wrought in our members to bring forth fruit unto *death*" (7: 5).
"I had not known sin except through the Law: for I had not known coveting except the Law had said, Thou shalt not covet. But sin, finding occasion, wrought in me *through the Commandment* all manner of coveting. . . . And the Commandment which was unto life, I found to be unto *death*" (7: 7–9).

Thus the holy Law given through Moses became a "law of sin and death"! So, when Paul now says, "The Spirit of life in Christ Jesus hath set me free", he means that the power of the inner betrayer which made keeping the moral law impossible has now been *broken*. This is meant to be the experience of *all* Christian believers, i.e. that the power of the hereditary selfish-and-carnal within us is consciously *broken*. Unless that is our experience we are still in chapter 7 with the "wretched man".

Next, Paul says: "That the righteous requirement of the Law

might be fulfilled in us who *walk . . . after the Spirit*" (8: 4). This indeed is realized holiness; no longer a weary struggle to keep the divine commandments yet failing because of captivity to innate contrariness, but keeping the Law with ease as the spontaneous by-product of "walking after the Spirit"! Oh, the sense of release and relief where this becomes real within the mind! This truly is the Christian "law of liberty" (Jas. 1: 25); not freedom *from* law, but freedom *in* it; that largest of all freedoms, a nature which is *one* with the Law, and delights in it as a large and happy place in which to live.

It is in this "walking according to the Spirit" that we begin to find a present fulfilment of those Old Testament promises, "I will put My law in their inward parts, and write it in their hearts" (Jer. 31: 33); "I will put My Spirit within you, and cause you to walk in My statutes" (Ezek. 37: 27). Only those who have experienced it know the soul-exhilaration of this inward renewal which turns the commands of the law from chains to wings.

To "walk according to the Spirit" is to live continually under His gentle persuasion, in glad one-mindedness with Him. How many of us, then, are "walking in the Spirit"? A walk is a reiterated step. There is a first step, followed by a continuity. So is it with this "walking in the Spirit"; there is a first step, or initial crisis, followed by an habitual response of mind. This issues in holy *character*; for, as someone has truly said, "character is consolidated habit".

It is in this consecrated "walking" with the Spirit that He "renews" our mind *itself*. For when (as John Fletcher says) there is a "total, irreversible, affectionate self-surrender to Jesus Christ as both Saviour and Lord", then (as Daniel Steele adds) "the Spirit of truth streams through and through the soul like a pencil of sunbeams, vitalizing, illumining, warming and cleansing". Not only is the power of "the flesh" (the selfish and animal) really broken, the soul itself has new health, and breathes the air of heaven.

Again, this mind-renewing "walk" in the Spirit lifts the mind right *above* "the flesh" to where the Holy Spirit can be a continuous Indweller. In verse 9 Paul says, "Ye are *not* in the flesh, but in the Spirit, if so be that the Spirit of God *dwell* in you". That word, "dwell", is wonderful here. It represents the Greek word for residing, or home-making. No longer is the Holy Spirit in us only as our new life; no longer is He only an occasional visitor to our awareness; He now makes the heart His *residence* as "the Spirit of *Christ*" (10). Self-consciousness becomes sublimated into Christ-consciousness. There is no eradication, for inhering sin-susceptibility is too subtle for that; but the dominant *direction* of the mind is now wholly toward that which is highest and holiest.

This indeed is the way of victory! This is the soul on wings! As Hannah Whitall Smith puts it, "Birds overcome the lower law of gravitation by the higher law of flight; and the soul on wings overcomes the lower law of sin and misery and bondage by the higher law of spiritual flying". "The soul that has mounted into this upper region of the life in Christ cannot fail to conquer and triumph."

This, also, is the way of transition from fear to *peace*. See verse 6, "The disposition [or minding] of the flesh is death, but the disposition [or minding] of the Spirit is life and *peace*". When the mind has become thus aligned with the will of God there is inner harmony instead of friction and discord. In the ultimate analysis there are just two things which prevent peace of mind— pride, and lack of love. Pride always carries the haunting fear of humiliating fall; and where love is lacking there can never be that rest of heart which comes only with perfect motive. I learned something about that years ago when I used to do a good deal of open-air preaching. At times, when Communists and other hostile persons in the crowd seemed likely to react violently, I would feel fear. Then I would say to myself, "If you were utterly down at the feet of Christ you could not possibly fear humiliation; and if you loved them as utterly as Jesus loves them you could not know fear, for 'perfect love casteth out fear' (1 John 4: 18)". It is a high point in the spiritual life when, cost what it will, we *submit* to the divine will; but the highest point of all is when the mind has become so renewed by the Holy Spirit that every *desire* is altogether *one* with that divine will. Oh, that is the way of "life and *peace*"! It is then that there comes the tranquil rest of which F. W. Faber sings—

> I worship Thee, sweet will of God,
> And all Thy ways adore;
> And every day I live, I seem
> To love Thee more and more.

I have no cares, O blessed Will,
   For all my cares are Thine ;
I live in triumph, Lord, for Thou
   Hast made Thy triumph mine.

Ill, by Thy blessing, is my good,
   All unblest good is ill ;
And all is right that seems most wrong
   If it be Thy sweet will.

Still further, this "walking in the Spirit" brings wonderful realization of the divine *fatherhood*. See verse 16: "The Spirit Himself beareth witness with *our* spirit that we are the children of God ; and if children, then heirs ; heirs of God, and joint-heirs with Christ". As plainly as words can show, this inward witness of the Spirit is real to the believer's *consciousness*. Otherwise it would not *be* "witness". It may not always be emotionally vivid, but it makes our fellowship with the heavenly Father, and our union with Christ, and our glorious hope as children of God, a living and luminous reality to the mind.

It must be added, too, that this "walking in the Spirit" brings a sense of heavenly *guidance* into all our life. See verse 14: "As many as are *led* by the Spirit of God, they are the sons of God". One of the most elevating of all experiences on this earth is to go through one's days and hours with an unbroken awareness of God-guidedness. Life is so complicated, so swift-moving today, and our huge, congested cities make the individual feel so lost in the crowd, that many now regard the idea of individual guidance from God, right down to details, as mere credulity. Yet some of the most unanswerable evidences of such guidance are those which these very days are supplying. When the Holy Spirit "*dwells*" in the mind, renewing, refining, and sensitizing it to His inner directing, such guidance becomes unmistakable. It is one of the most uplifting accompaniments of the Spirit-filled life.

A CONTINUOUS DELIVERANCE

Can there be an utter *death* of those selfish and animal propensities in us? I scarcely think we dare infer so. When the "wretched man" asks, "Who shall deliver me?" the verb is future indicative, denoting a continuing victory rather than a final extinction. So is it with Paul's concluding comment here on "the flesh"—

"So then, brethren, we are debtors, not to the flesh, to live after the flesh; for if ye live after the flesh ye shall die; but if ye through the Spirit *PUT TO DEATH* the doings of the body, ye shall live."

So this is *not* a completed death in the past, like our *judicial* death with Christ, as in chapters 6 and 7, but a *continual* "putting to death"; for the verb is in the present tense. Also, unlike the judicial death which our Lord died *for* us, this is a "putting to death" which we ourselves bring about; for the text says, "If *ye* put to death . . ." Furthermore, *this* "putting to death" is effected, *not* by union with our *Lord's* death, but by inward union with "the Spirit of *life*". And, once again, *this* "putting to death" is not death to some supposed "old man" or lump-evil in our being; it is a successive mortifying of distributed *activities* or "doings".

What, then, are those "doings of the body" which we are to put to death? Not its involuntary processes or normal functions, for *they* are not sinful, neither can they be "put to death" except by putting the body itself to death. Paul means activations of the body by the selfish-and-animal urges within us, and he calls them "the doings of the body" because the body expresses them.

And *how* do we "put them to death"? We do so (1) when the *will* says an implacable "No" even though unsanctified desire still lurks in the heart; and (2) even more so when the heart itself turns away unresponsively; and (3) most of all so when the will and the heart and the very "spirit of our mind" (Eph. 4: 23) unite in an *aversion* to them.

So this is not a death to sin *totally*, but a progressive death of unholy "doings" and the *urges* which activate them. Let me speak from my own experience. There are forms of sin which used to awaken vexatious response within me, but now (so far as I can tell) they have become utterly dead to me. Not only has my will always been resolutely set against them, but whatever desire there used to be toward them has apparently become extinct. But am I therefore dead to *sin*? No, alas. Why? Because as we become dead to *some* forms of temptation we become beset by others. This is simply because the inexhaustible versatility of sin corresponds with the exquisitely complex susceptibilities of our human constitution, and the super-sensitive interactions between spirit and mind and body.

We are eager to add, however, that this "putting to death" is not only continuous; it is definitely *progressive*. Not only is the power of "the flesh" really broken in the consecrated, Spirit-filled believer; unholy desires and responses more and more lose their power, and holiness is in continuous ascendancy. When we so truly live "*in* the Spirit" (9) that we "*walk* in the Spirit" (4) and habitually "*mind* the things of the Spirit" (5), then, that in itself continually "puts to death" the "doings" of the "flesh". That is the way of progressive deliverance and victory through "the Spirit of life in Christ Jesus". It is a true mortification of the *flesh* through a true sanctification of the *mind*. It is real victory, not by struggling against insinuating seductions down on their own level, but by living *over* them, through inward elevation of mind "in the Spirit".

All these considerations lead us to the following conclusion, which should henceforth be axiomatic in all our thinking about Christian holiness:

DELIVERANCE FROM SIN COMES, NOT BY CONTINUALLY STRUGGLING TO SUBDUE THE FLESH, BUT BY CONTINU-ALLY ALLOWING THE HOLY SPIRIT TO INFILL AND RENEW AND *TRANSFORM* THE MIND.

Now let us gather up our findings thus far. Christian holiness is a continuously full experience of Christ indwelling and purifying the mind through the Holy Spirit. It is the river of regenerating life in full flow. Sanctification is not a crucifixion of the basic human self, for as Paul says, "With the mind I MYSELF serve the law of God". It is not the basic human self which we need to crucify, but self*ism*. As Paul again says, in Galatians 5: 24, "They that are Christ's have crucified the *flesh*" (not the "self"). Nor is sanctification the eradication of a suppositionary "*old* self"; it is the sublimation of the *true* self. It is transition from egocentricity to Christocentricity.

Holiness is *restoration*. The New Testament persuasives to holiness are never invitations to some distant, foreign shore where we feel strangers. They are God's call to you and me to become our true selves. You may know that this is so, because deep down within you there is what can truly be called a *homesickness* for it. Holiness is the true homeland of the soul. The highest life which may be ours in Christ is in the direct line of our proper manhood. If the deepest currents of your being were not *for* holiness, would you be reading pages such as these? Holiness is the true man, the true woman, claimed through and through for God;

claimed, cleansed, filled, renewed, refined, so that the divine image again gleams lustrous through the consecrated personality.

Holiness is *fulfilment*. It is the quickening into their proper functioning of Godward capacities which are in the very nature of the soul. As the rising sun recalls a dark and seemingly dead hemisphere to new light and life and loveliness, so the sun-break of Spirit-wrought holiness within the mind suddenly uncovers responses, susceptibilities, capabilities which have lain there dim, dark, dormant. In spite of all else they are still there, and the Holy Spirit awakens them into new life. Holiness is no mere abrogation of evil within us; it is the flowering into fragrant, lovely completion of all that is truest in our moral being.

Holiness is *purity of heart*. The Holy Spirit comes not only to fill us, but to refine us in all our desires and impulses. He comes to burn away dross, in the holy flame of His presence. He comes to lift us out of the earth-bound into purifying fellowship with God such as we have never known before. We never sense how ugly sin is until we see it from those translucent heights of sanctification. We never guess what self-cheating folly prayerlessness is until we experience true heart-fellowship with God; for then we realize that *anything* which obstructs the streaming of that ineffable light into our being is fantastically wrong. We never fully know how wretched our bondage has been until we look back on it, freed from our chains and living in the spontaneous victory of hearts *renewed* into holiness. Well may we pray,

> Blessed Holy Spirit,
>   Heav'n-imparted Seal,
> Strike Thine inward impress
>   Deep and clear and real;
> By an inwrought insight
>   Cause my mind to see
> Cleansing, fulness, victory
>   Now in Christ for me.

How do we appropriate this provision, this holiness, this liberation through inward renewal? Is it something which we have to "claim"? Well, have you never found this, that you somehow cannot "claim" any of the higher blessings offered to us through Christ so long as any part of you remains unsurrendered? Your own heart will not allow you even to *start* seriously claiming so long as there is any reservation. The first thing is: LET THE

HOLY SPIRIT CLAIM *YOU*. It is a fundamental law of our spiritual life in Christ that we possess by *being* possessed. The possessors are the possessed. Once we are utterly and forever *His*, somehow there is scarce need for "claiming". The blessing is ours. The lovely miracle happens. The longed-for is ours, and we absorb it.

THE DEEPER WORK RE-DEFINED

"So each man strives to flee that secret foe
Which is himself. But, move he swift or slow,
That Self, forever punctual at his heels,
Never for one short hour will let him go."

Lucretius.

"Naturam expellas furca, tamen usque recurret.
(Though you drive out nature with a pitchfork
she will always return.)"

Horace.

"The law of the Spirit of life in Christ Jesus hath
set me free . . . that the ordinance of the Law
might be fulfilled in us who walk not after the
flesh, but after the Spirit"—Romans 8: 2, 4.

"Be renewed in the spirit of your mind"
—Ephesians 4: 23.

THE DEEPER WORK RE-DEFINED

PERHAPS we ought now to attempt a re-definition of this deeper Christian experience about which we are speaking. Holiness, however, is one of those qualities which are more easily described than defined. All great ideas remain elusive until they are expressed to us in some living form. Beauty is a mere abstraction until we see it smiling from some lovely flower. Music is a mere fantasy until some well-played instrument gives it speech. Art is ethereal until embodied in picture or sculpture. Even the meaning of love remains vague until we see it livingly aflame in some holy attachment or sublime behaviour. Similarly, holiness needs manifestation rather than definition if it is to be appreciated most perceptively.

Its perfect incarnation is seen in our incomparable Lord Jesus, the "chiefest among ten thousand", the "altogether lovely". Just as love is never defined in the New Testament, neither is holiness. When the Scripture would tell us what the divine love is, it must point to its *expression*—"Herein is love, not that we loved God, but that He loved us, and sent His Son to be the propitiation for our sins". Similarly, if we would see true holiness it points to Him, our Lord, "the Holy One of God".

Still, there is a place of definition. It can save our thinking from vague diffusion by gathering many deductions into useful concentration. So, when we think of the Holy Spirit's deeper work of sanctification in the Christian believer—what it is and what it does, we may give it useful focus in the following definition:

IT IS THAT EXPERIENCE, ORIGINATING AT THE CRISIS-POINT OF UTTER SELF-YIELDING TO GOD (NOT ALWAYS EMOTIONALLY VIVID BUT ALWAYS MOST DEFINITE) IN WHICH THE HOLY SPIRIT INFILLS THE HEART, MAKING FELLOWSHIP WITH GOD AND POSSESSION OF CHRIST REAL AS NEVER BEFORE, AND EFFECTING WITHIN THE FULLY CONSECRATED BELIEVER A MORAL AND SPIRITUAL RENEWAL INTO HOLINESS DEEPER AND FULLER THAN COULD EVER BE KNOWN OTHERWISE.

I do not claim that this definition is impeccably exact or adequate; but it is near enough to be called a true description, even though too brief to particularize incidental facets and individual variations of experience.

In no sense is this deeper work of sanctification our reaching a fixed point or line or terminus; for the self-surrender and triumphant faith of one splendid crisis-point cannot secure holiness for ever; but it *is* a point of new departure, a "crisis followed by a process"; the entrance to a richer quality and fulness of spiritual life; or, as we have elsewhere expressed it, an inwrought restoration to holiness in the sense of moral and spiritual FULNESS OF HEALTH.

In picturesque Scripture phraseology, it is a "mounting up with wings as eagles" into "heavenly places in Christ". It brings in full measure the "joy unspeakable and full of glory", the "peace which passeth all understanding", the "wisdom which is from above", and the love which "abounds yet more and more in knowledge and in all discernment". It is the life of realized "abiding" and "abounding" in Christ. Of temptation there is still incessant plenty, for there is no immunity on earth from that; but the *level* of temptation is now different, and the *strain* of it is eased by vivified awareness of endless resources in Christ.

Never is this inwrought sanctification maintained merely by human self-effort, though there is a necessary place for human vigilance and fulfilling of conditions. Never does it infix a once-for-all status of holiness. It may be forfeited through neglects; though it need not be even temporarily interrupted. It can be continuous, ever richer, deeper, sweeter, and is meant to be so. It never warrants anyone to say, "I am now without sin", but it *does* give the consecrated believer inwardly to know the "*FULNESS* of the blessing of Christ", the gracious inflooding of the Holy Spirit, and an inward renewal into holiness never known before.

Immersion in the Spirit

This experience may be further defined as *immersion in the Spirit*. The new "tongues" movement which is widely active today strongly emphasizes "the baptism with the Holy Spirit". Believers are urged to seek this "baptism", the first token of which (according to many) is speaking in "tongues". We do not wish to use space here in mere logomachy, but to set believers seeking the *"baptism"* of the Spirit is not strictly in accord with Scripture. If we adhere closely to the New Testament, the "baptism with the Holy Spirit does not mean *anything* which He does *now*. It refers exclusively to that long-ago historic "Day of Pentecost" which inaugurated the whole present dispensation of the Holy Spirit. Let this fact be duly appreciated, that in the New Testament the "baptism" in the Holy Spirit is pointed to only three times—

1. By John the Baptist: "He shall baptize you in the Holy Spirit" (Matt. 3: 11, Mark 1: 8, Luke 3: 16, John 1: 33).
2. By our Lord Jesus, repeating and confirming John's prediction (Acts 1: 5, 11: 16).
3. By the Apostle Paul, in 1 Corinthians 12: 13, "For in one Spirit were we all baptized into one body".

That this baptism in the Holy Spirit, foretold by John and our Lord, referred to Pentecost is settled by our Lord's word that it should be "not many days hence" (Acts 1: 5). And that the Corinthian verse refers *back* to Pentecost is clear because there is no other such collective baptism of all believers "into the one body". We cannot say it too insistently: the "baptism in the Holy Spirit" was that once-for-all Pentecost baptism of *all* believers by the "one Spirit" into the "one body"; the all-inclusive, all-anticipating immersion of the whole Church for the whole of the present age. Neither before nor after Pentecost does the New Testament anywhere speak of the baptism in the Holy Spirit as something which happens to a separate individual. Nor should *we*. To speak of someone as receiving the "baptism of the Holy Spirit" today is an anachronism. If we keep strictly to Scripture, there has been only the one, incorporative "baptism" in the Spirit, but as a result of its abiding efficacy there have been, and still may be, many individual *infillings* by the Spirit. In short: one "baptism", many "fillings".

That one "baptism" was an *immersion* of the whole Church. Such indeed is the literal meaning of the Greek word, *baptisma* (from the verb *bapto*, to whelm). But does this mean that every member of the true Church is *experientially* immersed in the Spirit? The obvious answer is, "No". Let me make a parallel. Our Lord is called "the Saviour of the world" (1 John 4: 14) who "bore away the sin of the world" (John 1: 29); but does this mean that all men are saved? No, for although the provision is universal it becomes savingly operative only in those who individually appropriate it. So is the whole Church included in the one immersion by the Holy Spirit (1 Cor. 12: 13) but that effusion becomes actual experience only in those who appropriate it by complete self-yielding and faith.

With far too many of us this flood-tide Christian experience is fond theory rather than proven truth. We refer to it with the usual glib cliches but in reality are strangers to it. Yet the gracious Spirit waits with the same condescending availability as ever to saturate the longing heart which will make way for Him.

Often this immersion takes the form of special fillings or enduings for special service or unusual need. The diary of Christmas Evans tells us how, one Sunday afternoon, on a lonely road to a preaching appointment, he became convicted on account of his seeming coldness in heart. He writes, "I tethered my horse and went to a sequestered spot, where I walked to and fro in an agony as I reviewed my life. I waited three hours before God, broken with sorrow, until there broke over me a sweet sense of His forgiving love. I received from God a new enduing of the Holy Spirit. As the sun was westering I went back to the road, found my horse, mounted it and went to my appointment. On the following day I preached with such new power to a vast concourse of people gathered on the hillside, that a revival broke out and spread through all Wales."

That great evangelist and Bible teacher, the late Dr. R. A. Torrey, has left the following remarkable account. "There was a time in the writer's ministry when he was led to say that he would never enter his pulpit again until he had been definitely endued with the Holy Spirit and knew it, or until God in some way told him to go. I shut myself up in my study, and day by day waited upon God for the filling with the Holy Spirit. It was a time of struggle. The thought would arise, 'Suppose you do not receive the enduement with the Holy Spirit before Sunday. How will it look for you to refuse to go into your pulpit?' But I held fast to my resolution. I had a more or less definite thought in my mind of what might happen when I was endued with the Holy Spirit, but it did not come that way at all. One morning as I waited upon God, one of the quietest and calmest moments of my life, it was just as if God said to me, 'The blessing is yours. Now go and preach'.

"If I had known my Bible then as I know it now, I might

have heard that voice the very first day speaking to me through the Word, but I did not know it, and God in His infinite condescension, looking upon my weakness, spoke it directly to my heart. There was no particular ecstasy or emotion, simply the calm assurance that the blessing was mine. I went into my work, and God manifested His power in that work. Some time passed, I do not remember just how long, and I was sitting in that same study. I do not remember that I was thinking about this subject at all, but suddenly it was just as if I had been knocked out of my chair on to the floor; and I lay upon my face crying, 'Glory to God! Glory to God!' I could not stop. Some power, not my own, had taken possession of my lips and my whole person.

"The writer is not of an excitable, hysterical or even emotional temperament; I had never shouted before in my life, but I could not stop. When after a while I got control of myself, I went to my wife and told her what had happened. I tell this experience, not to magnify it, but to say that the time when this wonderful experience (which I cannot really fully describe) came was not the moment when I was endued with the Holy Spirit. The moment when I was endued with the Holy Spirit was in that calm hour when God said, 'It is yours. Now go and preach'."

Never must we covet this infilling by the Spirit merely for the sake of an "experience". Our one motive must be the glorifying of our dear Lord through holy character and effective communication of Him to others. If that is truly our longing and motive, we may "ask and receive" that our "joy may be full".

Renewal of Mind

If there is one thing more than another which we have tried to recapture and re-emphasize in these pages it is that inward sanctification means a real renewing of the mind itself by the divine Spirit. If we stay closely with the New Testament, sanctification is no such peculiarity as a so-called "new nature" at last getting the upper hand over a so-called "*old* nature" which can *never* be sanctified. It is a renewal of our moral and spiritual nature as a whole. All over the New Testament we are shown that the sanctifying Spirit effects a very blessed change in what we constitutionally *are*.

When Luke 24: 45 says that our Lord "opened their understanding" it does not mean merely that He told them something out of His own understanding. He had already been telling them much which they could *not* understand. Luke means that now, by the Holy Spirit, our Lord did something to their *minds*.

When Peter reports how the Holy Spirit had descended on the household of Cornelius, he describes it in Acts 15: 9 as a *"puri-fying of their hearts"* by faith. Not only was there a judicial cleansing from guilt through the atoning blood of Christ, there was an inward purifying of their moral *nature* by the fire of Pentecost.

When Hebrews 13: 21 speaks of God as "working *in* you that which is well-pleasing in His sight", it means something significantly different from merely working *"on* you" or *"for* you" or *"by* you".

So we might go on, for the New Testament epistles are pervaded by this idea of interior renovation of the believer. To holiness-hungry hearts it is the gladdest of glad news. Dear Christian, *you* may be changed. You cannot but remain the same distinctive "you", for you are preciously unique to God; but the Holy Spirit can work a deep-going inward renewal by which you become fundamentally *disposed* to holiness. He can refine you to such love of the pure, and to such sensitive detest for the unholy, that the power of "the flesh" drops away, and, in the words of Charles Wesley, the soul becomes "rooted and fixed in God".

Mind you, the Holy Spirit does not effect this wonderful transformation in suchwise that thereafter it can continue apart from Himself. He and His sanctifying work are one. Think back to your conversion. When the Holy Spirit regenerated you into new spiritual life, He did not impart a life which would henceforward go on apart from Himself. Somehow, besides imparting the life, He Himself *is* the life. So is it with sanctification. The inwrought renewal cannot continue apart from His own continuous infilling of the heart. Let us be affectionately grateful for this. It is one of our heavenly Father's gracious ways of keeping us in continual *fellowship* with Himself.

How glowing are the testimonies of those who have known this deeper ministry of the Spirit! Frances Havergal described it as "a sudden, luminous mind-opening and heart-cleansing". Professor Daniel Steele speaks of it as a shedding of the "all-victorious love of Christ" within him, and adds, a long while afterward, "After years of life's varied experiences, on seas sometimes very tempestuous, in sickness and in health, in tests of exceeding severity, there has not come up out of the depths of either my conscious or my unconscious being anything having the ugly features of sin"! Such testimonies might seem unbelievable to many. Yet never was there a saner or sincerer testifier than Dr. Daniel Steele.

We might add more such testimonies, but space forbids. All I would do here is call special attention to three texts the wording of which makes the possibility of thorough-going moral renewal unmistakable.

"Be ye transformed [*metamorphosed*] by the renewing of your mind" (Rom. 12: 2).

"We are being transformed [*metamorphosed*] into the same image [i.e. of our dear Lord] even from the Lord the Spirit" (2 Cor. 3: 18).

"Be renewed [lit. *being* renewed] in the spirit [*pneuma*] of your mind" (Eph. 4: 23).

Those three representative texts give us truly Scriptural teaching. There is not the faintest hint of any area, such as a so-called "old nature", which *cannot* be sanctified. A thorough moral metamorphosis is indicated; and the last of the three texts goes right through the mind to the *pneuma*, the very "spirit" which is the originating fountain of our thought-life. That, indeed, is inwrought holiness.

Deep-going Renovation

In our companion volume, *A New Call to Holiness*, we have lingered over the first two of those texts. They open the gate to wonderful transfiguration of character. But even more penetrative is Ephesians 4: 23, "Be renewed in the spirit of your mind".

First, in the Greek that verb, "Be renewed", is *passive*, indicating, not something which we ourselves do, but something done *to* us and *in* us by an activity of God. Such inward renewing is *always* the work of God Himself within us, as in Titus 3: 5, "The renewing of the Holy Spirit".

Next, the verb is in the present tense, indicating, not an isolated operation, but a *continuing* renewal of our moral nature—as in 2 Corinthians 4: 16, "Our inward man is being renewed day by day".

Next, the Greek word translated as "renewed" does not mean

"new" in the sense of a new beginning, but a renewedness in *condition*. It is the word which would be used if we said that a decrepit old man had been renewed into *youth*. Even so, *we* are to be renewed into fresh, vital, moral *health*.

Nor is that all. This inwrought renewal is not merely in the mind, but "in the *spirit* of your mind". The apostle here draws a clear distinction between the mind (*pseuche*) and the spirit (*pneuma*). Both are part of man's spiritual being, but the mind or soul is the thinking human *self*, whereas the spirit is the inmost and most mysterious *attribute* of it.

How deeply penetrating, then, is "Be renewed in the *spirit* of your mind"!—not just renewal in the mind itself with all its thought-activities (wonderful as that would be), but a divine renewing of the very "spirit" which predetermines the *moral quality* of thought! The mind, so to speak, is the lake or reservoir: the "spirit" is the spring or stream which feeds it. If the spring is impure, so is the reservoir. If the spring is *pure*, so is the reservoir. This is the inmost secret of victorious holiness, not by an exhausting struggle to repress, but through cleansing and renewal at the very *springs* of thought, impulse, desire, motive and will!

How often have we sighed, "If only this non-stop, restless sin-toward mind of mine with its alarmist imagination, truant memory, subtle cravings, inventive excuses—if only this *mind* could be cleansed, quieted, changed, renewed! Well, in the words of Ephesians 3: 20, the divine answer is "exceeding abundantly above all that we ask or think according to the *power* that worketh *in* us". It is a moral renewal which goes through and beyond the mind, beyond imagination and will, to the very "*spirit*" of the mind. If that does not mean a deep, thorough renovation, what words could? And, of course (mark yet again) it gives utterly no recognition to any supposed "old nature" inside us which *cannot* be renewed. Yes, this is the true way of holiness: a full union with our Saviour in His risen life, bringing to us this inwrought renewal into His own dear image.

Sanctification of Character

I dread lest at any point in these studies we should make over-fine distinctions. Yet I think there is ground for discriminating between enduement for service, and renewal into holy *character*. There is a coming of the Spirit *upon* us as an equipment for witness-bearing or other Christian activities; whereas sanctification is His deep-going work *within* us to develop Christlike *character*. There may be many such comings of the Spirit *upon* us, as we see in the Acts of the Apostles (2: 4, 4: 8, 31, 13: 9); whereas entire sanctification is a *continuous* experience. If that does seem a rather fine distinction, I only refer to it in order to emphasize that what we are to seek is not some isolated "visitation" of the Spirit, but His *abiding* fulness to sanctify. Most of those Christian converts who comprised the churches in Apostolic days had known some super-normal envelopment by the Spirit about the time of their conversion, yet in the Epistles they are exhorted to seek the Spirit's further and more penetrating ministry of character-transfiguration.

One of the most significant Scriptural emblems of the Holy Spirit is *fire*. He is the "Spirit of burning" (Isa. 4: 4) whose action is like "the refiner's fire" (Mal. 3: 2). When He came in fulness at Pentecost, He came not only like a "rushing, mighty wind" as the new heavenly *power*, but in "cloven tongues like as of *fire*" to be the new inward *purifier*. Fire is the most penetrating *tester*. Fire is the intensest *cleanser*. Fire is the most thorough *refiner*. The sin-intolerant flame often hurts when it first begins its testing, searching, cleansing, of our hearts, but as it burns up "the dross of base desire" it brings the pure joy of a heart-radiance and fellowship with God such as we scarcely dreamed possible this side of heaven. Oh, it is with good reason that we pray with Charles Wesley,

> Refining Fire, go through my heart,
>   Illuminate my soul;
> Scatter Thy life through every part,
>   And sanctify the whole.

"*Love in its Fulness*"

Supremely, this deeper work of the Holy Spirit in us may be described as the experiencing of *LOVE IN ITS FULNESS*. That phrase, "love in its fulness" we borrow from Moffatt's delightful translation of 1 John 4: 18, "Love in its fulness drives all dread away".

Yes, "*love in its fulness*"; not love, however, merely as a subjective sublimity of feeling, but as a compassionate outreach to others; not merely as a luxury-emotion, but a self-emptying otherism which gives and gives and gives itself to bless others. That is the love which floods us with the "joy unspeakable", because it never seeks to *get* joy, but only to *give* it. This "love in its fulness" is *life* in its fulness. It is the love of God Himself "shed" copiously within us by the Holy Spirit, ensphering, purifying, enriching, enlarging our own human love until the divine and the human completely blend in a gracious, continuous outgoing of goodness toward the human need all around us.

This *"love in its fulness"* is the dynamic secret behind the character-transformation of all those penmen who wrote our New Testament for us. Who needs to be reminded that all the writers of those immortal pages were Jews (with one exception: Luke). Those old-time Jews were the most exclusive and bigoted race in the world. To them the Gentiles were "dogs", and the Romans, in particular, were "jackals". Those Jews not only despised the Gentiles, they jealously begrudged any thought that the Gentiles should ever have "a part or a lot" in the covenant privileges of Israel. After the attempted lynching of Paul by the Jerusalem mob (Acts 21), when he made his "defence" to the crowd, they tolerated him up to the point where he related how God had said, "I will send thee far hence *unto the Gentiles*". That finished him! The whole crowd was in a frenzy of anti-Gentile rage (22: 21–24). All the Apostles and first Christians were Jews. If we would see how prejudiced Peter was, we only need to read the opening verses of Acts 10. If we would see the flaming hatred of Paul we only need turn to the opening verses of Acts 9. Yet it was those Jews, the most bigoted and prejudiced people on earth, who gave to the world the one and only "whosoever" and universal faith!

Think of Saul, the conceited, strait-jacket Pharisee; a mass of anti-Gentile prejudice, madly determined "in the name of God", to stamp out the blasphemous Nazarene heretics; and then read these amazing words of his: "Unto me, who am less than the least of all saints is this grace given, that I should *proclaim among the Gentiles* the unsearchable riches of Christ" (Eph. 3: 8). "For I speak to you *Gentiles*: inasmuch as I am an apostle of the *Gentiles*, I glorify [or glory in] my ministry" (Rom. 11: 13). "I have you in my heart" (Phil. 1: 7). "Ye are written in our hearts" (2 Cor. 3: 2). "I will most gladly spend, yea be *spent out*, for your souls, even though the more *abundantly I love you* [Gentiles!] the less I am loved" (12: 15).

Can we ever forget?—it was from that erstwhile disdainful Pharisee and his obstinately Jewish co-Apostles, and those many other once-bigoted Jewish evangelists, that we Gentiles received the glad tidings which brought us salvation, and founded Christianity among us. And, wonder of wonders, so magnanimously concerned were those Jews to share their Gospel with us, so eager to welcome us as partners in their God-given covenant promises, that they willingly suffered whippings, scourgings, stonings, clubbings, starvings, drownings, burnings, imprisonments, tortures and excruciating deaths for the sake of it! *Why?* The whole answer is found in words like these: "The *love of Christ* constraineth us" (2 Cor. 5: 14); "The *love of God* is shed abroad in our hearts by the Holy Spirit" (Rom. 5: 5); "*We love* (i.e. others) because He first loved us" (1 John 4: 19). The revolutionary miracle is all in that one little phrase, "*LOVE IN ITS FULNESS*" (1 John 4: 18).

"Love in its fulness." How clear and wise was John Wesley in always coming back to this, that the principium and primary proof of the second blessing is pure love to God and neighbour! "*Love* is the sum of Christian sanctification" (*Sermons*, vol. 2: 221). "What I want is holiness of heart and life . . . that is, loving God with all our heart, and serving Him with all our strength" (to Mr. Venn, 1765). "Rapturous joy, such as is frequently given in the beginning of entire sanctification, is a great blessing; but it seldom continues long before it subsides into calm, peaceful love" (*Letters*, 6: 269). J. A. Wood, who carefully analysed all John Wesley's characteristic phrases, says, "He used the term, '*renewed in love*' more frequently than any other" (*Christian Perfection*, 103).

This is the acme, the zenith, the sunlit top-peak, "*love in its fulness*". This is holiness, entire sanctification, "*love in its fulness*". This is that longed-for something which somehow includes all the others, "*love in its fulness*". This is the biggest, gladdest, richest reality in the second blessing, "*love in its fulness*". This is what the many who have experienced it have been trying to tell us: it is "*love in its fulness*". This is no dreamy mysticism so occupied in getting without the "self" that it becomes psychopathically self-occupied! This is a self-forgetting love for God and man which overflows in practical godliness and goodness. It is Christianity at flood-tide: "*love in its fulness*".

A heart in every thought renewed
    And *filled with love divine*:
Upright and pure, sincere and good,
    A copy, Lord, of Thine.

Can it really be? Yes, it really can! And that, in its truest
and most Christ-like expression, is Christian holiness. In these
pages we have spoken of the second blessing as "inwrought
holiness", "entire sanctification", "infilling by the Holy Spirit",
"moral and spiritual renewal", "transfiguration of character";
but that which is truest and deepest and highest and most God-
like of all, and that which crowns all else is just this—

"LOVE IN ITS FULNESS"

I ask, dear Lord,
    A heart renewed and clean,
Reflecting Thee,
    With not a cloud between ;
A heart all Thine,
My King divine,
    A heart with Thee aglow ;
In me, dear Lord,
    A heart like this bestow.

I ask, dear Lord,
    A soul on fire for Thee;
A soul endued
    With heavenly energy;
A willing mind,
A ready hand,
    To do whate'er I know ;
To spread Thy light
    Wherever I may go.

TWO DEEP-GOING QUESTIONS

"Whether we call it a Second Blessing or not, that is what it is. It is distinct from regeneration, and subsequent to it. Those who contend that they received all that is involved in salvation when they were 'born again' do not distinguish between potentiality and conscious possession."

Samuel Chadwick.

There are those whose minds are once-for-all closed to the idea of a "second work of grace" in the believer, whatever name may be given to it. My own contacts with them seem to indicate that few of them have really thought the thing through with minds able to evaluate the total Scripture evidence unprejudicially. Yet I am not doubting for one moment their sincerity. As one put it to me recently, they believe in "progression rather than crisis." He pointed me to the progress indicated in 2 Corinthians 3:18, "from glory to glory". But why for one text shut out the evidence of so many others? We ourselves preach the progressive metamorphosis indicated in 2 Corinthians 3:18, but does that text contradict the various others which indicate a post-conversion crisis-point *into* that progressive transformation? Not at all. Does that progressive metamorphosis really take place at all in any *but* the entirely sanctified, i.e., the entirely yielded and Spirit-possessed believer? The evidence seems to say, "No". How, then, do we reach that point of entire set-apartness? Do we gradually slide or slip into it? Evidence says, "No". Do not most of us need some sort of a decisive after-conversion crisis to bring us to it?

J.S.B.

TWO DEEP-GOING QUESTIONS

BY NOW, perhaps, some who may have persevered through these pages could be asking: Is this deeper work of the Holy Spirit in believers the experience which used to be called (and not infrequently still is) the "second blessing"? With certain reservations our answer is: Yes, though we are not one bit anxious either to resurrect or to perpetuate a mere name for it—not unless there is real value in so doing.

Older persons who may have chanced on these chapters may recall how, in their younger years, that phrase, "the second blessing", was current coinage on most holiness conference platforms, especially in England. Nowadays it has lapsed into comparative disuse; but is that because holiness teaching itself is in disrepair?

One thing is still alive, and that is the strong resentment which many show toward the expression, "second blessing"! They exclaim disdainfully, "Why, there are hundreds of blessings; not just two!" Yet such reply is merely throwing dust into the air. The vital question is: Does Scripture teach, and does experience confirm, that there is a deeper work of inwrought holiness in Christian believers which begins with such a post-conversion crisis that it merits this distinctive name, "the second blessing", or some other equally distinguishing designation?

An alternative expression has been, "the second work of grace"; and if what these studies have shown from Scripture and experience is true, then perhaps we have reached a point where we may well ask with new seriousness whether this controverted "second work of grace" in the believer is, after all, mere illusion, or believable reality.

Wesley and His Successors

Those who toss the matter aside with off-handed scorn dishonour some of the greatest leaders whom our Lord has given to His Church during the past two centuries. I name here only one:

John Wesley, who originated the phrase, "second blessing". How much does all Christendom owe to that great Methodist! If ever a man was "great in the sight of the Lord", John Wesley was. If ever a man was great in the nobleness and enduring worth of his legacy to succeeding generations, John Wesley is. He has been impartially pronounced, "the greatest force of the eighteenth century". The late T. R. Glover, recently Public Orator of Cambridge University, links Paul, Augustine, Luther, and Wesley as the four outstanding figures of evangelical history. Hundreds of those who have followed in the Wesley "second blessing" tradition have been exceptional leaders known far and wide for their consistent, all-round godliness; and, as A. M. Hills observes, with some understandable resentment, "These are . . . the great army of saints who are called 'holiness cranks' by people scarcely worthy to touch their shoe-latchets."

A Practical Doctrine

A collateral feature which deserves unbiassed reconsideration is, that the representative sons and daughters of this Second Blessing lineage, other than being unpractical introverts, have been energetic Christian *workers*. Again I revert to John Wesley as prototypal of this. None of the would-be debunkers of his Second Blessing doctrine could ever insinuate even a hint of dreamy mysticism in *him*!

What a worker he was! In more than forty years of horse-back travel on the road, he covered more than a quarter of a million miles, and preached some forty thousand sermons. He crossed the Irish Sea over fifty times, and the Atlantic from England to America and back several times. Referring to his horse-back itinerations he tells us, "History, philosophy and poetry I commonly read on horseback, having other employment at other times". (He had a small desk fitted behind the horse's neck.) Somehow he found time to pen some two hundred and thirty larger and smaller works, including several histories, a book on logic and one on physics, an English dictionary, a Hebrew grammar, a Greek grammar, and a French grammar! All that from a man who in middle years seemingly had tuberculosis, and wrote his own epitaph in expectation of an early demise!

Since Wesley's days the scenery of life has greatly changed in our Western hemisphere. Such copious literary output, along with such manifold ministerial labours, amid such old-fashioned conditions, could never be duplicated in anyone afterward. Yet he "fixed the type", so to speak. All his spiritual successors in the Second Blessing line have been eminently of the spiritual-*practical* sort. Whatever quirks of teaching or method may have been alleged against them, they have been men and women who have "adorned the doctrine" by zealous "good works" and practical philanthropies. Therefore to let haughty prejudice without fair enquiry antagonize us to the doctrine of the Second Blessing is unworthy evasion.

So, then, the second blessing, as a deep and definite post-conversion work of God in the soul: is it reality or illusion? To begin with, let me mention a remarkable peculiarity which bears on this.

A Warfield Peculiarity

At the time of his death in 1921, the late Dr. Benjamin Brecken-ridge Warfield, Professor of Didactic and Polemic Theology at Princeton Theological Seminary, was pretty generally regarded as the leading Calvinistic theologian of the English-speaking world. Through the Oxford University Press, an Editorial Committee published his contributions to theological thought in ten volumes, of which volumes 7 and 8 embody his massive treatise on *Perfectionism*; a work of over one thousand large pages. I know of no more compendious or searching scrutiny of successive schools on the subject. There is a scholarly logic about his writings which is a stimulating tonic to those who think alike with him, but which bears down like an armoured war-horse on dissident theories.

Now no one can read those two tomes without seeing that Dr. Warfield is no friend of the Second Blessing idea. As the Irish-man would say, he is "*agin* it". We might even say in Scottish parlance that he has a *scunner* against it. Wherever he can strike a blow at it he does, and there are opportunities not a few. Yet here is the remarkable thing: from beginning to end of those thousand pages I cannot find one place where he gives us any real *argument* against it. Again and again there are strong thrusts and objections in connection with extremist positions; and with many of them I am bound to agree; but cogent *argument* I cannot find even once against the Second Blessing itself as a deeper work of the Holy Spirit in the regenerated, distinguishable though not severable from regeneration, and usually though not necessarily subsequent to it. That Warfield peculiarity speaks rather loudly to my own mind.

An Alternative Emphasis

Not only have those in the Wesley lineage taught the "second blessing". Equally definitely, though more cautiously, has the Keswick Convention. Less frequently has Keswick used the actual phrase, "second blessing" (wisely so, I think) lest Keswick teaching should ever be confused with the eradicationist theory. That gifted master of the Keswick formula, Evan H. Hopkins, prefers to put it that sanctification comes as a distinctively further or second experience which he calls "a crisis followed by a process". From his various references to it I cull the following which appear in the *Keswick Week* of 1907.

"There are few things connected with the Keswick movement which have so much puzzled people as the apparent contradiction—that the blessing is both instantaneous and progressive. Those who have been brought into definite blessing, along the line of sanctification by faith, have borne witness to the fact that they had been brought into an experience of what the Lord Jesus can be to them for holiness, with a suddenness that has been as striking as the change has been blessed and soul-satisfying."

"He [God] does not do it gradually ; it is done instantaneously. This is what has taken place in the case of hundreds of souls in this very Tent. In a few brief moments the whole inner being has been adjusted. First, spiritual adjustment, and afterwards spiritual enduement."

Frankly, I myself am no committed advocate of the term "second blessing", yet neither can I be over-bigotedly against it, provided it represents a genuine experience corresponding to that name. My own preference is for the Scriptural phrase, "the *fulness* of the blessing of Christ".

In our early chapters on "Old Testament Pointers" and "New Testament Patterns", and "Real or Imaginary?" we surely saw enough evidence, both in Scripture and in creditable biography, to indicate that there is indeed a further, deeper, more or less crisis experience through which believers come to know entire sanctification ; a renewing work of the Holy Spirit inseparable from prior regeneration yet distinct and powerful enough to be reasonably called the "*deeper* blessing". Agreeing, then, that this *is* a reality, in what *sense* can we still believe in it?

Ideas No Longer Tenable

(1) No longer can we believe in the "second blessing" as an *eradication* of all sin-proclivities in human nature.

(2) Nor can we believe in it as any kind of surgery on a suppositionary "old nature" which (theoretically) co-exists with a so-called "new nature" in the regenerate. As we have seen, the notion of "two natures" in the believer is phantasmal.

(3) Nor can we believe in it as an inward crucifixion with Christ, a supposedly "making real" in present experience of something done once for all, two thousand years ago. The Christian's identification with the Cross *judicially* was never meant to be re-enacted (and *cannot* be) interiorly, i.e. inside the believer's moral nature. Such a "mystery" concept of sanctification by simulated uni-crucifixion is alien to the New Testament, as we have shown.

(4) Nor can we believe in the "second blessing" as such a take-over of the consecrated believer by Christ that the human personality itself is superseded. Any teaching which strains yieldedness to Christ into *absorption* by Christ, so that the human self becomes *substituted* by Christ, is a mystical excrescence utterly extrinsic to Scripture. To misplay the words, "Christ liveth in me" (Gal. 2: 20) into meaning, "Christ liveth *instead* of me", or the words, "Christ is our life" (Col. 3: 4) into "Christ is *ourselves*", is hyper-spiritual exoticism, not sane exegesis.

(5) Nor can we henceforth think of the "second blessing" in any way which separates it too acutely from *conversion*. That teaching which divides all the born again so that they live either on one or the other of two rigidly demarcated levels: (1) saved but not sanctified, (2) saved *and* sanctified, is astray from the New Testament highway. There are *degrees* of sanctification.

(6) Nor must we think of this deeper work in us as "the *gift* of the Spirit". I have heard enthusiasts of the new "tongues" movement say, "Until you speak in tongues you are without the 'sign' which always accompanies the 'gift of the Spirit'." Such talk is the wildfire of error. It blisters many and blesses none. The first promise Christianity ever made when it came out on to the platform of publicity was, "Repent ye, and be baptized every one of you in the name of Jesus Christ unto the remission of your sins; and ye shall receive the gift of the Holy Spirit" (Acts

2: 38). That promise was made to *unconverted* persons, contingently upon their receiving Jesus as Saviour. Apart from any "second work of grace" or speaking in "tongues", all the born again *have* the life-giving Holy Spirit.

(7) Nor, finally, can we believe in the "second blessing" as in any sense a once-for-all elevation to top-level spiritual experience with a built-in guarantee of life-long permanence. There is no such intrinsic permanence in it as there is in *justification*. Our justification, resting on the finished work of Christ, is absolutely changeless despite fluctuations in ourselves; but obviously an inward *condition* can have no such unvarying fixity, for it is contingent (intendedly so) upon maintained consecration and communion with God.

A Revised Presentation

But now, after these eliminations, does there still remain a sanctification experience epochal enough to be termed in unmistakable distinction the *second* blessing? May we not reply a cautious *Yes?* If the second blessing is a genuine reality it will survive all such strippings away of the false, and become the more authentic by its disentanglement from error.

This, then, is what remains: In response to our utter self-yielding, longing, trusting, appropriating, the Holy Spirit unobstructedly fills us, suffusing heart, mind, personality with Himself, and communicating to us from then onwards, in a way never knowable before, a deep-going sanctification of our moral and spiritual nature. Let me repeat our definition:

> IT IS THAT EXPERIENCE, ORIGINATING AT THE CRISIS-POINT OF UTTER SELF-YIELDING TO GOD (NOT ALWAYS EMOTIONALLY VIVID BUT ALWAYS MOST DEFINITE) IN WHICH THE HOLY SPIRIT INFILLS THE HEART, MAKING FELLOWSHIP WITH GOD AND POSSESSION OF CHRIST REAL AS NEVER BEFORE, AND EFFECTING WITHIN THE FULLY CONSECRATED BELIEVER A MORAL AND SPIRITUAL RENEWAL INTO HOLINESS DEEPER AND FULLER THAN COULD EVER BE KNOWN OTHERWISE.

Yes, that is it. That is the deeper blessing. It is deep enough, distinctive enough, *epochal* enough to be called in a unique sense *"the* deeper blessing"—different in its transforming effect from all other "blessings" of the Christian life. When once it is inwardly experienced, not all the dogged logic of all the scholarly objectors who ever wielded the pen can syllogise away the blessed reality of it!

In an earlier chapter I submitted several testimonials as to the reality of the blessing. There were two defects clinging to most of them: (1) they were from persons now deceased, (2) they were mainly from adherents of the eradicationist theory. So let me here give the experience of two well-known Christian leaders who are still with us, and who have no public connection with the two main holiness platforms. In both these testimonials there are expressions with which our present re-study of New Testament teaching will not let us agree; but they none-the-less serve to show the crisis-nature and experiential reality of this second and distinctive work of God in the soul.

The first is from the pen of the widely known Dr. E. Stanley Jones. We quote from his *Victorious Living*, page 20.

"I was a Christian for a year or more when one day I looked at a library shelf and was struck with the title of a book, *The Christian's Secret of a Happy Life*. As I read it my heart was set on fire to find this life of freedom and fulness. I reached the forty-second page when the Inner Voice said very distinctly, 'Now is the time to find'. I pleaded that I did not know what I wanted, that when I finished it I would seek. But the Inner Voice was imperious, 'Now is the time to seek'. I tried to read on, but the words seemed blurred. I was up against a Divine insistence, so I closed the book, dropped on my knees and asked, 'What shall I do?' The Voice replied, 'Will you give Me your all—your very all?' After a moment's hesitation, I replied, 'I will'. 'Then take My all, you are cleansed,' the Voice said with a strange inviting firmness. 'I believe it,' I said, and arose from my knees. I walked around the room affirming it over and over, and pushing my hands away from me as if to push away my doubt. This I did for ten minutes, when suddenly I was filled with a strange refining fire that seemed to course through every portion of my being in cleansing waves. It was all very quiet and I had hold of myself—and yet the Divine waves could be felt from the inmost centre of my being to my finger-tips. My whole being was being fused into one, and through the whole there was a sense of sacredness and awe—and the most exquisite joy. . . . My will was just as much involved as my emotion. The fact is, the whole of life was on a permanently higher level."

The second culling is from a little book, *The Fulness of the Holy Spirit*, by George S. Ingram. On page 23 he says:

"Never had the Devil so tempted me to doubt God, as when He gave me grace to trust Him to sanctify me wholly according to His promise in 1 Thessalonians 5 : 23, 24. Before I had risen from my knees he attacked me, and day after day as I waited for God's inward assurance that He had cleansed my heart from all sin, the Devil again and again attacked me with doubts that nothing had happened because I felt nothing. And every time, God enabled me to hurl that promise which He had given me at the Devil; and every time, he left me, defeated by the Word. And then in God's own time came His deep inward assurance that He had cleansed my heart from *all* sin, and *filled* me with His Holy Spirit, and that inward assurance has remained with me through the years as a very precious possession."

No one would ever associate the name of the famous C. H. Spurgeon with any doctrine of the second blessing. Spurgeon was a Calvinist and a Puritan in theology and expository cast. Yet even Spurgeon says, "There is a point of grace as much above the ordinary Christian as the ordinary Christian is above the world."

Truly understood, the second blessing has (intendedly) as real and distinctive a place in our experience of salvation as the entering into Canaan had for the Israelites long ago. Besides the *exodus* from Egypt there was the *eisodus* into Canaan. That exodus and that eisodus were the two outstanding crises in the one "so great salvation". The earlier preachers of the deeper blessing, especially in the radical, extinctionist sense, were sometimes charged with preaching a "second conversion", or with magnifying the *second* blessing to the depreciation of the *first* (i.e. conversion); but the *true* doctrine emphasizes the oneness of the two. Disembarrassed from eradicationist and other curious accretions, the *true* doctrine of the deeper blessing correctly preserves the meaningful parallel with those two capital crises in that long-ago salvation of Israel: (1) the Red Sea crisis, i.e. *exodus* out of Egypt, to new life and liberty; (2) the Jordan crisis, i.e. into Canaan, to bounty, rest, victory—the subjugation (but not eradication) of all foes. Let us mark this fact carefully: it is that Egypt-to-Canaan period of which 1 Corinthians 10: 11 says,

"Now all these things happened unto them as TYPES (*tupoi*); and they are written for *our* admonition."

That entrance into Canaan was not a second salvation, but it *was* a complemental second *part*. It was so in a conspicuous and emphatic sense as the *second* of those two major events compared with which all others were only incidental. It was the big *SECOND BLESSING* to which those people of the Covenant had been pointed ever since their coming out of Egypt. Yes, that is the Old Testament type. The New Testament *anti*type is that wonderful deeper blessing in the Christian life through which, in answer to our complete self-yielding and our appropriating faith, the Holy Spirit infills all our human capacities, making the mind His very sanctuary, breaking all inward bondage to sin, bringing to us new consciousness of Christ, lifting us into new fellowship with God, and thenceforward, as never before, renewing us into holiness, that is, *fulness of moral and spiritual health*.

IS IT "CHRISTIAN *PERFECTION*"?

There is one further question which we think should be asked and briefly answered here. What is meant by "Christian *perfection*"? Perhaps younger readers may not have come across that phrase often as yet, but many others know how closely it has been associated with teachings on holiness. Believers have been taught to seek "Christian *perfection*" as the goal of holy character in this present life. They have been pointed to verses such as Colossians 4: 12, "Perfect and complete in all the will of God"; or Hebrews 6: 1, "Let us go on unto perfection".

At any rate, in case anyone who reads these pages should ever come under perfectionist teaching, I think it is good to confront the question here: Does the New Testament teach the possibility of a moral and spiritual sanctity in this present life which might be accurately called "Christian *perfection*"?

The phrase, "Christian perfection", sprang into vogue through the voice and pen of John Wesley. From then until recently it has been the most alluring yet the most controversial of all holiness watchwords. The special doctrine which the phrase focalized and crystallized was regarded by Wesley as the "grand depositum" which God had committed to and through the Methodist movement.

To any thoughtful mind in quest of sanctification the phrase, "Christian perfection", is at once arresting, magnetic, hope-inspiring. It lifts the eyes to what seems like a shining plateau of spiritual "finish" firmly above the fogs and shadows and alternations of lower levels. Even those with the most Jacob-like inward duality of carnal versus spiritual feel sure that here is the gate to an inward Paradise—"Christian *perfection*".

But what is the real truth about "Christian perfection"? Is there such a reality in this present life? What do John Wesley and his followers mean by it? Why has it been so controverted, so denounced by others? Those are important questions if we would get finally clear on this subject of Christian holiness.

Resentment against the doctrine of Christian perfection there certainly has been in plenty, right from the first. At one time criticism was so acute that Wesley wrote to his brother Charles, "I am at my wits' end"; and a month later,

"Shall we go on in asserting perfection against all the world? Or shall we quietly let it drop? We really must do one or the other; and, I apprehend, the sooner the better" (*Letters* 5 : 88).

Yet, as W. E. Sangster says, that was "only a mood". "The great little man took a firmer grip of his pen and battled on." Although he wrote Dr. William Dodd, "I have no particular fondness for the term", he *had*, for he clung to it and championed it to the end. Only three months before he died, he wrote Dr. Adam Clarke,

"If we can prove that any of our Local Preachers or Leaders, either directly or indirectly, speaks against it, let him be a Local Preacher or Leader no longer" (*Letters* 8 : 249).

Why, then, did Wesley adhere so perseveringly to his oft-maligned doctrine of "Christian perfection"? It was because he believed sincerely that it was Scriptural. Why has it persisted from then until now? For the same reason. Many of the devoutest saints, including keen scholars, have gloried in it as highest-level sanctification.

But *is* it truly Scriptural? Our reply is a cautious, No. We have carefully examined all the sixty places where the words, "perfect", "perfected", "perfecting", "perfection", "perfectly", "perfectness" occur in our New Testament (Authorized Version). They translate to us a variety of Greek words, and the fact is, that not one of those Greek words means perfection in the stricter meaning of our English word. To save burdening our pages here we have transferred the showing of this in detail to an Excursus: *Is "Christian Perfection" Scriptural?* (see p. 225). The one point which we emphasize here is, that not one of those Greek words means perfection in the exact English sense: therefore there is *no* true doctrine of so-called "Christian perfection". The phrase should be dropped altogether, as a misleading by-product of inexact translation into English.

Nowhere does New Testament nomenclature teach holiness as centering in an abstract principle of perfection. Nowhere in its pages is the goal of Christian holiness a fixed level of ethical perfection. As vapours vanish in the light of a glorious sunrise, so all human philosophies of perfection give way before the revelation of the Absolutely Divine and Altogether Lovely, our Lord Jesus. *HE* is perfection incarnate. *HE* is the goal of Christian holiness. In the light of that sunrise let us cease talking about "Christian perfection", and talk of *LIKENESS TO HIM*. The only Christian perfection is that of our perfect *standing* in Christ before God. That, however, is positional, not experiential. Any idea of a standardized "perfection" in individual character let us repudiate as foreign to the New Testament.

My own guess would be that Wesley clung so tenaciously to the phrase, "Christian perfection", despite the calumny and irritation which it provoked, because it was a kind of necessary twin to his eradication theory. Believing, as he did, that there were "two natures" in the born again—the incurably sinful *old,* and the necessarily sinless *new,* he held that once the old was eradicated sin was gone. He evidently felt he dare not claim the *actuality* of such sinlessness, yet with such premises how could he preach less than the possibility of it? Galatians 2: 20, "I am crucified with Christ", means (see Sermon 40) "My evil nature, the body of sin, is destroyed". Apparently it never occurred to him that Galatians 2: 20 says nothing at all about a crucified "old nature"!

In reality, however, Wesley's argument (see Sermons 40 and 76) is for perfection in name only. He begins by explaining that Christian perfection is not that of angels, nor that of unfallen Adam, nor is it without defects even moral. He says, "This is the sum of Christian perfection: it is all comprised in that one word, Love". In another place Christian perfection is the undivided "fruit of the Spirit". In another it is to be "created anew", and in another "entire sanctification", and in another, "salvation from sin, from all sin"—"the root as well as the branches". Yet after all it is only an accommodated perfection, and therefore not really perfection at all. At one time Wesley wrote to his brother Charles, "I still think that to set perfection *so high* is effectually to renounce it". Such "Christian perfection", as Lutheran theologian, Dr. Günther Dehn comments in his *Man and Revelation*, "largely consists in recognizing that a man *cannot* be perfect".

Or, to quote Dr. B. B. Warfield again, "it differs from all other kinds of perfection precisely in this, that it is not real perfection . . . and provokes the jibe that one may be a perfect Christian without being a perfect man".

So, in this perfection which is *not* perfection, which is made to seem so Scripturally obvious yet is such a tangle of exegetical faultiness, *how far did John Wesley really go?* We may answer in his own phraseology, "Christian perfection" is the "destruction of all inward sin", so that "the evil root is destroyed, and inbred sin subsists no more." It is to be "renewed into His [God's] whole image", and to be "so far perfect as not to commit sin". It is to have the soul "all love", to be filled with "pure love, expelling sin, and governing both heart and life."

Was such "perfection" ever really experienced? Wesley said he knew hundreds of whom it was true: "I think I see five hundred witnesses of it." Yet writing to Miss Jane Hilton in 1769, he laments, "Although many taste of that heavenly gift, deliverance from inbred sin, yet so few, so exceeding few, retain it one year; hardly one in ten; nay, one in thirty." (How account for this drop-back into sin if the "evil nature" had been eradicated into non-existence?)

Why was there such disappointing reaction? It was because John Wesley's doctrine of perfection through eradication overshoots the Scripture. Does any one of the New Testament writers anywhere claim sinlessness? No. Does any one of them anywhere claim perfection? No. Does John Wesley himself ever dare to make such a claim? No. He writes in a letter to Dr. William Dodd, "I tell you flat, I have not attained the character I draw." W. E. Sangster says, "The most convinced adherents of his teaching have been unable to discover him making this bold claim for himself." (*Pathway to Perfection*, 161.)

For two decisive reasons, then, the expression, "Christian perfection" should be now and forever renounced: (1) the relevant Greek words of the New Testament give no warrant for it; (2) John Wesley, its progenitor, means no more by it, on his own confession, than an *imperfect* perfection, which is not perfection at all. Many thousands have been allured, stirred, challenged, drawn, deceived, mocked, and afterwards dashed down by it into heart-rending doubt. It is a false banner. Let us march under it no longer.

But now, finally, if we cannot retain *that* banner, is there a new and truer standard which we can upraise in its place? There is. Never must we let our criticisms of John Wesley's perfectionist theory blind us to his magnificent new insistence on the Scriptural imperative and *experiential reality* of entire sanctification. All the way through he is bearing witness to a further and deeper and special work of the Holy Spirit in the already born-again; a real and verifiable experience of inwrought holiness. He may call it by a wrong name; he may explain some of its aspects in a wrong way—as eradication or sin-extinction, but the *experience itself* is genuine and boundlessly meaningful. There *is* such a "second blessing". What is more, we cannot be too grateful for John Wesley's glorious emphasis on *love* as its crowning positive. I refer again to Moffatt's delightful translation of 1 John 4: 18, "*Love in its fulness* drives all dread away". That was what John Wesley continually stressed as the crowning reality and beauty of entire sanctification: *"LOVE IN ITS FULNESS"*.

Yes, let us peal it out again: *"LOVE IN ITS FULNESS"*. That is holiness in its most radiant dress. That is holiness most after the image of Jesus. Hear the Scripture: "Love worketh no ill to his neighbour" (Rom. 13: 10)—is not *that* holiness? "Therefore love is the fulfilling of the Law" (Rom. 13: 10)—is not *that* holiness? "For all the Law is fulfilled in one word, even in this: Thou shalt love thy neighbour as Thyself" (Gal. 5: 14)—is not *that* holiness? "God is love: he that dwelleth in love dwelleth in God, and *God in him*" (1 John 4: 16)—is not *that* holiness?

Oh, Christian believer, that is the holiness to seek: the love of the heavenly Father and the Redeemer-Son flooding into the surrendered heart, engulfing all the true, natural affections and sublimating them into truly Christlike virtues. In this (as we have said) the Holy Spirit is the Executive of the Godhead, even as Romans 5: 5 declares—"The love of God is *shed abroad* in our hearts by the Holy Spirit". Or as Weymouth translates it, "God's love *floods our hearts* through the Holy Spirit". That is the sanctification to seek. It is that which works the gracious miracle of interior renewal and transformation: love at flood-tide in the heart. Christian, wait on God; *keep* waiting on Him, till you *know* that you are a "living sacrifice" to Him. Then ask Him (if it does not come *without* your asking) to give you the "witness" of this immersion in sanctifying love.

During my youthful years I used to revel in the little books written by Col. S. M. Brengle of the Salvation Army. *He* certainly knew the "sacred thrill" of the deeper blessing. He held on eagerly to the Salvation Army theory (the John Wesley eradication theory) of the second blessing, and in that we cannot agree with him; but what a radiant, consistent testimonial he was to the reality of a second and distinctive crisis-work by the Holy Spirit in the believer! He had no doubt as to the moment when it happened or the deep transformation which it effected. His little book, *Helps to Holiness,* begins, "On January 9th, 1885, at about nine o'clock in the morning, God sanctified my soul". He thus describes its initial impact:

"It was a heaven of love that came into my heart. I walked out over Boston Common before breakfast, weeping for joy and praising God. Oh, how I loved! In that hour I knew Jesus, and loved Him till it seemed my heart would break in love. I loved the sparrows, I loved the dogs, I loved the horses, I loved the little urchins on the streets, I loved the strangers who hurried past me, I loved the heathen—I loved the whole world."

That experience was no emotional "flash in the pan". It was the inflooding of that "perfect love" which "casteth out fear" and sanctifies the heart and transfigures the character, as Colonel Brengle proved through many a day afterwards. Our explanations of the deeper blessing may need considerable revision, but the deep and blessed experience itself is *real;* and it is so against all the cavils which have ever been flung at it. Let our prayer be that of seventeenth-century Paulus Gerhardt:

> Oh, grant that nothing in my soul
>   May dwell, but Thy pure love alone!
> Oh, may that love possess me whole,
>   My joy, my treasure, and my crown:
> Strange fires far from my heart remove;
> Each act, word, thought, be holy love!

LET US GO UP AND POSSESS

"I suppose that if, when we made our acts of consecration, we could actually see Him [our Lord] present with us, we should feel it to be a very real thing, and would realize that we had given our word to Him, and could not dare to take it back. Such a transaction would have to us the binding power that a spoken promise always has to a man of honour. What we need, therefore, is to see that God's presence is a certain fact always, and that every word spoken in prayer is as really spoken to Him as if our eyes could see Him and our hands could touch him."

Hannah W. Smith

LET US GO UP AND POSSESS

IT HAS been pointedly observed that despite the present-day emergence of a "scientific mind" and an "educated public", our twentieth century is being moulded far more by prejudice than logic. It is equally true that prejudice rather than open-minded appraisal of evidence decides the attitude of many Christians to what has been named, from John Wesley's time onwards, the "second blessing". The reaction of many may be expressed in the ironic cameo often fixed on party politics: "My mind is made up; do not confuse me with facts". Others, not a few, use the term, "second-blessing", as a satirical soubriquet describing religious eccentrics.

Throughout these present studies we have made ourselves clear as to this: We believe that Scripture and experience unite in attesting a deeper, richer, fuller experience of salvation than most Christian believers today seem to know; an experience distinct from regeneration, though inseparable from it, and complemental to it, and usually (though not necessarily) subsequent to it, in which the Christian believer is lifted into a spiritual victory, liberty, fulness and fellowship with God never known apart from it. It is generally entered by a post-conversion *crisis*. In the New Testament it is referred to as entire sanctification. It brings gracious infilling by the Holy Spirit; a purifying renewal of the moral nature; and enduement of power, wisdom, grace, spiritual gift, for special service or need.

If such an experience of salvation in Christ is indeed indicated in Scripture and endorsed by experience, should not *all* Christian believers be taught so, and seek the reality of it for the service of Christ and the glory of God? If the promise is really there, in the Word, does not Hebrews 4: 1-11 become a searching challenge?

"Let us therefore fear, lest, a promise being left us of entering into His rest, any of you should seem to come short of it. . . . Let us therefore give diligence to enter into that rest, lest any man fall after the same example of disobedience [as Israel's]."

Dear Christian believer whom it is now my privilege to address, have you yet entered that "promised land" of entire sanctification? If you happen to be one of those who rebel against the designation, "second blessing", let me re-word the question: Are you really living in the *"fulness* of the blessing of Christ"? If you are *not*, then in repudiating a mere name for the blessing are you masquerading behind an evasion, and thus grieving the divine Spirit?

Of most who have read these pages, however, I am sure we may use the words of Hebrews 6: 9, "But, beloved, we are persuaded better things of you". Are there not many of us who are convinced as to the authenticity of that "better thing" (Heb. 11: 40) which God has provided for us? and are we not asking the way into it?

Long ago, when the Israel tribes reached the border of Canaan, they appointed twelve "spies" to reconnoitre and report. All twelve concurred that it was "an exceeding good land", "flowing with milk and honey", but ten of them said, "We be not able to go up against the people, for they are stronger than we" (Num. 13: 31). Thus they dispirited the Israelites. But the other two "spies", Caleb and Joshua, said, "Let us go up at once and possess it". The ten had their eyes on the *human*; the two had their eyes on the *divine*. The ten had their eyes on the *problem*; the two had their eyes on the *promise*. That is ever the difference between doubt and faith.

> Doubt sees the difficulties
>   Faith sees the way ;
> Doubt sees the darksome night,
>   Faith sees the day ;
> Doubt dreads to take the step,
>   Faith soars on high ;
> Doubt whispers, "Who believes?"
>   Faith answers, "I".

When at last Israel *did* enter Canaan, after thirty-eight years of delay, it was by what may be truly called the *crisis* of the Jordan crossing. There was no entering the promised land piecemeal or graduatedly. The *whole* of Israel crossed over in one crisis of committal, and saw the divided Jordan waters flow together again behind them, cutting off retreat.

The *principle* of occupation was, "Every place that the sole of your foot shall tread upon, that have I given you" (Josh. 1: 3). In the terms of the Abrahamic covenant, the whole land was already theirs by God-given right of possession; but possession is not the same as *occupation*. That which was provided must now be *appropriated*. They would actually occupy only what they took: "Every place that the sole of your foot shall *tread upon, that have I given you.*"

It is the same now in relation to the deeper Christian life of "entire sanctification". It is truly given to us in Christ, and the Holy Spirit waits to make it real; but we ourselves, each of us individually, must "go up and possess", planting our feet by faith upon the clear promises of the Word. To be more specific, there are seven steps in the *crisis* of "going up to possess", as follows.

I. BELIEVE IT IS A GIFT

Believe that sanctification, in the sense of inward renewal, is a divine *gift*. Obviously, if any real change is to be wrought in our moral nature, only God can effect it. Self cannot change self. There *is* a human side to it, but sanctification as an inwrought purifying is exclusively the work of the Holy Spirit; therefore it is a gracious gift. A gift is to be received. We do not earn it, win it, merit it, attain it; we *receive* it.

Get hold of that firmly for it has been denied. The learned Dr. B. B. Warfield is very blunt: "When it is said that sanctification is by faith, 'without works of law'—that, to speak frankly, is nonsense" (*Perfectionism*, vol. 2, p. 94). But Dr. Warfield is wrong. The very fact that salvation *is* salvation means that it must be *received*. And how *can* it be received but by *faith*? Forgiveness is a gift. Cleansing is a gift. Justification is a gift. Regeneration is a gift. And they are *all* received by *faith*. As Dr. Daniel Steele says, "In truth, faith is man's only capacity to receive God. He cannot enter us through the senses, for they report only material things. Nor can the Spirit enter the soul through the reason, which apprehends only relations, not realities. Therefore faith is the only door by which the Holy Spirit comes into the human spirit."

Dr. Warfield's mistake is his confusing of the human with the divine in sanctification. There *is* a human side of "works", i.e.

of obedience to the divine law and the divine will; but *those* delightful "works" are not in order to *become* sanctified; they are a *result* of it. They are our grateful human response in order to *remain* sanctified through the unhindered work of the Holy Spirit within us.

Dear Christian, believe it against all that well-meaning disapprovers say. Sanctification is *God's* work within you. That is why 1 Thessalonians 5: 23 says, "The God of peace Himself sanctify you." And that is why it is to be received as His *gift*. Of ourselves you and I simply cannot *achieve* it; but through consecration and faith we may indeed *receive* it.

2. BE RECEPTIVE TO IT

Have we not seen, in these studies, that the promise is written plain in the Word? If we fulfil the requirement of a loving and complete hand-over of ourselves to Christ, will the divine promise fail us? Are you tempted to think that because God is not visibly manifested to your eyes, such a transaction as taking sanctification by faith is unreal? When you came to Him for salvation, for forgiveness, for cleansing from guilt through the atoning blood of Christ, for the new birth which only the Holy Spirit can effect in the soul, could you see God standing before you? No. But did you believe? Yes. And did you receive? Yes. *Why?* Because your sense of need was so acute, and you were so persuaded of His promise in the Word, that you *acted* upon it. As Hannah Whitall Smith says, "Just as you believed at first that He delivered you from the guilt of sin because He said it, so now believe that He delivers you from the power of sin because He says it. Let your faith lay hold of a new power in Christ." Yes, believe that He *can*; that He *promises*; and that He *will*.

3. HAND OVER COMPLETELY

This utter yielding of everything to Christ corresponds with Israel's crossing through the Jordan long ago into the *place* of promised blessing. It is our crossing over from self-management to Christ-monopoly; and it puts us in the *place* where He can fully bless us.

This consecration must be an unconditional surrender, with not even a wisp of legalism in it—such as doing it in order to *deserve.* It must be because we love our adorable Lord so dearly and deeply that we want holiness for *His* dear sake as well as our own; a holiness which, besides answering our own longing, will bring joy to *Him,* and make us true reflectors of our Lord to others.

Perhaps here again we encounter difficulty because our dear Master is invisible to us. I sometimes think it is easier to receive an invisible Christ as Saviour than to hand over everything to Him as an invisible Master. With most of us, when we received Christ as Saviour, there was an inward registration of it. We knew and *felt* that He had come in, according to His promise, "If any man open the door, I will come in." But to hand over *everything* to Him, without being able to see that He takes it, and without any registration of it in our consciousness, is often far from easy. Yet it has to be so, or faith would not *be* faith. Besides, this believing that He *does* take what we give, despite His invisibility, is the very thing which begets the faith by which we thereupon trust Him to make good His promise of inward sanctification.

4. WELCOME THE DIVINE WILL

One of the strangest things is the fear which many Christians have of the divine will. It would seem as if some of us are more afraid of it than of anything else! There is a subtle suspicion that if we give ourselves up utterly to Him, He will take advantage of us, and cause all manner of disagreeable testings and trials to overtake us which we miss by not being *too* much under His control! There are those who seem to think that all our heavenly Father wants is a chance really to "get them" so as to make them miserable by taking away things which they do not want to give up. And they vaguely imagine that by holding on to their *own* will they hinder Him from doing this!

Oh, what folly and mix-up! Nearly all their troubles come because they keep getting *out* of God's will. How *can* we forget that the will of God is the will of our *FATHER,* and the will of our *SAVIOUR,* and the will of the heavenly *COMFORTER*? It has been said only too truly, "Could we but for one moment get a glimpse into the mighty depths of His love, our hearts would spring out to meet His will and embrace it as our richest treasure; and we would abandon ourselves to it with an enthusiasm of gratitude and joy, that such a wondrous privilege could be ours."

Dear Christian, fling away for ever all doubts about God's will for your well-being. His will is utter love and goodness. Let your heart *welcome* it.

5. ANTICIPATE THE BEYOND

This may seem strange advice. No; it is given thoughtfully. Realize that everything here, in this present life, is part of a brief prelude to an immeasurable destiny. Everything here is intended character-preparation for high ministry *there*. It matters comparatively little whether you are rich or poor; whether you are academically educated or have had little schooling; whether you are big or small according to the world's standards. In *God's* sight you are special. You are one of His redeemed; one of the "elect". He calls you to a unique and exalted ministry reaching on from your last day on earth through the timeless eons of eternity. Once He can *fully claim* you, through your own free-willed and loving all-surrender to Him, He will truly set you apart, sanctify you, give you to know the *abiding* of His Spirit within you; renew you inwardly, and enrich your heart, and beautify your character. Yes, anticipate the Beyond! *All* Christians wish they had been *utterly* yielded to Christ when they are passing from here to there.

6. BE FINALLY CLEAR

Be clear as to what you are asking. You are *not* asking for the "eradication" of an evil "old nature"; for the written Word does not promise any such internal surgery, nor does it dichotomize your moral being into "two natures". Nor are you asking that an "old nature" may be "crucified with Christ" so that you may "reckon yourself 'dead indeed' unto sin"; for Romans 6: 11 refers to our *judicial* identification with the Cross two thousand years ago, not to some *counterpart* crucifixion of an "old nature" inside us now.

What you *are* asking is: (1) that you may be enabled to yield yourself utterly to Christ, whatever the consequences; (2) that the Holy Spirit may *infill* you and be pleased to give you the inward *evidence* of it; (3) that He may so *renew* you in the inmost springs of your moral nature as to make this renewal unmistakable within you, breaking all bondage to the "flesh", making His renewal of your mind the deepest reality within you, and flooding your heart with the love of God Himself; (4) that you may be enabled to count your covenant of utter self-surrender sealed in Heaven, and to *receive,* by simple, appropriating faith, the sanctifying fulness, whether at once attested emotionally or not.

7. NOW ACT AND POSSESS

And now, actually *give* yourself to Christ. Really *believe* that He takes what you give. Are you still afraid? Does it seem like a leap in the dark, or like stepping off a precipice into space? You are only one of millions who have felt the same. You can *now* become one of those millions who have actually *done* it, and whose joyful testimony is the same without exception—faith "falls on the seeming void, but finds the rock beneath". Give your all to Him. Cease looking inside yourself to see whether you *have* faith. Cease doubting your own sincerity. *Do it.*

Maybe during past months you have given yourself to Him again and again, in intention, but each time you have doubted whether you had *really* done so, because you did not *feel* anything. Shake off that bondage to feeling once for all. Consecration is *not* a matter of your feeling, but of His *taking.* Remember His own words, "The altar sanctifieth the gift" (Matt. 23: 19), and know that the very minute you give Him your *all* you are thus set apart by Him.

How can you know, even though you do not yet have any inward, supernatural attestation of it? Well, for one thing, if you are saying "I am now His altogether, *whatever the consequences*" that is a good token. But do not stop there. Say, "Lord, so far as I know my heart, I have now given Thee my all, with all my problems, longings, possibilities and relationships. I therefore believe that Thou dost now sanctify me. I do believe Thy promise. I trust Thee now to give me that infilling of the Holy Spirit which brings inward renewal to holiness. I ask Thee to give me some inward witness to this, deep in my consciousness; but even if that does not come in the way I imagine it, give me that equally true token—a fixed faith in Thy promise, *apart* from feelings."

Then reckon that as done, and *continue* to reckon it so. Let that crisis-step become a walk. *Live* your consecration and faith.

Pray as never before (for no crisis or blessing of the Christian life ever develops into permanence apart from habitual prayer). You need not keep re-enacting your consecration, but keep *renewing* the sacred covenant you have made with your Lord. Keep trusting that the "witness" of the Spirit will flame within you; yet do not for one moment let its seeming absence deter your faith. Keep trusting that His renewing, sanctifying work is now going on within you (for it *is*); and you will begin to *prove* it so. Yes, you will know it and *feel* it in ways which no words of mine could here express. Whether you have delightful earth-quakes of emotion or not, you will find yourself lifted into a consciousness of victory and liberty, of spiritual expansion and fellowship with God, which themselves will be a witness to you.

What more need we add? We have reached a point where further advice is a superfluity if the Holy Spirit Himself does not lead you to this complete hand-over of yourself to Christ, and to your receiving "the fulness of the blessing" by *faith*. May His gentle but persuasive pressure bring you there even now.

Some time ago I wrote a hymn expressing the longing of my own heart. Perhaps it may now become the language of yours as well. It is a prayer; a prayer for fullest inward renewal and enduement; a prayer which I believe the Holy Spirit waits to answer in every truly consecrated heart.

Come, heavenly Spirit, breathe upon me here;
Heart, mind and soul in Thy pure life ensphere.
Breathe now the fragrance of Thy love divine,
And my whole nature permeate with Thine.

Live in my living; think through all my thought.
Will through my will till only Thine is wrought.
Move through each impulse; temper each desire;
Cleanse all my motives in Thy heavenly fire.

Speak through my speaking; love in all my love.
Shed through each feeling fragrance from above.
Come, blest Shekinah, flame throughout my mind,
Till, cleansed from dross, I am as gold refined.

Come, most of all, for my dear Saviour's sake,
And my whole life His worthier dwelling make;
Come heavenly Fire, O sin-consuming Flame,
And for His temple my whole being claim.

SUPPLEMENTARY

1. WHO IS THE "WRETCHED MAN" OF ROMANS 7?

2. IS THE TERM "SECOND BLESSING" VALID?

3. IS "CHRISTIAN PERFECTION" SCRIPTURAL?

WHO IS THE "WRETCHED MAN" OF ROMANS 7?

PERHAPS our earlier reference to the "wretched man" of Romans 7 will become more meaningful and convincing if we amplify it here. The point which we make is, that if the *sixth* chapter teaches a present, inward experience of deliverance from indwelling sin (as is generally assumed and taught in the usual theories) then surely it is awkwardly *misplaced* in the progress of the epistle. That is, if chapter 6 teaches an inward deliverance from "the body of sin" and a being experientially "dead *indeed* unto sin", how comes it that right after it, here in chapter 7, we are back again at "Oh, wretched man that I am! Who shall deliver me from the body of this death?"

What, then, are we to say about that "wretched man"? Does he not make us feel that either chapter 6 or chapter 7 is misplaced? He certainly is a subject of debate among expositors, one of whom actually complains that it was inconsistent of Paul not to introduce the "wretched man" earlier! Perhaps, here, it may be useful to glance at some of the ways in which that "wretched man" of Romans 7 has been "explained".

First: he is a vivid Pauline picturing of that pitiful phenomenon, coextensive with fallen humanity, the continued inward collision of conscience and conduct; of "I ought" with "I don't"; of "I ought not" with "alas, I did"; of "I will" with "I can't".

Second: he is a spiritually awakened but still unconverted man who now suddenly sees himself exposed by the divine law as a self-condemned monstrosity of moral contradiction, and is startled, ashamed, helpless, dismayed.

Third: he is a half-regenerate soul, struggling on its way from darkness to light, stumbling across a border zone between the power of Satan and the kingdom of God; deeply convinced of sin, but battling against it in the old impossible way after all, of meeting self with self.

Fourth: he is a Christian believer, truly converted and regener-

ated, but not yet consecrated and sanctified by the destruction
or subduement or nullifying of the old Adam-nature within
him.

Fifth: he is a fully developed Christian, converted, consecrated,
living in the Spirit, but ever reminded that right to the end of this
present life in the body, the battle with inward evil must go on,
many a time evoking, despite moral victories, the humbling cry,
"Oh, wretched man that I am!"

Sixth: he is a synopsised spiritual history of Paul himself, (a) in
his unregeneracy, up to verse 11; then (b) spiritually awakened
and alarmed, up to verse 15; then (c) discerning that the inward
struggle is really between an inmost sympathy of the "mind" with
the holy "law of God", and a contrary "law of sin" within him,
up to verse 23; then (d) utter despair in self, offset by the hope of
victory "through Jesus Christ our Lord" (24, 25).

Each of these "explanations" is vulnerable to exegetical demoli-
tion from the context itself; but there is little need to go into
detailed criticism. Whichever of the six we prefer, they all leave
us with a strange anti-climax, an illogical drop-back, if (as is
supposed) chapter 6 teaches a decisive *inward* deliverance from
"sin that dwelleth in me". Yes, indeed, what a contradictory
reversal!—for whereas the exulting cry of chapter 6 is, "Being
then *set free* [aorist] from sin . . ." (18), the despairing groan
of chapter 7 is, "I see another law in my members . . . bringing
me into *captivity* to the law of *sin* which is *in my members*" (23).

To my own mind, the most artificial "explanation" of all is
that which is given by one of the most beloved and original
exponents of the counteraction theory. I mention it separately
here because it exposes how passages become diverted or accommodated to fit current theory, even by such able and well-meaning
teachers. Of the passage in question (Romans 7: 14–25) he speaks
thus: —

"I say that we have here the description of a Christian man. But a
Christian man *regarded in himself*, apart from faith in Christ. 'But
how can such a condition be possible?' You say, 'It is utterly inconceivable'."

We readily appreciate what the speaker is driving at; but is
not his comment cloudy? "A Christian man regarded in himself,
apart from faith in Christ", is only a verbal round-about for "A
Christian regarded as *not* a Christian", which is absurd. The

speaker himself has to admit that his hearers will rejoin, "But how can such a condition be possible?" "It is utterly inconceivable."

Having told us that the "wretched man" is a Christian regarded as *not* a Christian, the speaker has to suppose that the whole passage is parenthetical.

"The passage is in parenthesis in the line of argument, and for a moment the apostle is contemplating himself as a converted man, and yet as apart from Christ."

But the passage (14–25) is *not* parenthetical, as anyone can see, for there is direct connection between the verse next *before* it (7: 13) and the verse next after it (8: 1). Paul never put it in brackets, for the obvious reason that it logically and progressively continues his main line of reasoning.

Next, in pursuance of this idea, the author misunderstands the *sayings* of the "wretched man". See verse 22: "*For I delight in the law of God after the inward man*". We are told that, "The natural man could never have said this, and the sinner, however deeply awakened, could never have used such language". Now I can contradict that comment from my own experience, for before ever I was converted I had a deep appreciation of the Ten Commandments, and even more for the Sermon on the Mount, along with a genuine desire to live up to them. However, Paul himself contradicts the theory, for in this same Romans epistle, chapter 2: 14, he says, "For when the Gentiles, which have not the Law, do by nature the things contained in the Law, these . . . show the work of the Law *written in their hearts*, their conscience bearing witness therewith". Some well-known lines from Ovid leap to mind in concurrence with this:

> "My reason *this*, my passion *that*, insists,
> I see the right, and I approve it too ;
> Condemn the wrong, and yet the wrong pursue."

Moreover, all over the Jewish world there were devout souls who, although they knew nothing about regeneration in the Christian sense, "delighted" in the law of God "after the inward man". Josephus, in writing *Against Apion*, says of his fellow Jews, that from their earliest years the sacred teachings of that Law were "engraven on their souls". Thousands had chosen death rather than be disloyal to those teachings. Thousands, too, were acutely conscious of the painful irony which plagued the "wretched man" of Romans 7, namely, that the very Law which was their "delight" *morally* was their condemnation *legally*.

Even stranger is our speaker's further comment: "By the 'inward man', I take it, we must understand that part of his being which had been born from above. The language, therefore, is the language of a Christian man." Is it not unallowable, however, to speak of *"that part* of his being which had been born from above"—as though regeneration is merely partial, and not a renewal of the whole person? Any such part-regeneration is foreign to the New Testament.

What Paul meant by the "inward man" which delights in the law of God (22) is made clear by the words which immediately follow: "With the *mind* I myself serve the law of God". The "inward man" is that innate moral sense which is in every normal human being; and by the "mind" here Paul means the moral reason.

And when Paul speaks of "delighting" in the law of God he is speaking of what every godly Jew did, after the pattern of the godly man in Psalm one: "His delight is in the law of Jehovah". When will some of us learn that although the natural man is *spiritually* dead, he is not *morally* so. If all the unconverted were *morally* dead they would be utterly incapable of making any response whatever to the Gospel, and the preaching of it would become a theatrical unreality implying insincerity in God. For some time before my own conversion I truly "delighted" in many Bible truths, especially in the beautiful character and self-sacrificing love of Jesus. Later, when I realised acutely my need of salvation, even when I was struggling against conscience and inward "conviction" by the divine Spirit, I knew that my "inward man" was all on the side of "the law of God". Was that kind of experience peculiar to myself? No; it is the testimony of millions. Therefore, not only does Paul himself refute the above error as to the "inward man", but common experience does so as well.

Even that is not all. The theory further "explains" that although Paul uses the present tense all through the passage, "he is not speaking from the standpoint of present *experience*". Let me further quote: "When I say, 'Fire burns me', I do not mean precisely the same thing as when I say, 'The fire is burning me'. In the first case I am simply describing the property of fire; in the second I am giving a description of the present action of fire within the sphere of my consciousness." But Paul's present tense in the "wretched man" passage is not merely that of "Fire burns me"; it is the *very* present tense of "The fire is *now* burning me"—

"I see another law in my members, warring against [present participle] the law of my mind, and bringing me into captivity [present participle] to the law of sin which is in my members."

Surely that should settle it: Paul is telling of something going on within the "wretched man" in a vivid *present* sense.

Another questionable comment here on the "wretched man" is: "Sin is stronger . . . than all his holy tendencies upward, which he has by virtue of his new birth." Can that be right? Is it not that same new life in Christ which, in chapter 8, is said to *conquer* all the downward pull of sin? To make quite sure that I am not misunderstanding our speaker's meaning, I have looked up what he says about the "wretched man" passage in at least one other publication where he deals with the same subject, and in it he says the same thing just as peculiarly.

"The 'law of sin' in their members is stronger than their renewed nature" (p. 42).

Now is not that disturbing and surprising?—this law of sin within me is not only stronger than my natural will and noblest strivings; it is even stronger than the new life of regeneration which has come to me in Christ!

Again, what does the speaker mean by the "renewed nature"? One would assume that he means my nature after it has become regenerated, for the New Testament plainly tells me that I, as a human person, *need* to be "born from above", and that through faith in Christ I *am* thus born again, or regenerated. But no, our author does not mean that, for a few lines later he says that I now have "*two* natures"—

"I myself am conscious of a miserable condition of internal conflict, between two opposite tendencies—the two natures; thus one consenting to the law that it is good, delighting in it, and desiring to fulfil its requirements; the other drawing me in the contrary direction, and, *being the more powerful of the two,* actually bringing me into captivity to the law of sin, and thus resulting in a condition of *condemnation*" (italics ours).

So, after all, I do *not* truly have a "renewed nature" as the theory said, for there is a part of me that is *not* renewed, which now becomes one of "*two* natures" inside me, and is "the more powerful of the two"! Nor can the *other* "nature" (the good but supposedly weaker one) be in reality a "*renewed* nature", as the theory calls it, for *that* nature is the "new" nature from God—and how can that which never fell *need* "renewing"? I speak respectfully, but surely that reasoning is a flat tyre with punctures of its own making!

Strangest of all, perhaps is the observation on the "I myself" of verse 25.

"The 'I myself' is one thing, but the 'Christ-life' is another. There are multitudes of Christians who are living the 'I myself-life'. They know what pardon is . . . but they are living the 'I myself-life' instead of the 'Christ-life'."

Yet as we earlier pointed out, Paul himself makes no such contrast between the "I myself" and the so-called "Christ-life". Paul is *commending*, not condemning, the "I myself", i.e. the real, true, human self, the mind, the intellect, as being altogether on the side of the divine Law. The contrast which *Paul* makes is between the "I myself" and the "*flesh*". He says, "So then, with the mind 'I myself' serve the law of God; *but with the flesh the law of sin*".

Dr. Daniel Steele, one-time Greek professor at Boston University, saw right through this misfeaturing of that "wretched man" into a regenerate man representing an unregenerate. Let the "wretched man" be either one or the other, but no such hybrid! Dr. Steele himself sees him as an *un*regenerate man; and his comment is worth quoting:

"The best scholarship discredits this chapter as the photograph of a regenerate man. The Greek Fathers, during the first three hundred years of church history, unanimously interpreted this Scripture as describing a thoughtful moralist endeavouring without the grace of God to realise his highest ideal of moral purity. Augustine, to rob his opponent Pelagius of the two proof-texts, originated the theory that the seventh of Romans delineated a regenerate man. Luther and Calvin followed him. The trend of modern scholars is to return to the view of the Greek Fathers" (*Half Hours With Paul*, p. 74).

We have neither space nor need, here, to re-examine the verdicts of those Greek Fathers or of Augustine. The point is: whether we make that "wretched man" of Romans 7 either a converted man or an unconverted man, he remains a chagrining flop-back, an unaccountable regression in Paul's exposition—*if Romans 6, just beforehand, has taught an inward crucifixion and death (or disabling) of the (so-called) "old nature"*. Why is there this relapse into seemingly worse wretchedness than ever, if "sin which dwelleth in me" has already been "crucified" and "done away" or "rendered inoperative"?

Yet a Needless Problem

What then? Why this: that "wretched man" is in his right place, and need have been no expository trouble, if only chapter 6 had been interpreted with due regard to the structure of the epistle. From chapter 1: 18 to chapter 3: 20, Paul has shown us that we need a twofold salvation: (1) from *sins*—the legal aspect; (2) from *sin*—the moral aspect. Then from 3: 21 to 5: 11, he has shown us how the Gospel deals with the first of these two needs, i.e. the problem of *sins*—

> (a) judicially 3: 21 to 4: 25.
> (b) experientially 5: 1 to 5: 11.

And now, from chapter 5: 12 onwards, he shows how the Gospel answers the *second* big problem, i.e. of *sin* as an hereditary corruption. He follows the same order as before: first the *judicial* aspect (5: 12 to 7: 5), then the *experiential* (7: 6 to 8: 39). By the time he comes to chapter 7: 6 he has expounded *three* profound Gospel deliverances—

> 1. From sins, judicially (3: 21 to 4: 25).
> 2. From sins, experientially (5: 1 to 5: 11).
> 3. From *sin*, judicially (5: 12 to 7: 6).

It is wonderful indeed to have those three deliverances. But there is yet one more which I need, as a member of the old Adam's fallen race; I need deliverance from this horrible thing, "sin that dwelleth in me". And *that* is why Paul introduces the "wretched man" *here*, in the final section of these eight chapters on "How the Gospel saves the Sinner". It is to show that the Gospel has an answer even to *this* problem, this inward perversion, or "sin that dwelleth in me". The answer, of course, is chapter 8, with its climactic contribution on deliverance through the indwelling

Spirit: *"the law of the Spirit of life in Christ Jesus hath set me free from the law of sin and death"*. The wretched man wailing at the end of chapter 7, "who shall deliver me?" is found exclaiming, at the end of chapter 8, "We are more than conquerors through Him that loved us!"

That "wretched man" of chapter 7, therefore, is *not* meant to depict a Christian believer, born again but still unsanctified; or a "half-regenerate soul" struggling in a "border-zone"; or a legalistically minded Christian supposedly trying to keep the moral law by self-effort; or even an unconverted man in contrast with the Christian believer. He is simply a *representative human being*, exhibiting what is the experience of any human being at the stage which Paul has now reached in his progressive exposition of "How the Gospel saves the Sinner". He represents all those who know three out of the four deliverances from sin which are provided in the Gospel, but who still need to know the *fourth*, i.e. deliverance from indwelling sin *experientially*. He must pass from chapter 7 to chapter 8, and learn dynamic deliverance through the inward operation of the Holy Spirit, a deliverance which Paul calls, "the glorious liberty of the children of God" (8: 21).

When we see Paul's "wretched man" in *that* way we see that he is introduced exactly where he belongs, that is, just after chapter 6. But as soon as we start making chapter 6 teach *sanctification*, in the sense of inward crucifixion, inward death to sin, inward destruction of "the body of sin", *then* the "wretched man" is strangely out of place; he is a sudden denial of all that Paul has just said, and an exegetical enigma. The fact is (let us say it again) that Romans 6 was *never meant* to teach any such inward crucifixion and deliverance from inbred sin as is usually supposed. What it teaches is our *judicial* identification with Christ in His Calvary death. Those two expressions, "our old man" and "the body of sin", are not names for our so-called "old nature" at all, but Paulinisms for the whole Adam race.

IS THE TERM "SECOND BLESSING" VALID?

THE understanding of inwrought sanctification as a distinctly second work of grace can be found prior to John Wesley, but the actual definition, "second blessing", seems to have originated with him. It occurs, for instance, in his counsel to Jane Salkeld, "Exhort all the little ones that believe to make haste and not delay the time of receiving the second blessing". That he preached this "second blessing" as bringing eradication of inbred sin we have sufficiently exhibited elsewhere. From then onwards the phrase became current among all who followed in the Wesley line of teaching, and among other groups too.

SOME CONSCIENTIOUS OBJECTIONS

In many instances the only sure way of knowing the strength or weakness of a position is to test it under attack. It is also true that we often learn more from those who oppose us than those who amen us. So it may be wise and useful if we here pay some attention to voices which contradict us, and deny the reality of the second blessing, the more so because in this case they are all voices with a clear ring of sincerity in them.

I turn to Dr. Warfield's great work on *Perfectionism*. Some of my quotations from it are not necessarily Dr. Warfield's own views, but are those of others, whose theories he is examining. One recurrent objection asks:

"If when we enter into Christ by faith . . . we receive . . . all that He has and is, what remains to be obtained by a second act of faith as a 'second blessing'?" (vol. 1: 355).

The fault in this objection is its confusion of all that is appropri*able* at conversion with the mere modicum which most of us then appropriate. All Canaan belonged to Israel right away on Israel's leaving Egypt: but did Israel *occupy* Canaan right away? No, there was a long gap. Yet could not Israel have

occupied Canaan *without* any such gap? Yes, indeed, but the
gap is there, nevertheless, as a matter of *fact*; and it is with this
gap in full view that Paul says, "These things happened unto
them as *types*."

A further objection comes from Dr. Warfield himself. He
agrees that the New Testament makes at least a *"conceptional*
distinction between justification and sanctification", but not any
such separation as allows sanctification to be a "second blessing".

"It [the New Testament] is absolutely impatient of their separation
from one another, and uniformly represents them as belonging together . . . in the one, unitary salvation which is received by faith"
(Vol. 1: 363).

But the difference between justification and sanctification is
not merely "conceptional". Flatly against Dr. Warfield, the New
Testament *does* separate them. If justification and sanctification
are inseparably received together by faith, why does Paul exhort
the already justified to *become* sanctified? It is because at our
conversion we become justified *completely* through the Saviour's
finished work *for* us, whereas we become sanctified only *in-
cipiently* through the beginning of the Spirit's work *in* us. Our
justification in Christ is absolute; our inward sanctification is
procedural, in proportion to our consecration and faith. Hence
Paul exhorts those who have the new *life* of the Spirit to know
the *infilling* of the Spirit, and those who are regenerated to become "sanctified wholly".

Along the same line, Dr. Warfield represents Jellinghaus of
Germany as objecting thus:

"When we enter into 'mystical' union with Christ, we receive in Him
all that He is and has, *all at once*. It may be possible to make room
for a progressive realization [of this] but . . . there is no room for
those who are already in Christ . . . by a *new* act to enter into Christ
and to obtain as a *second* benefit from Him something entirely new"
(Vol. 1: 364).

The big fallacy in that objection is the unfair cleavage drawn
between the second blessing and our union with Christ at
conversion. Not even the most drastic eradicationist would make
the second blessing a "new act to *enter* into Christ". Once you
have entered into a country (as, for instance, Columbus into
America) you need not go out and come in again in order to make
some big discovery further inland! Once you are in, and pressing

further in, you may find a wonderful region of wealth or beauty the existence of which you never guessed at from the shoreline. The inward sanctification which becomes a living experience through the deeper blessing is just as united *to* as it is distinct *from* the regeneration which precedes it. In fact, "entire sanctification" *is* regeneration in fuller operation. It is a development, not a disjunction, as may be illustrated by the caterpillar and the butterfly. See the development from the larva or caterpillar stage through the pupa transition until the same little creature emerges from the chrysalis in its imago condition as a florid butterfly. How different the butterfly from the caterpillar! Yet there is the same identity all the way through. It is the same life, received at the beginning, but now expressing itself in higher, lovelier manifestation *through a second major crisis*.

A further and subtler suggestion against the second blessing is that there would be no such vivid crisis at all if only we Christians, from the time of our conversion, were more consecrated than most of us are—just as "sudden conversions" to Christ are "less to be expected in the case of those who grow up in good Christian nurture".

"When surrender and trust have been complete from conversion, and have grown evenly side by side and soundly, then a distinct, renewed surrender, which would change the inward condition essentially and suddenly for the better, and notably advance it, would not be possible, precisely because it would be already existent" (Vol. I, p. 367, quoting Jellinghaus).

Are there not three mistakes here? (1) "Sudden conversions" *often* occur among "those who grow up in good Christian nurture" (my own was such), and are all the more astonishing to the converted person because right to the moment when the Gospel truth is made savingly luminous by the Holy Spirit the soul has been "so *near* yet so *far*". (2) The deeper blessing *often* comes most overwhelmingly to those who through months or years have been slowly drawing nearer to it by a *gradually* increasing consecration. Such was the case with the saintly Frances Ridley Havergal, on whom it at last broke as a sudden luminous mind-opening. (3) This argument against the deeper blessing rests on the gratuitous assumption that it is only a *human* crisis, and not a special intervention of the Holy Spirit. Let us be clear once for all: either this deeper blessing *is* a special divine operation in the soul, or it is not. If it *is*, then every syllable of serious argument about it is more than worthwhile; but if it is *not*, let us desist at once; why waste time pursuing a mirage or investigating a phantom?

However, if what we have gathered together in these pages is true (and with all my heart I believe it is) then the deeper blessing is *real;* and it is so as a deep-going work of *God* in our moral nature. Moreover, there is a clear reason why the deeper blessing frequently occurs in just as gladly startling a way to those who arrive at it *gradually,* by seriatim steps of further-and-further consecration, as it does to others who have hitherto been in a more or less backslidden condition. We fill a kettle with water, and put it on a fire or stove in order to boil the water. We start, let us say, with the water at 70 degrees Fahrenheit. It gets warmer and warmer, hotter and hotter: 80 degrees, 100 degrees, 200 degrees, but it still is water. It heats right up to 211 degrees, and still is water. But at 212 degrees a sudden transmutation happens: the water begins turning into steam. Well, it may illustrate only imperfectly, but it illustrates what is perfectly true. Even in those cases where there is a gradatim process of self-yielding, there is eventually a completive crisis-point (corresponding with that 212 degrees) at which consecration becomes *utter,* and the lovely miracle of *full* pervasion and renewal by the Holy Spirit then begins.

What is more, even if it could be proved with mathematical precision that *some* devout believers graduate into the "fulness of the blessing" *without* any such pin-pointed crisis, as smoothly as the sun moves from nadir to zenith, or as a rose develops from bud to full bloom, it would not alter the fact that *most* regenerated Christian believers *do* enter the "fulness" by a memorable crisis. It would be only another case of exceptions proving the rule.

But now, a yet further objection to the second blessing is voiced by those who argue that the "baptism of the Holy Spirit" takes place *at conversion,* and is never to be thought of as a *"second* experience".

"The New Testament nowhere requires a second sudden baptism with the Holy Spirit for all believers. In the case of the most, the deeper filling with the Holy Spirit comes gradually, with sufferings, humiliations, and marvellous answers to prayers, and deliverances through the deeper experience of the power of Christ's death and resurrection.

He who teaches that every Christian must have the experience of the eradication of his sinful nature, and of sinlessness through a second baptism of the Holy Spirit, is an anti-Biblical fanatic and a victim of delusion" (Vol. 1, p. 368).

That is strong language but weak argument. (1) It confuses the second blessing with eradication and sinlessness. (2) It incorrectly identifies *regeneration* with the "baptism of the Holy Spirit" (the author, Jellinghaus, actually adds, "the baptism with the Holy Spirit *is* regeneration"). Now as for regeneration being identical with the "baptism of the Holy Spirit", we might easily rebut that mistake by referring to the Apostles, whose regeneration *preceded* Pentecost. To them the "baptism of the Holy Spirit" certainly came as their "second blessing". Foregoing that, however, I insist that if we adhere closely to the New Testament, "the baptism of the Holy Spirit" does not mean *anything* which the Holy Spirit *now* does, either in regeneration or sanctification. It refers exclusively to that historical "Day of Pentecost" which inaugurated the whole present dispensation of the Holy Spirit. (See again our comments on this on pages 168–170.)

Closely allied with this is another objection to the Second Blessing, namely, that the believer's *sanctification* dates from conversion, which fact rules out any thought of sanctification as a later or "second blessing".

"*A sharp separation of two distinct sorts of sanctification* [i.e. one at conversion and the other later] *we do not find in the Bible*. It cannot be taught on Biblical grounds that we must all first be justified and regenerated, and then we must all later, at a definite time and by a sudden, definite transaction, be sanctified in complete fashion" (Vol. 1: 370, quoting Jellinghaus).

We note two errors here. (1) The unfair use of the word "must". Careful exponents of second blessing truth do *not* teach that the believer's full sanctification "*must*" be later; it need not be, even though in the generality of cases it is so. (2) The ambiguous use of the word "sanctified". There is *positional* sanctification; and there is *experiential* sanctification in character. The former becomes ours *completely* at our conversion; the latter *cannot* come to us completely; it progresses as the new life develops in us. So, despite the foregoing quotation, there *are* "two distinct sorts of sanctification".

In volume two of Dr. Warfield's spacious survey, most of the criticisms directed against the second blessing are his own; and I think we are being strictly fair to him if (to save further page-space) we sum them up as follows. (1) The same, or nearly so, as those already noticed. (2) Objection to the separating of sanctification from justification. (3) Objection to the teaching that sanctification comes "all at once" through a separate act of faith.

Of course, all the way through, Dr. Warfield mixes up *positional* sanctification (which is absolute) with *experiential* sanctification (which is relative). One tires somewhat of his masterly drumming that practical sanctification is an always inconclusive "lifetime" struggle largely dependent on "the expenditure of time-consuming effort". Does not Dr. Warfield also hold, like the rest of us, that practical sanctification progresses arm-in-arm with the believer's *consecration to Christ*? Yes, his two volumes indicate so. Consecration and sanctification progress *pari passu:* the one determines the measure of the other. Very well, must there be a life-long inconclusiveness about our *consecration* to Christ? Can there not be a point at which, with adoring love and meaningfulness, we yield ourselves in *entire* consecration? There can; and when that point of entire consecration is reached there can be "entire *sanctification*", as faith gratefully grasps the Scriptural promise of it (1 Thess. 5: 23, 24). No doctrine of progressive sanctification can be truly Scriptural which refuses to admit that there can be a *special* divine work of inwrought sanctification in response to entire consecration and faith.

Some Later Comment

I do not seem to find any new objection since Dr. Warfield laid down his powerful quill, except perhaps in form of statement; but I think perhaps we should notice two or three recent writers who know how to pen such criticism persuasively.

Dr. Chester K. Lehman, in his trenchant little book, *The Holy Spirit and the Holy Life,* lists twelve Scripture passages which he says are the principal passages given by Wesley and later writers in support of a second crisis-work in Christian experience, and then observes, "The crucial question before us is this: Do these Scriptures speak of a normal second crisis having the nature of entire sanctification, of perfection, of holiness?" (p. 157, 158). Dr. Lehman says, "No."

Now with warm respect to Dr. Lehman, *is* that the crucial

question (whether we take his 12 texts or W. E. Sangster's 30)? Surely the crucial question is: Do these (and other) Scriptures indicate a spiritual level and fulness which all too many Christians do *not* experience? and if so, how do Christian believers enter upon it?—gradually? or by a further crisis? Even though no particular one of all the cited texts didactically teaches entrance by crisis, what do all of them together "add up to"? Again and again, from many texts taken together we extract some important truth which is not actually *stated* by any one text in particular. The equality of the Holy Spirit with the Father and the Son; the salvation of those who die as infants; the mutual recognition of our departed Christian loved ones in the Beyond (not to mention other instances); where do we find direct statements on those? Yet a collation of all the Scripture data leads us to decidedly positive conclusions. Just so; and I maintain that an open-minded survey of all the Scriptural data on which we must decide Yes or No as to the deeper blessing will require a twofold verdict: (1) The New Testament teaches an experience of inwrought holiness and spiritual fulness to which very many Christians are more or less strangers. (2) The only way by which most of them ever can or ever will enter into it is by a reciprocal crisis of uttermost self-surrender and faith on *their* part, with a corresponding response of unprecedented inward renewal by the Holy Spirit.

But Dr. Lehman expresses himself more freely against the second blessing in this next quotation.

"We have found in earlier chapters that a number of experiences converge into the one grand moment which we may call conversion. Conviction of sin, change of mind and attitude toward sin, confession of sin, forgiveness of sin, the new birth, baptism with the Holy Spirit, union with Christ, commitment to discipleship—all these are aspects of a single experience which marks the beginning of the Christian life. This is definitely *the* crisis experience of the Holy Spirit's encounter with a sinner. It is this experience which issues in salvation. From this moment onward the Holy Spirit dwells in the believer. As a son of God he has the Spirit of Christ; he is led by the Spirit of God; he walks by the Spirit; he is filled with the Spirit; he fights with the sword of the Spirit; and he prays in the Spirit. There is no second crisis to be experienced with the Holy Spirit. What crisis experience could transcend baptism with the Spirit which brought into being the new life in Christ Jesus? There is no Biblical language that speaks of experiences with the Holy Spirit which surpass these just mentioned. With all respect to the sincerity and zeal of those who profess a second crisis of entire sanctification wrought by baptism with the Holy Spirit, it must be said that this baptism is the crisis experience which marks the beginning of the Christian life. All later experiences have their origin through the energizing of the indwelling Spirit" (pp. 177, 178).

Now amid much that is grandly true in that quotation, it is still off-focus as a criticism of the second blessing if for no other reason than that its description of conversion is unallowably overdrawn. Conversion is *not* the "baptism with the Holy Spirit", as the quotation says. We have already shown why it cannot be. Also, when the quotation adds that "from this moment onward" (i.e. conversion) the believer is "*filled* with the Spirit", it is simply not true to experience. Surely Dr. Lehman must have realized, even though he wrote those words, that thousands of Christians, on their own testimony, do *not* have that experience. Surely, too, he must have reflected that a multitude of others have joyously witnessed that they *did* eventually experience that "fulness" through a post-conversion *crisis*. Somehow, I cannot help thinking that able writers like Dr. Lehman and other sincere critics of the second blessing are bothered by the assumption that second blessing teaching must *necessarily* involve eradicationist and perfectionist theories, which it does not, as we have tried to show in these pages.

For a final quotation I turn to Bishop Stephen Neill's thought-provoking contribution, *Christian Holiness*. Here we have, not so much a sledge-hammer blow at the second blessing, as rather a smooth "explaining away". Describing "a very large number" of those who become converted, he says:

"They believe themselves to have entered into a new world, in which all things have become new; and there is much more than illusion in this belief. What they may have failed to notice is that they have brought with them into the wonderful new world an old and recalcitrant nature. . . . What is going to happen with the first serious lapse into sin, when circumstance and habit resume their power? . . . It is at this point that a second experience of Christ may be needed, and, if granted, may come with the force of a second miraculous deliverance. What the Christian soul at this point discovers is the adequacy of God's provision in Christ for all the needs of man. . . . Then, the fact of the Holy Spirit leaps out of the dead print of the Creed as a burning reality. In this sense holiness really is received by faith. Anxiety is replaced by trust and confidence. A new development of Christian personality is possible, and one of the signs of this new development is ethical victory in areas where previously defeat was the rule. No doubt Christians ought to know all these elementary truths from the day . . . of their rebirth. It is just a fact that they do not know them, and that the discovery or revelation of them is greeted with touchingly grateful astonishment" (pp. 33, 34).

So, according to this further explanation, the so-called second blessing is merely what *should* have been realized at conversion but only happens later. We appreciate its delightful clarity, but does it represent what the deeper blessing *really* is? Even when that which should have happened at conversion does happen later (according to the quotation) it is scarcely more than a fuller apprehension of it on the *human* side; whereas the true doctrine of the second blessing is that God Himself *does something* deep and transforming in the very basis of the human personality.

There is one further aspect of the matter which perhaps we should mention. Some may ask: If the theory of eradication or of inward death to sin is *error*, why is it that thousands who have misguidedly sought the second blessing as *including* eradication or death to sin have had such wonderful divine response in mighty deliverances and inwrought sanctification? There are at least several good reasons for it.

First, their seeking of the deeper blessing in suchwise has brought them to the point of complete consecration to Christ. Next, it has intensified their abhorrence of sin into a painful longing to be freed from it. Again, it has kept the now fully-yielded believer steadily, urgently hanging on in prayer for divine answer. Furthermore, despite exegetical error in the idea or *theory* of the second blessing, God has honoured that fundamental part of it which has been the truth of His Word. And, once more, in answer to human consecration, longing, believing, appropriating, the Holy Spirit has indeed mightily visited the soul with the inflooding love of God, bringing new expulsive power against sin, renewing the desires and motives, and lifting the believer into cloudless new fellowship with God.

As we have said and repeated in these pages, the experience itself is indeed real, but the *definitions* given of it by many who have rejoiced in it, especially during their early wonder at it, have frequently been unintentionally inexact; and some of the witnesses have later corrected themselves. Many have presumed that an eradication had taken place, only to find later that they were mistaken. Such miscomprehensions have occurred because the mind was wedded to a particular theory. All the way through any re-thinking of this subject, we must distinguish between theory and reality. As for the former, we should seek to clear it from all which will not square with Scripture. As for the latter, i.e. "the *fulness* of the blessing of Christ", let it be our prayer that in these days there may be a widespread revival of new interest in it through all our evangelical churches.

IS "CHRISTIAN PERFECTION" SCRIPTURAL?

THE phrase, "Christian perfection" might well suggest a triumphant culmination; but it is a misnomer. It was coined by John Wesley. During forty years he used it and preached the doctrine which it represented, despite the fact that it aroused more opposition than any other aspect of his teaching. In Sermon 40 he tells us why he clung to it.

"Some have advised [us] wholly to lay aside the use of those expressions ['perfect' and 'perfection'] 'because they have given so great offence'. But are they not found in the Oracles of God? If so, by what authority can any messenger of God lay them aside, even though all men should be offended?"

But *are* those expressions found in Scripture? and *is* Wesley's doctrine of "Christian Perfection" truly Scriptural? Believing, as I do, in Wesley's unimpeachable sincerity, I would be the last man ever to suggest "special pleading" on his part; yet the way he appropriates or handles some of his supposed proof-texts is as innocently gratuitous as it is utterly sincere. I mention just one instance here. In his *Plain Account of Christian Perfection*, he thus appropriates Matthew 5: 48 ("Ye therefore shall be perfect, as your heavenly Father is perfect"):

"They wanted, they sought, occasion against me; there they found what they sought. 'This is Mr. Wesley's doctrine! He preaches perfection!' He does: yet this is not his doctrine any more than it is yours or anyone's else who is a minister of Christ. For it is His doctrine, peculiarly, emphatically His! It is the doctrine of Jesus Christ. Those are His words, not mine: Εσεσθε οὖν ὑμεῖς τέλειοι ὥσπερ ὁ πατὴρ ὑμῶν ὁ ἐν τοῖς δύρανοῖς τελειὸς εστιν. 'Ye shall therefore be perfect as your Father in heaven is perfect.' And who says ye shall not; or at least, not till your soul is separated from the body? It is the doctrine of St. Paul, the doctrine of St. James, of St. Peter and St. John; and not otherwise Mr. Wesley's than as it is the doctrine of every one who preaches the pure and the whole gospel. I tell you, as plain as I can speak, where and when I found this. I found it in the oracles of God, in the Old and the New Testament when I read them with no other view or desire but to save my own soul."

Now it is obvious that our Lord, exhorting that long-ago mixed crowd in Galilee, before Calvary and Pentecost, could not possibly have meant "perfect" in the Wesley sense of eradication and entire sanctification. There is not a syllable in the context to suggest so; nor would those people have understood it even if that *had* been what He meant, for the Spirit was not yet given at Pentecost, nor were the people of that promiscuous multitude what we would call "born again" persons. Nor could our Lord have meant perfection in the strict meaning of our *English* word, "perfection". Nor does the Greek adjective, *teleios*, in itself mean perfection. And even if the Greek word *had* meant perfection, our Lord did not use it to exhort those people to a *complete* human perfection, but only in one particular way, i.e. in impartiality of kindness to friend and foe alike, even as God sends the rain "on the just and on the unjust". If John Wesley was determined to make this text serve his doctrine of "Christian perfection", then in all consistency should he not have acknowledged that the text calls us to be perfect *even as God is*—which is an impossibility?

In our English New Testament (Authorized Version) the words "perfect", "perfected", "perfecting", "perfection", "perfectly", "perfectness", occur a total of sixty times. These translate to us a variety of Greek words, which may be classified as follows:

1. The adjective τέλειος (*teleios*) with its noun and other forms; also (twice) ἐπιτελέω (40)
2. The verb καταρτίζω (*katartizo*) and the two noun forms. (9)
3. The noun ἀκρίβεια (*akribeia*) with adjectival and adverbial forms. (7)
4. The noun ὁλοκληρία (*holoklēria*)|(Acts 3: 16, physical wholeness). (1).
5. The adjective ἄρτιος (*artios*) (2 Tim. 3: 17, "complete", A.S.V.). (1)
6. The verb πληρόω (*pleróō*) in its passive participle="fulfilled" (Rev. 3: 2). (1)
7. The verb διασώζω (*diasozo*) in its aorist passive form (Matt. 14: 36). (1)

The big query is: Do these Greek words hold out the possibility of a present moral perfection in the strict meaning of our English word, "perfection"?

To begin with, we can delete number 7. That verb does not mean to make perfect, but to preserve or save or keep safe. In the only place where the King James version translates it as "perfectly" (Matt. 14: 36) both E.R.V. and A.S.V. drop it.

Equally we may discard number 6. The verb and its cognates all have the idea of *full*, but never of perfect. Out of all its many occurrences, only once is it translated as "perfect" and even there the E.R.V. changes it to "fulfilled".

Similarly we may exclude number 5. It definitely does not mean perfect. Its central idea is that of being freshly ready. Its only occurrence is 2 Tim. 3: 17, and both E.R.V. and A.S.V. translate it, "complete".

Again, number 4 may be eliminated. Its only occurrence is Acts 3: 16, where it refers to physical soundness. It comes from *holos* which is translated 42 times as "whole" (e.g. "the whole city"), 66 times as "all", once as "altogether", twice as "every whit", and once as "throughout". Its main idea is wholeness or altogetherness. Nowhere does it refer to moral condition except twice in an adjectival form:

"That ye may be . . . *entire*, lacking in nothing" (Jas. 1: 4).

"Your spirit and soul and body be preserved *entire*, without blame at the coming of our Lord Jesus Christ" (1 Thess. 5: 23).

In the first of these two texts (Jas. 1: 4), as the context shows, the entireness is that of *faith* developed through endurance of *trial*. It has absolutely no reference to an inwrought condition of holiness. In the second (1 Thess. 5: 23) the entireness is that of area: "spirit and soul and body", not of moral perfection. The words, "without blame", and "sanctify you wholly" will come up in connection with the word *teleios* (number 1).

As for number 3, *akribeia*, it may be dismissed at once. None of its seven occurrences refers to our human moral nature. Nor does the word mean perfection, but *exactness*; and in most of its seven occurrences the E.R.V. and A.S.V. alter the translation accordingly.

So is it with number 2. That it should have been translated anywhere by our English word, "perfect", is misleading. Its force is that of a thorough repairing or readjusting, as is shown by the way it is elsewhere translated, i.e. "fitted", "framed", "mending", "prepared", "restore".

Of course, there is a popular (as distinct from exact) way of using our word "perfect", as when we say, "It was a perfect meal", or "He has perfect health", or "He makes a perfect husband", not to mention slang uses such as "perfect misery". Therefore some of the above Greek words may perhaps be allowably translated by our English word, "perfect", so long as it is understood that our word, "perfect", is not to be taken in its *strict* sense.

The trouble is, however, that the average reader of our English New Testament, not knowing Greek, assumes that our word, "perfect", represents a *Greek* word meaning perfect in the *strict* sense; and thus a wrong idea of New Testament teaching on holiness is given. Little does the average English reader suspect that our New Testament word, "perfect", in its various occurrences, represents *seven* different Greek words, in over a dozen different forms, not one of them meaning perfection in the *strict* sense.

But now it is time to examine that Greek word τέλειος (*teleios*) which, in its several grammatical forms, is translated no less than forty times as "perfect", "perfection", etc. This adjective, with its kindred noun, verb and adverbial forms, derives from a primitive verb, *tello,* which means to set out for a definite point or goal, but with emphasis on the point aimed at as a limit. From this the noun, *telos,* means a termination-point or accomplished end; a completion or fulfilment or issue. Thus our Greek adjective, *teleios,* carries the meaning of *completed,* entire, fulfilled, full-grown. Only in those modified senses does it mean perfect.

An interesting confirmation of this is, that *teleios* was a word associated with the old Greek mystery cults, where (says Lightfoot) it "seems to have been applied to the *fully instructed* as opposed to novices." Philo also (B.C. 20?–A.D. 42?) and the Alexandrian philosophical Judaists used it considerably. Philo distinguishes between the "fully initiated" (*teleioi*) and the merely "advancing" (*prokoptontes*). He allegorises Jacob into typifying the latter, and Israel the former! In ordinary common use, *teleios* meant "full-grown", or "grown men", in contrast to "children".

The very fact that it and its cognates are translated, "of full age", "finish", "performance", "accomplish", "expire", will settle it that *teleios* in itself does *not* mean perfect in a fixed or strict sense. Whether in any given instance it *implies* perfection in the strict or absolute sense has to be decided by the context.

So now, from the 40 instances where *teleios* is translated "perfect", let us pick out the 16 places where it refers to *human* condition or possibility; for those are the occurrences which specially concern us. They are as follows.

(1) Matthew 5: 48, "Be ye therefore *perfect*, even as your Father which is in heaven is perfect." The paragraph teaches *impartiality* in kindness to both neighbours and enemies. Although we are so ear-tuned to the usual translation that any alteration sounds strange, a true rendering (with the word, "impartial" in italics) would be, "Ye therefore shall be entirely *impartial*, even as your heavenly Father is entirely so."

(2) Matthew 19: 21, "Jesus said unto him, If thou wilt be *perfect*, go and sell that thou hast, and give to the poor. . . ." This has no real bearing on inwrought holiness, but rather to a legal righteousness through a fulfilling of the Law. The rich young ruler had apparently kept the Law "to the letter". Our Lord now tests him as to implementing the *spirit* of it: "If thou wilt be *complete*", i.e. to the true limit of fulfilment.

(3) 1 Corinthians 2: 6, "Howbeit we speak wisdom among them that are *perfect*". All later versions translate this as "full-grown" or "mature".

(4) (5) Philippians 3: 12 and 15, "Not as though I . . . were already *perfect*". "Let us therefore, as many as be *perfect*. . . ." If anything could show that the Greek word does not mean perfection, this twice-occurrence does, in which Paul says he both *is* and is *not* "perfect". There is no contradiction, but only a contrast between a *future* completion through resurrection, and a *present* completeness through justification. The fact is, verse 15, "Let *us* . . ." connects right back to verse 3, "*We* . . . glory in Christ Jesus, and have no confidence in the flesh". All the intervening verses (4–14) are in the singular "I", with Paul himself as the illustration of "no confidence in the flesh" (4–8), glorying in a *present* completeness in Christ (9, 10), and in a *future* completion through the coming out-resurrection (11–14).

(6) Colossians 1: 28, "That we may present every man *perfect* in Christ". The presenting is at the return of Christ, our "hope of glory" (27). Here, the truer translation would be "complete", instead of "perfect".

(7) Colossians 4: 12, "*Perfect* and complete in all the will of God". If we follow the Revised Text, the true rendering here is,

"Complete and fully assured in every will of God". There is no thought of outright perfection.

(8) Hebrews 6: 1, "Let us go on unto perfection". Here, again, the idea is that of going on to a point of full development. The E.R.V. and A.S.V. margins give "full growth".

(9) (10) Hebrews 10: 14 and 12: 23, "For by one offering He hath *perfected* for ever them that are sanctified" (10: 14). "The spirits of just men who have been *perfected*" (12: 23). These are the only two places, so far, where (as it seems to me) the use of our English word, "perfected" is warranted by force of context. The Greek verb, in itself, still means no more than completion; but inasmuch as it here refers to the completion of a faultless sacrifice *for ever*, completion equals perfection. So does it in 12: 23, since in those "just men" it refers to the full accomplishment of a purpose consummated *in heaven*.

(11) James 1: 4, "Let patience have her *perfect* work, that ye may be *perfect* and entire . . ." A better translation would be, "Let endurance have its complete effect, that you may be complete and entire", i.e. free from deficiency.

(12) James 3: 2, "If any man offend not in word, the same is a perfect man (*anēr*) and able to bridle the whole body". The very fact that James here uses the word, *anēr*, for man (=a male of full age and stature) indicates the sense of "perfect". If any man stumble not in word, he is the complete gentleman, or the *thoroughly manly man*, "able to bridle the whole body".

(13 to 16). "But whoso keepeth His Word, in him verily is the love of God *perfected*" (1 John 2: 5). "If we love one another, God dwelleth in us, and His love is *perfected* in us" (4: 12) "Herein is our love made *perfect* . . ." (4: 17). "There is no fear in love; but *perfect* love casteth out fear" (4: 18).

Context settles it that the first of these (2: 5) means *our* love of God; so the sense is, "In him love for God has become complete". I have hitherto regarded the other three verses (4: 12, 17, 18) as meaning *God's* love, but Alford and others weightily insist that it is *ours*. Thus verse 12 says that "love of Him is *completed* in us"; and verse 17, "Love is completed in this, that we have boldness about the day of judgment". Moffatt delightfully gives the sense of verse 18, "Love in its fulness drives all dread away".

Of course, all these four verses *imply* that God's own love is "shed" within us (Rom. 5: 5), and that it is the originating cause of *our* new loving ("*we* love because *He* first loved: 1 John 4: 19); but his new love in our hearts is not merely God's own love loving Him back, it is our own human love, cleansed, renewed, enriched, permeated and enkindled by His; so that *we* do indeed love *Him*; yes, and love others in a new way, with the love of God Himself also expressing itself *through* our love. However, whichever way we read the verses, our English word, "perfect", in its strict meaning, has no rightful place.

I have just read again Wesley's famous sermons, number 40, "Christian Perfection", and number 76, "On Perfection". Knowing Greek as he did, one wonders why he clung so doggedly to either the phrase or the word. Number 40 begins, "There is scarcely any expression in holy writ which has given more offence than this. The word *perfect* is what many cannot bear." His reply is, "Whatsoever God hath spoken, that will we speak", as though the English version, not the Greek original, were the final authority! He sums up the first part of his sermon, "Christian perfection, therefore, does not imply . . . exemption from ignorance, or mistake, or infirmities, or temptations. Indeed, it is only another term for holiness. They are two names for the same thing. Thus, every one that is holy is, in the Scripture sense, perfect. Yet we may lastly observe that neither in this respect [i.e. holiness] is there any absolute perfection on earth." That is surely a doctrine of *im*perfect perfection.

John Wesley is the last man one would ever want to charge with sophistry; yet one cannot help feeling, in Sermon 40, that his fine eagerness outruns his judgment, as though to help God's Word say a bit more than it actually does. The way he gets round 1 John 1: 8, "If we say that we have no sin, we deceive ourselves", by making it mean no more than "sinned" as in verse 10, and then informing us that neither verse says that we *do* sin now, is cute even if not convincing! To argue from Luke 6: 40 ("Every one who is perfect shall be as his master") that Christians are made "free from all sinful tempers" because our Master, Jesus, was free from all such, is certainly strange, since the "master" or "teacher" in Luke 6: 40 is not our Lord Jesus, but the "blind guide" who leads "every one that is perfected" (i.e. fully taught) of him, "into the pit"! His comments on certain other texts (e.g. Mark 7: 21 and 1 John 1: 7) are equally naïve; but he eventually gets to his interim conclusion, namely, that Christians "are now in such a sense perfect as not to commit sin, and to be freed from evil thoughts and evil tempers."

There are other sincere inconsistencies. Though Wesley is at pains to convince us that by Christian perfection he means "no more than . . ." he yet in fact means "*much* more than". For instance, in one of his letters he says that it is "loving God with all our heart, and serving Him with all our strength"; to which he adds, "Nor did I ever say or mean any *more* by perfection than thus loving and serving God". Yet he *did* mean more, much more. Wrapped up invisibly in that simple manifesto of his is his doctrine of eradication; the complete destruction of the "old nature", the utter extinction of "inbred sin", the instantaneous cleansing away of all evil thoughts and tempers—all based on a misunderstanding of Romans 6: 6, 1 John 1: 7, and on an inadequate view of sin.

This, however, should always be borne in mind, that although we may disallow phrases like "Christian perfection" because not truly Scriptural, we do not thereby negate the reality of the blessing itself which the phrase misnames. Nor must we ever forget Wesley's magnificent emphasis that the *essence* of entire sanctification is the infilling love of God begetting in the heart of the Christian believer pure love to God and man. Nor do our frank comments on the aforementioned features of Wesley's teaching betoken any less admiration for that glorious man of God. The more we reflect on Wesley, the more do we see his greatness of stature. What millions of us owe to him, under God, tongue simply cannot tell.

APPENDICES

NEW TESTAMENT VERB-TENSES AND THE BELIEVER'S DEATH TO SIN

NOT ONLY must Romans 6: 6 be interpreted according to its location in the total structure of the epistle, it must be seen along with all the other New Testament references to the believer's death to sin. Not once in the New Testament is the believer's death with Christ, or death to sin, spoken of as taking place in the present, or *inside* the believer, or as being a continuous *dying*. The references are given below. If there are others, which are they? In each instance we give the Authorized Version, and alongside of it the truer rendering of the English Revised and American Standard Versions. Much as we cherish our dear old Authorized Version, it is considerably responsible for that widespread misinterpretation of Romans 6 which lies behind the error that the believer is to experience, here and now, an *inward* co-crucifixion with Christ.

	Authorized Version	*The Truer Rendering*
Romans 6: 2	"How shall we that are dead to sin live any longer therein?"	"We who *DIED* to sin, how shall we any longer live therein?"
6: 4	"Therefore we are buried with Him by baptism unto death".	"We *WERE* buried therefore with Him through baptism into death."
6: 7	"For he that is dead is freed from sin".	"For he that *DIED* has been justified from sin."
6: 8	"Now if we be dead with Christ . . ."	"But if we *DIED* with Christ. . . ."
6: 10, 11	"For in that He died, He died unto sin once. . . . Likewise reckon ye also yourselves to be dead indeed unto sin."	"He died unto sin *once for all* . . . Even so [i.e. once-for-all] reckon ye also yourselves dead unto sin."
7: 4	"Wherefore, my brethren, ye also are become dead to the law. . . ."	'Wherefore, my brethren, ye also *WERE MADE* dead to the law"
2 Cor. 5: 14	"We thus judge, that if One died for all, then were all dead."	"We thus judge that One died for all, therefore all *DIED*".
Gal. 2: 19	"For I through the law am dead to the law."	"For I through the law *DIED* to the law."
Col. 2: 20	"Wherefore if ye be dead with Christ from the rudiments of the world . . ."	"If ye *DIED* with Christ from the rudiments of the world . . ."
Col. 3: 3	"For ye are dead, and your life is hid with Christ in God."	"For ye *DIED*, and your life is hid with Christ in God."
2 Tim. 2: 11	"For if we be dead with Him, we shall also live with Him."	"For if we *DIED* with Him, we shall also live with Him."
1 Pet. 2: 24	"That we being dead to sins, should live unto righteousness."	"That we, having *DIED* unto sins, might live unto righteousness".

I have not included 1 Corinthians 15:30, 31, "Why stand we in jeopardy every hour? . . . I die daily . . . What advantageth it me, if the dead rise not?"—for the reference here is solely to *physical* dying. So also is it in 2 Corinthians 4:9, 10, "Persecuted but not forsaken; cast down but not destroyed; always bearing about *in the body* the dying of the Lord Jesus, that the life also of Jesus might be made manifest in our body" (i.e. in the "mortal flesh", see verse 11).

So far as I know, there we have all the data; and what must we deduce? Is it not provenly clear that Romans 6 does *not* teach a present, experiential death or dying to sin, in the believer? Is it not equally clear that the usual holiness teaching based upon that chapter is wrong and harmful?

So Near Yet So Far!

It is a strange wonder to me how *near* some of the greater Christian teachers have come to seeing the real truth of Romans 6, yet even then have missed it through the misleading supposition that they must also somehow *make* it describe the experiential *as well as* the judicial and positional. For instance, take the following observations of John Wesley on Romans 6:

> "Now, the Word of God plainly declares, that even those who are justified, who are born again in the lowest sense, 'do not continue in sin'; that they cannot 'live any longer therein'; (Rom. 6:1, 2); that they are 'planted together in the likeness of the death' of Christ; (verse 5); that their 'old man is crucified with him', the body of sin being destroyed, so that henceforth they do not serve sin; that, being dead with Christ they are free from sin; (verses 6, 7); that they are 'dead unto sin, and alive unto God'; (verse 11); that 'sin hath no more dominion over them', who are 'not under the law, but under grace'; but that these, 'being free from sin, are become the servants of righteousness' (verses 14, 18)."

Think of it: the "old man crucified" and the "body of sin destroyed", and "dead with Christ", and "dead unto sin", and "free from sin"; and all these, so Wesley frankly agrees, are true of *all* the "justified". One would have thought that since all these phrases admittedly describe *all* Christians, right from their *justification* in Christ, Wesley would have stumbled into the realization that they could refer only to the *positional*, not to the experiential; yet having drawn so near, with such firm tread, he limps lamely away with the curious comment, "The very least which can be implied in these words is, that the persons spoken of therein, namely, all real Christians, or believers in Christ, are made free from *outward* sin". Thus does Wesley miss by an inch and wander a mile!

Coming much nearer to our own time, American evangelism never produced a finer popular-type Bible expositor than the late Dr. Arthur T. Pierson. He is one of my favourite authors, and I have profited much from his pen. In his book, *Vital Union with Christ,* he says:

"Enough has been written perhaps to introduce us to the great thought first presented in this sixth chapter of Romans. When Paul asks, shall we continue in sin? his first reply is, How shall we that have died to sin live any longer therein! Know ye not that so many of us as were baptized into Jesus Christ were baptized into His death? Therefore we are buried with him by baptism into death.

"It is perfectly plain that these words can be understood only *judicially*. We are all of us conscious of no such actual identification with Christ in death and burial. We have never yet really died or been laid in the grave. The only way to interpret these words is to interpret them, not only as expressing a historical fact, but a *judicial* act, something counted or reckoned or imputed to our account by the sovereign mercy and grace of God. That they are so to be interpreted is plain from the whole argument preceding. The first direct mention of a *judicial* righteousness found in the New Testament is in the opening chapters of this Epistle."

Could anything be more robust than that? Surely Dr. Pierson has seen clearly enough that what Romans 6 teaches is a joint-death with Christ to sin in a once-for-all *judicial* sense. Yet when he comes to verse 11: "Likewise reckon ye also yourselves to be dead indeed unto sin", his eyes suddenly become strangely blurred to the evidential build-up of the context. He spends practically the whole of chapter 3 "beating around the bush" so ineffectively with illustrations which do not illustrate that I could only feel sorry for my beloved author vainly struggling to prove the unprovable. Dr. Pierson himself agrees that to reckon oneself dead indeed to sin seems like reckoning the impossible, and then gives over ten pages "illustrating" such faith; but the illustrations simply do *not* illustrate Romans 6: 11; and at the end, all he can feebly say is, "God would have you count yourself dead to sin and hence living no longer therein. . . . If you expect to sin you will sin, and if you expect *not* to sin, because you reckon yourself no longer under sin's mastery, but under God's, you will find that expectation itself a security." So the "reckoning" has not given us death to sin after all, but only an "expectation" which armours us against committing it.

Other such examples might be given. Scholarly expositors have been obliged to acknowledge this exclusively judicial aspect in Romans 6, yet have strangely fallen prey to the allurement that they must *also* make it teach a present, inward *experience* supposedly necessary to Christian sanctification. Always this has led to self-contradiction. For instance Dr. E. W. Bullinger, in his dissertation, *The Two Natures in the Child of God* says:

"The first object of this section (Romans 5: 12 to 8: 39) is to teach us that though we still see the fruits, we are to regard the old tree as though it had died, and to reckon that we died in Christ's death. No change has taken place. The root still remains. The change is in our standing before God."

Is there not palpable contradiction in such teaching? Think of it: the "fruits" of the so-called "old nature" are still continuing; yet although the "old tree" thus proves itself very much alive, we are to "regard" it as dead! We are "to reckon that we *died* in Christ's death"; yet *how* did we die in any inward sense, if as Bullinger's next sentence says, "*No* change has taken place" *inside* us, and "the root still remains"? And why try to make the passage mean an *inward* change at all, if, as Bullinger adds, its sole meaning is: "The change is in our *standing* before God"? What confusion there is here between spiritual *state* and positional *standing*!

It is sometimes noticeable, too, how those who force this exper- iential interpretation upon Romans 6 have a way of substituting a word of their own in place of the actual words in the text. Take this further comment by Dr. Bullinger:

> "In spite of the fruits which we see from time to time, we believe God when He tells us that the tree, in His sight, is *CONDEMNED*."

We have put that word, "condemned" in capitals to draw attention to this common expedient of bending the meaning by changing the wording. God does *not* say that the "old man" is merely "condemned"; he was "*crucified*". Nor does God say that the "body of sin" is merely "condemned"; the Scripture word is, "*destroyed*". Dr. Bull- inger simply dare not use the actual words of Romans 6:6, because, although he struggles to make Romans 6:6 refer to an intended in- ward *experience*, he insists over and over again that the "old nature" or "old tree" or the "flesh" *remains* within the Christian believer to the very end of mortal years on earth. How could anyone ever find poise or comfort on the horns of such a dilemma?

It sounds brave when the worthy Doctor says, "We believe God when He tells us that the tree, in His sight, is *condemned*". It has a "we-go-all-the-way-with-God" ring about it; but in reality it is an evasion. So is his further word on Romans 6:11:

> "Observe, it does not say that we are to *feel* ourselves as dead, or that we are to realise it; but to 'reckon' it as being really so in God's sight, *AS THOUGH* it were an accomplished fact."

Mark again the words which we have put in capitals. That softening phrase, "as though", is completely foreign to Romans 6:11. That text does not tell us that we are to reckon "*as though*" dead (a make- believe reckoning) but to reckon ourselves dead "*INDEED*"!

We might fill pages with equally round-about and facile ambiguities from preachers and writers who expound the usual "holiness" theory of Romans 6; but we desist, lest by further such quotings we should seem disrespectful or becloud what we are desiring to clarify. Do not all the forementioned factors converge on one conclusion? Romans 6 does *not* teach a present, inward joint-crucifixion with Christ. From beginning to end, the passage of which it is a part refers to the *judicial* aspects and bearings of our union with Him, and *only* to them.

THE IDENTIFICATION THEORY AND HUDSON TAYLOR

It almost causes a wry smile to see how some of the most beloved among our Lord's servants have held on to an interpretation when all the time, deep in their hearts, they have *known* that it was not true to experience. Take the following testimony (and admission) from that glorious missionary, Hudson Taylor. (We fully realize that to a certain type of admirer, Hudson Taylor is too sacrosanct to be criticized; as for ourselves, we esteem him far too highly to allow him any such immunity). He says:

"I am no better than I was before (may I say, in a sense I do not wish to be, nor am I striving to be); but I am dead and buried with Christ—aye and risen and ascended, and now Christ lives in me and 'the life that I now live, I live by faith in the Son of God who loved me and gave Himself for me.' I now believe that I am dead to sin. God reckons me so and tells me to reckon myself so. He knows best; all my past experience may have shown that it was not so; but I dare not say it is not so when He says it is. I feel and know that old things have passed away. I am as capable of sinning as ever, but Christ is realized as present as never before. He cannot sin, and He can keep me from sinning. . . . And further, walking in the light, my conscience has been more tender, sin has instantly been confessed and pardoned, and peace and joy (with humility) instantly restored."

Surely any Christian heart reacting genuinely to that testimony must feel that in part it is sadly misguided. The words, "I am no better than I was before . . . nor am I striving to be", strike a jarring discord. They betray a warped idea of sanctification, arising from the "identification" theory, and are *not* in accord with the actual teaching of Scripture. We must never allow any theory to becloud the Scripture teaching that we are to *develop* in Christlikeness of *character*.

Hudson Taylor's, "I am no better", indicates a delusion, not a blessing; for any "blessing" which does not better what I *am* is spurious. The Holy Spirit designs to renew *me*, not just a part of me to the exclusion of a so-called "old nature" which supposedly *cannot* be regenerated, and has to be imaginatively "reckoned" dead (even though, as Hudson Taylor sadly admits, experience shows it to be still alive!). The Holy Spirit, I repeat, comes to sanctify the *whole* of me—"spirit and soul and body" (1 Thess. 5:23). I ask again: if that triune specification, "spirit and soul and body" does not mean my whole *being*, and every part of my *nature*, then what language could? Any thought of a part within me which *cannot* be "sanctified" and made "blameless" (i.e. a supposed "old nature" or "old self") is thereby disqualified.

As for Hudson Taylor's words, "nor am I striving to be", why, as the New Testament epistles teach us again and again, the Holy Spirit's inward working and our own prayerful striving are to go together in a progressive approximation of our character to the lovely "image" and "stature" of our heavenly Master (2 Cor. 3: 18, 7: 1, Eph. 4: 13, 15). We are to "strive", to "increase", to "grow", to "go on", to "press forward", to "abound more and more", not to mention other similar expressions, all of which are aspects of godly "striving" after conformity to Christ.

I am far from suggesting that Hudson Taylor was unaware of all these. Nay, was there ever a more energetic aspirer after true holiness than he? All I am saying is, that his viewpoint on sanctification was warped by this "identification" theory, this theory that a so-called "old nature" is supposedly crucified and buried with Christ in a present, inward operation. Did Hudson Taylor find that his "reckoning" the old self dead was ratified in experience? No; with a sadly comic touch he has to say, "I now believe that I am dead to sin. . . . All my past *experience* may have shown that it was *not* so; but I dare not *say* it is not so, when He [God] says it is." In other words, the misleading theory compels him to accept as a divine truth something which he knows in experience is not true at all! *That* is not good even for a saintly giant like Hudson Taylor. It did not help him. It hindered and puzzled and disappointed him. The blessing which came to him through his surrender-crisis came through the surrender, not through the "identification" astigmatism—for *that* part of the "blessing" did not work!

SCOFIELD VERSUS ALLIS ON THE "TWO NATURES" IN THE BELIEVER

Among Evangelicals this supposition of "two natures" within the born again is so general that its Scripturalness is assumed unquestioningly. So inextricably interwoven does it seem to be with the standard pattern of holiness teaching that perhaps we ought to give this further consideration to it here.

Where, then, does this "two natures" concept come from? It derives, so I believe, from the misinterpretation of a certain few verses in the Pauline epistles, and secondarily from the continual emphasizing of this misinterpretation by holiness platforms which urge our experiential identification with the crucifixion of Christ.

In our chapter on the subject we referred to the Scofield Bible note on the "wretched man" of Romans 7.

> "The apostle personifies the strife of the two natures in the believer, the old or Adamic nature, and the divine nature received through the new birth (1 Pet. 1: 23, 2 Pet. 1: 4, Gal. 2: 20, Col. 1: 27). The 'I' which is Saul of Tarsus, and the 'I' which is Paul the apostle are at strife, and 'Paul' is in defeat."

Not one of those four texts which the Scofield note cites says that a new *nature* is "received through the new birth". Glance through them.

The first (1 Pet. 1: 23) says that "believers" (21) have been "begotten again" of incorruptible "seed" through "the word of God".

Mark well: it is we ourselves who have been "begotten again" by a "seed" communicated through "the word of God". That communicated life regenerates *us*; it does not merely *add* a new "nature", leaving what we humanly *are* unchanged. Common as it may be, that idea is exogenous; it is not in the text. A regeneration which does not regenerate *me*, but only transplants into my being a so-called "new nature" which is not really the "me", and which is always distinct from what I am in myself, is not regeneration at all.

The second Scofield text (2 Pet. 1: 4) says that through the "promises" we become "partakers of the divine nature". But this common sharing of *His* nature does not mean that *we* each have a "new nature" planted in us, a nature which is not really our own self. A parallel text (Heb. 6: 4) says we are made "partakers of the Holy Spirit", but does that mean a separate Holy Spirit transplanted into each of us? Nay, does it not mean that the one holy life is shared by us all? If a band of migrants, languishing through thirst, all eagerly drink from one and the same suddenly discovered reservoir, does the liquid draught become a separate little reservoir inside each one of them? No, it revives the participants by renewing *their own* nature.

In Second Peter 1: 4, that word, "nature" means the *life*. That life of our divine Lord is to be continually drawn upon by all His people; but how far is that from meaning a separate "new nature" in each of us, a superinduced entity which is not our own human nature at all! If such were the teaching of the text, then my receiving the so-called "*new* nature" would make all that I now am the so-called "*old* nature" which, according to the usual holiness teachers, "*cannot* be regenerated". Therefore, this doctrine of "the two natures" negates the true meaning of regeneration, for it leaves the human "I" (my real self) not regenerated at all!

As for the other two texts in the Scofield note (Gal. 2: 20, Col. 1: 27), comment is scarcely needed, so obviously do they *not* teach any such imparting of a "new nature".

In our chapter on the subject we referred to Ephesians 4: 22–24 and Colossians 3: 9, 10, where the "putting off" of the "*old* man" and the "putting on" of the "*new* man" is supposed to indicate two natures. But, as we said, this simply cannot refer to two natures, for *we* are utterly unable either to "put off" the hereditary evil in us, or to "put on" a regenerate new life. If we would know when and what that completed act of "putting off" and "putting on" *was*, there are references which clearly tell us. As to the "putting *on*" see Galatians 3: 27,

> "For as many of you as were *baptized* into Christ did *PUT ON* Christ."

Both the verbs here, i.e. "were baptized" and the "did put on" are aorists, indicating completed acts identical in time. As to the "putting *off*", see Colossians 2: 11,

> "In the *PUTTING OFF* of the body of the flesh . . . . buried with Him [Christ] in *baptism,* wherein also ye are risen with Him."

In both instances the reference is to the initiating rite of baptism, wherein those believers of the early days had publicly *professed* their having "put off" the old way of life in Adam, and their having "put on" the new way of life in Christ. Thus, even more clearly, we see that the putting off of the "old man" (i.e. living for the old creation in Adam), and the putting on of the "new man" (i.e. living for the new creation in Christ) have nothing to do with the misleading invention of "two natures" in the believer.

Professor Oswald T. Allis has a comment on the Scofield note to Ephesians 4: 24 which is well worth quoting here. It occurs in his *Prophecy and the Church,* page 44.

"Stated bluntly this amounts to saying that the Christian has a dual personality. He has an old nature, the old man, which can do nothing but sin, and a new nature, the new man, which cannot sin. Scofield tells us in commenting on Ephesians 4: 24, that 'the new man is the regenerate man as distinguished from the old man', and 'in no sense the old man made over or improved'. This is a dangerous miss-statement of a precious truth. The new man is *not* the old man improved. He *is* the old man made over. The Christian is 'renewed in the whole man after the image of God'. That renewing, that gradual change of the old man into the new man, is progressive sanctification, which is the work of the Spirit of God. As the new man grows stronger, the old man must grow weaker. For Paul refers 'not to two distinct natures properly so-called, but to two distinct conditions of one and the same nature'. Were this not the case, the distinction between the old man and the new would practically amount to saying that Paul the Pharisee and Paul the apostle were two distinct persons, and that Christ did not save Paul but rather substituted Paul for Saul and left Saul (the old nature) to perish in his iniquity. But Paul was acutely conscious that he was the very Saul who had persecuted the Church and had been met and conquered by Christ on the way to Damascus. And every Christian, even the most saintly, knows that he is the very same lost sinner whom Jesus sought and saved."

DR. E. W. BULLINGER ON THE "TWO NATURES" IN THE BELIEVER

First let me pay tribute to the many excellent things which have come to us from this unusual scholar's pen. Also let it be understood that although some of my reactions here are severe, my respect for the ministry and memory of Dr. Bullinger are unwavering. His thesis on *The Two Natures in the Child of God* is a typically didactic product. To deal with it as lengthily as it deserves would run away with far too many pages here. Representative quotations must suffice, our purpose being solely to show how insupportable the "two natures" theory is when examined critically.

His first chapter is on the *Names and Characteristics of the Old Nature*: and (supposedly) its first name is "the flesh".

"The flesh, as we have it in John 3: 6, 'That which is born of the flesh is flesh'. It comes by birth as generated by a fallen begetter. Concerning this flesh we are told: it 'cannot please God' (Rom. 8: 8); it 'profiteth nothing' (John 6: 63); there is in it 'no good thing' (Rom. 7: 18)."

Is not that a strangely fallacious beginning? The word "flesh", is treated as the same in all four texts, yet clearly, those texts use the word in three different senses! In John 3: 6, "flesh" means simply the *physical*—in answer to Nicodemus's question as to physical birth. It has no moral (or evil "old nature") reference at all.

Next, in John 6: 63 the word, "flesh", means the merely *natural*. There is no *moral* (or evil "old nature") reference whatever. Our Lord says, "The bread that I will give is My flesh", and then explains that His reference is from the outward to the inward: "It is the Spirit that quickeneth; the flesh profiteth nothing."

The other two texts (Rom. 7: 18 and 8: 8) *do* have a moral bearing; but to say that even they refer to the "flesh" as an evil "old nature" is sheer presuming. Here, however, all I point out is the preliminary bungle of texts; for if first premises are so wrong, can conclusions be right?

Indeed, Dr. Bullinger *does* draw a fatally wrong conclusion from those bungled premises. Having wrongly made the word "flesh" in John 3: 6 mean a supposed evil "old nature" in us, he says, "The first thing we learn is: It (the 'flesh') cannot be changed. 'That which is born (or begotten) of the flesh is flesh', and remains flesh. . . . Neither education nor religion can alter the old nature." Thus, the idea that the "flesh" (a supposed name for a supposed "old nature") cannot be changed, Dr. Bullinger deduces from a text in which "flesh" has no such reference! But that is not all. It leads Dr. Bullinger to a further eccentricity:

"No! the nature of the old man cannot be changed. . . . When once this fact is realized, it becomes impossible for us to pray, 'Make clean our hearts within us'; for the question naturally arises, which 'heart'? The old one, or the new one? If the old, it cannot be cleansed. If the new, it needs no cleansing."

So now, according to this "two natures" theory, there are two *hearts* in the Christian, the one unclean beyond cleansing, the other so clean that is never needs cleansing; and the ever-filthy and the ever-clean must live together in the same human being to the day of death!

How wrong it is to make the word, "heart", mean a so-called "old nature" we have shown on earlier pages. The word is used in Scripture of the whole thinking human ego, often with special reference to the desires, emotions, and will; but never is it used of either an old or a new "nature" supposedly residing in us without being actually ourselves.

What can this Bullinger "heart" vagary say about verses like Acts 15: 9? That verse tells how the Holy Spirit came on a group of Gentiles at their conversion—*"PURIFYING THEIR HEARTS* by faith". Now *which* "heart" was purified? It could not have been the "new", for (says the theory) that one was only just being received (and that one never *needs* purifying); so it *must* have been the (so-called) *"old* heart" which was "purified". Yet Dr. Bullinger says that the "old" one *"cannot* be cleansed". Which, then, are we to believe: theory, or Scripture? But again:

> "The second thing we learn is that it (the 'flesh') has only one end. Its end is death! . . . *'In Adam all die'* (1 Cor. 15: 22)."

Yet the words, "In Adam all die", are part of a passage dealing *only* with the death and resurrection of the *mortal body*; they have nothing to do with the "flesh" as a supposed evil "old nature" within us.

We turn over a page, and another peculiarity waylays us. Dr. Bullinger quotes 1 John 5: 18, with bracket and comment, thus:

> " 'We know that everyone that has been begotten of God does not sin; but he (i.e. the new man) that was begotten of God keepeth him, and the evil one toucheth him not.' . . . The new nature is personified and spoken of in the masculine gender. It cannot refer to the believer as a whole . . . for the new nature is born of God and does not sin."

Is not that a manoeuvre with words? The pronoun, "he" is the so-called "new nature" in masculine gender, not "the believer as a whole". But besides the "he" there is a "him" which the "he" is said to "keep" from the evil one. So here we have the comical contrariety of the new nature "keeping" the old nature, and keeping it so well that Satan cannot "touch" even that wicked *old* nature! Yes, that is what is implied, for Dr. Bullinger himself says that the new nature is *"unable* to sin", and it therefore needs no guarding, whereas "the believer as a whole" *does*! What queer streets we get into as we track this "two natures" theory!

Of the *new* "nature" Dr. Bullinger says it is "divine" and "perfect", which leads to this brash annotation: "When once we really learn and believe this blessed fact it becomes difficult if not impossible for us to pray: 'Take not Thy Holy Spirit from us'." But surely that is a sad presumption. Dr. Bullinger fails to distinguish between the Holy Spirit's giving us new *life* by regeneration, and His enduing us with spiritual grace and power for Christian *fellowship or service*. Christians can "grieve" the Spirit away (Eph. 4: 30) even though they do not lose their regenerate *life*. I have known ministries, once powerful, from which the Spirit has departed; and I shall ever pray that He may not be withdrawn from my own.

However, the most disturbing of these Bullinger lucubrations occur in his chapter on the *Conflict between the Two Natures.*

"The two natures thus dwell side by side in one personality. Like the graft of a rose on a briar, or an apple on a crab-apple, it is one tree; but all that is brought forth above the graft is a new kind of fruit, while all that is brought forth from the old stem, below the graft, is of the nature of the old tree."

What a nugatory picture of regeneration! A graft is a mere insertion, not fundamental stock. The tree itself is not changed. There is no new life set coursing through it; and even the new graft must receive its life from the old tree in order to bear fruit! In other words, at conversion to Christ the human person itself is not regenerated; but only a so-called "new nature" engrafted; and even that must receive its life from the "old"! How can able Bible scholars deviate so, when the Word says: "If any man be in Christ, he is a new creature, old things are passed away; behold, *all things are become new*"!

But Dr. Bullinger adds more about this theoretical co-occupancy of the two "natures":

"The experience is so interlaced that it is difficult for man's word to describe it or explain it. Only "the Word of God" can do that; nothing else. 'It is able to divide what is of (the) soul' (i.e. soulical or natural, the old nature), and what is 'of (the) spirit' (i.e. the new nature); and is able to judge (yes, and to condemn) the thoughts and intents of the heart (i.e. the old nature)" (Heb. 4: 12).

Yes, indeed, this "interlaced" co-habitation *is* difficult "for man's word to describe"! Nor can even the Word of God describe what has no reality. Dr. Bullinger's slovenly misadaptation of Hebrews 4: 12 (part omitted, part paraphrased) is futile. To say that "soul" means the old nature, and "spirit" the new, is analytically faulty, as a further glance at the text confirms. There are three pairs of entities: (1) "soul and spirit"; (2) "joints and marrow"; (3) "thoughts and intents". The Word of God is said to "divide" or "discern" between each pair. If then the first pair are forced to represent the supposed old nature and the new, then the second pair, the "joints" are the old, and the "marrow" is the new; while in the third pair the "thoughts" are the old, the "intents" the new; and exegesis becomes travesty. The real truth is, that the three duals have nothing to do with the supposed two natures in a believer, as the context shows.

But the most dismaying concomitant of all, in Dr. Bullinger's elaboration of the "two natures" supposition, is its *dogmatic defeatism.* Not only is there no discharge from this war of the "two natures", but there can be neither "deliverance" nor "victory" to the end of our mortal years! That is what the following excerpt emphatically avers. (Note the confusion in its use of the word, "flesh"):

"A certain class of modern holiness teaching in this sphere of truth robs it of all its beauty and its power. It realises the fact of the conflict within us, but would have us engage in the hopeless task of improving or eradicating the old nature. It would thus, at the best, occupy us with ourselves, and would have us ignore the emphatic assurances from God's Word that the old nature, or the flesh, can never be changed into spirit. And, supposing it could be eradicated, where is it to go? What is to become of it? It is 'flesh'; and nothing can end the burden of the 'flesh' but death and resurrection, or rapture. No amount of surrendering, or believing, can get rid of 'the flesh'. . . . The Scripture word is 'deliverance' and 'victory', and this, not victory over 'sins' as such, but over 'sin' itself, over this death-appointed body. This 'deliverance' will be experienced *only in rapture or resurrection.*"

Think of it: no "deliverance" except through death or translation! Surely, for the learned sponsor of this dreary news to speak of its "beauty" and "power" is of all euphemisms the most eccentric. What a deviation is his doleful pessimism from the triumphant note of the New Testament—"The law of the Spirit of life in Christ Jesus *HATH SET ME FREE* from the law of sin and death"!

These criticisms of Dr. Bullinger's treatise are longer than I intended, but shorter than it deserves. Everywhere its inconsistencies catch the eye. In the following abbreviated extract note the misleading usage of the pronoun, "we", and the noun, "persons", as synonymous with "the old nature".

"Even so, it is our first bounded duty to reckon that *we* are (as regards the law and all its claims on us) as though we were dead *persons*. . . . So that our first responsibility as to the *old nature* is . . . to reckon it as having died with Christ when he was crucified" (italics ours).

Yes, Scripture does say that *"we"* (as whole *"persons"*) died with Christ in the judicial reckoning of God; but it does *not* teach that only a *part* called the "old nature" was crucified with Him. Dr. Bullinger has synonymized terms which greatly differ. So do all our holiness brethren who hold the "two natures" theory. Dr. Bullinger himself tilts at them, but in so doing trips over his own toes:

"Special meetings and 'missions' and 'conventions' have been introduced with the expressed object of 'deepening the spiritual life'. . . . But it shows a forgetfulness of the Word, which declares that this new nature is 'perfect' and 'divine', and therefore cannot be 'deepened' or increased."

Thus there emerges a grimly comic predicament: the old nature is "evil" beyond possibility of regeneration, while the new nature is divinely "perfect" beyond possibility of being made more so. The Christian life becomes a conundrum, and our conventions for the "deepening of the spiritual life" a wishful superfluity.

That is the self-contradiction at the centre of all holiness movements which teach the "two natures" theory, unless they capitulate to the eradicationists, and agree that the old nature may be removed. A usual teaching, as we have seen, is that the so-called old nature can neither be extirpated nor regenerated. It may be "counteracted", but it lives within us to the end. So, in a "Convention for the Deepening of the Spiritual Life", *what* is to be "deepened"? It cannot be the "*old* nature", for (we are told) the "flesh" cannot possibly become "spiritual". Yet neither can the "*new* nature" be spiritually "deepened", as it is already "divine" and "perfect".

Could it be, then, that although the "new nature" cannot be improved in *quality*, it can be increased in *quantity*? No, not even that for the "old nature" cannot be reduced by any *partial* eradication. It may be reckoned "crucified" and "dead", yet (psycho-pneumatic mystery!) it remains *alive* with us to the end, as the old "self". So there is no further territory within the human person in which the new nature *could* expand! The old can never become new, and the new can never eject the old; so where are we?

It is a perplexity to me that this "two natures" phantasy has for so long dominated and dislocated evangelical holiness teaching. Exegetically it is a distortion; and in experience it makes sanctification an agony instead of a glad release. It makes the condition of the believer even more "wretched" than that of the average unconverted person. Dr. Bullinger himself says as much in his comment on the *result* of the warfare between the (supposed) two natures:

"The result of this unceasing warfare is the *wretchedness* which leads the ego in the next verse to cry out, in broken gasps: 'O wretched-I-man!' . . . He (God) will deliver all who have this conflict, in the only possible way; by Death, Rapture, or Resurrection."

Yet Dr. Bullinger sees no inconsistency in adding, as his final counsel:

"Cease all efforts either to improve the flesh or to get rid of it. Feed the new nature regularly with the divinely prepared food, *and everything else will fall into its own proper place*" (italics ours).

This paradoxical blend of gasping "wretchedness" with "everything" happily falling into its "proper place" (including wicked "old nature"!) may well make one wonder what feats of sanguine credulity scholarly Bible teachers can perpetrate.

Various other incongruities of the "two natures" theory might be quoted, but we forbear. This hunting-out of its inconsistencies becomes much too like a hare-and-hounds affair; only in this instance, instead of one hare and many hounds, it is a solitary hound trying to round up more naughty hares than it can comfortably cope with! Surely what we have tracked down already is enough to show that the "two natures" theory is unscriptural, self-contradictory, and baneful. Christian holiness teaching, at long last, should discard it.

IS SANCTIFICATION NECESSARILY INSTANTANEOUS?

Most decidedly John Wesley taught that entire sanctification is necessarily instantaneous. A characteristic argument, in his *Plain Account of Christian Perfection,* is, "God usually gives a considerable time for men to receive light, to grow in grace, to do and suffer His will, before they are either justified or sanctified; but He does not invariably adhere to this; sometimes He 'cuts short His work'; He does the work of many years in a few weeks; perhaps in a week, a day, an hour. He justifies or sanctifies . . . those who have not had time for a gradual growth either in light or grace. And may He not do what He will with His own? Is thine eye evil because He is good?"

Tyerman, the Methodist historian, tells us that for about half of his long ministry Wesley made instantaneous sanctification a leading emphasis (see his *Life and Times of Wesley,* pp. 346, 416, 444).

Most forcibly of all (see *Journal of Hester Ann Rogers,* p. 174) he writes, "You may obtain a growing victory over sin from the moment you are justified. But this is not enough. The body of sin, the carnal mind, must be destroyed; the old man must be slain, or we cannot put on the new man, which is created after God (or which is the image of God) in righteousness and true holiness; and this is *done in a moment.* To talk of this work as being gradual, would be nonsense, as much as if we talked of gradual justification."

In his later years, Wesley felt it necessary to modify certain points of his earlier teaching, and to clarify others. Those readjustments were marks of honesty and maturity, not of unreliability. I incline to think they have been unduly magnified by some of his critics. Think of it: his many writings on sanctification are distributed through sermons, journals, articles, letters, over a stretch of sixty-six years. Is it over-surprising that contradictions, either seeming or real, appear here and there? For my own part, I am grateful that he tarried on earth long enough to revise, in a ripe old age, certain incidentals of his earlier teaching. It adds the value of seasoned judgment and experience to his testimony as a whole.

But whatever incidental emendations Wesley made, he never moved from teaching that entire sanctification is *instantaneous.* J. A. Wood, who compiled a useful little manual of Wesley's teachings, says, "Mr. Wesley repeatedly denies any radical change in his views, although he admits a few overstatements and less distinctness during a part of his early ministry. It may be safely averred, that while he gives us no case of gradual sanctification by growth, he does positively teach *instantaneous* sanctification by faith, and gives us several thousand such instances. He also asserts that he never knew a case of *gradual* entire sanctification." (*Christian Perfection*, p. 178.)

Mr. Wood further comments that Wesley "taught *instantaneous* sanctification by faith, twenty years before the great revival of holiness in 1761-63, and afterwards on to the close of his life in 1791". In confirmation of this, see Wesley's letter to Bell and Owen (Journal, Oct. 1762): "You have over and over denied instantaneous sanctification to me; but I have known and taught it (and so has my brother, as our writings show) above these twenty years."

C. W. Ruth, also, is a more recent representative: "If sanctification were by growth, then time would be a factor; for all will admit that it requires time to grow. Suppose an individual might be said to grow into sanctification in two years; and suppose that this individual should die at the expiration of one year, just half way to sanctification; would not the next half of sanctification, of necessity, have to take place instantly? And if the last half of sanctification might be completed instantly, why not the first half? To hope for sanctification by growth is hoping in a theory that can never be realised. Sanctification is plainly a 'divine act' obtained instantaneously by an entire consecration and faith. As well speak of growing into justification as growing into sanctification" (*ibid.*, p. 23).

Editor Thomas K. Doty writes: "Some teach that entire sanctification is a gradual work only. . . . Others teach that it is both gradual and instantaneous. . . . And yet others teach, quite correctly, that like conversion it is always and altogether wrought in a moment. No examples of the blessing received by the first two methods are known to exist; but by the last there are many—they are numbered by the thousand. Holiness work dies out in the hands of the teachers of gradualism; but it thrives under the efforts of those who know nothing but instantaneous sanctification" (*Lessons in Holiness*, p. 41).

Looking back over more than forty years (in a printed sermon prepared shortly before his death) John Wesley tells how he was first led to believe in the reality of inwrought sanctification. It was through the tried and tested witness of several persons in London and others in Bristol. He arranged a meeting with those in London, of which meeting he says, "When we met, first one of us and then the other asked the most searching questions we could devise. They answered every one without hesitation, and with the utmost simplicity, so that we were fully persuaded, they did not deceive themselves."

Wesley then continues, "In the years 1759, 1760, 1761, and 1762, their numbers multiplied exceedingly, not only in London and Bristol, but in various parts of Ireland as well as England. Not trusting to the testimony of others, I carefully examined most of these myself; and in London alone, I found six hundred and fifty-two members of our society who were exceedingly clear in their experience, and whose testimony I could see no reason to doubt. I believe no year has passed since that time, wherein God has not wrought the same work in many others; but sometimes in one part of England or Ireland, sometimes in another—as 'the wind bloweth where is listeth'—and every one of these (after the most careful inquiry, I have not found one exception either in Great Britain or Ireland) has declared that his deliverance from sin was *instantaneous*; that the change was wrought in a moment. Had half of these, or one third, or one in twenty, declared it was *gradually* wrought in *them*, I should have believed this, with regard to *them*, and thought that *some* were gradually sanctified and some instantaneously. But as I have not found, in so long a space of time, a single person speaking thus; and as all who believe they are sanctified declare with one voice that the change was wrought in a moment, I cannot but believe that sanctification is commonly, if not always, an *instantaneous* work."

Bound up with Eradication

As we pointed out on page 93, this insistence that entire sanctification must come instantaneously is bound up with the "eradication" theory. For instance, since entire sanctification is said to bring "freedom from *all* sin", C. W. Ruth naturally says, "To teach that the divine work of sanctification in the purifying and cleansing of the heart *from all sin* is a gradual work would be to admit that a heart might be a little holy, more holy, and most holy; so that it might become exceeding difficult to know just in what degree of holiness the individual experience might be located" (*Entire Sanctification*, p. 30). His point is, of course, that a complete excision of the sin-bent leaves no room for degrees such as "more" or "most". It is a sheer case of "Yes" or "No".

Thomas K. Doty, after distinguishing between the cleansing away of *guilt* at conversion, and the later cleansing away of inbred *depravity* by entire sanctification, says, "Not a hint can be traced [i.e. in Scripture] of cutting into pieces our 'old man' or the 'body of sin'. . . . What the Christian requires to have cleansed from his heart is simply 'sin', or the 'carnal mind'." Therefore, consistently with teaching such an *utter ablution* of sin from the heart, he later adds, "It is unscriptural to teach growth as a substitute for cleansing" (*Lessons in Holiness*, pp. 30, 42).

Viewed as a divine surgery in the soul, or as an utter ablution of sin from the heart, we agree that entire sanctification *must* be instantaneous. Even if we make it a *series* of surgical operations, it is the *last* operation in the series which effects *entire* sanctification and makes it thus instantaneous. Or viewing it as a "*death* to sin" it is just as apparently instantaneous; for (reverting to John Wesley) if sin actually "ceases" in the soul, then "there must be a *last* moment of its existence, and a *first* moment of our deliverance from it"—that is, an instantaneous transition-point.

Inconsistencies

Even if the eradication theory were right, however, which it is not (as we have shown), the inconsistencies of those who teach the necessary instantaneousness of entire sanctification disqualify their dictum. We have referred to this in chapter 5, but we may mention here that another cause of their self-contradiction is their large emphasis on the *negative* aspect of sanctification (i.e. the destruction of inbred sin). It seems to me that the *positive* aspects of sanctification, namely, inward renewal, fulness of heaven-imparted life and love, enduement by the Holy Spirit, all imply that there can be *gradualness* in sanctification; for there assuredly *can* be and (as we all know) there certainly *are* degrees in such inward renewal and in the experience of that imparted life.

Is it not plain to all of us that the fulness which entirely sanctifies is a maximum of something already possessed in *degree*? Again and again Wesley is obliged to acknowledge this, despite his usual insistence on the instantaneousness of sanctification. He says, "They know [the Methodists] indeed that at the same time a man is justified, sanctification properly begins. For when he is justified, he is 'born again', 'born from above', 'born of the Spirit', which, although it is not (as some suppose) the whole process of sanctification, is doubtless the gate of it." (*Sermons*, vol. 2, p. 390.) So the *process* of sanctification *does* begin at conversion!

With a touch of interesting peculiarity he avers, "Certainly sanctification (in the proper sense) is 'an instantaneous deliverance from all sin', and includes 'an instantaneous power then given, always to cleave to God'. Yet this sanctification (at least in the *lower degrees*) does not include a power never to think an unclean thought, nor ever speak a useless word" (To Miss Purly in 1762). So there are *"lower degrees"*!

With another touch of this peculiarity he writes, "I have so often explained this that I cannot throw away time in adding any more now; only this, that the moment a sinner is justified, his heart is cleansed in a low degree; but yet he has not a clean heart, in the full, proper sense, till he is made perfect in love" (*Works*, vol. 5, p. 284). So there is a *"low degree"*!

There is no getting away from it: when we view entire sanctification as the *crowning* experience of the Christian life, which indeed it is, we are bound to admit that sanctification may be gradual as well as instantaneous. At the first Methodist Conference, in 1744, it was asked: "Is faith the instrument or the condition of sanctification?" The answer was: "It is both the condition and the instrument of it. When we begin to believe, then sanctification begins; and as faith increases, *holiness increases*, till we are created anew" (Tyreman, vol. 2, p. 147).

An Incorrect Equation

Yet again, those who insist that entire sanctification is necessarily instantaneous make (so it seems to me) a fallacious equation of entire sanctification with the "enduement of power from on high". I will not over-press this, but to my own thinking the enduement with "power" has to do with service, especially *witness-bearing* (Luke 24: 48, 49; Acts 1: 8) whereas entire sanctification is a renovation deep down in

one's *nature*. Am I too finely discriminating if I say that the enduement of power is a coming of the Holy Spirit *upon* us as an equipment
for specific service, whereas entire sanctification is His deep-going
work *within* us, to transform character? There may be many such
comings of the Spirit *upon* us, as we see in the Acts of the Apostles
(2: 4, 4: 8, 31; 13: 9), whereas entire sanctification is a *continuous*
experience of *inwrought holiness*.

I frankly confess that in making fine distinctions such as these,
apprehension besets me lest we should seem to complicate what we
seek to clarify. We have no wish to "strive about words to no profit"
(2 Tim. 2: 14). Yet we *should* make precise distinction where otherwise there can be hurtful confusion. When holiness expositors aver,
without qualifying their phraseology, that "entire sanctification" is
identical with the "enduement of power" or the so-called "baptism
of the Spirit", it seems to me that they easily engender misunderstandings. A single illustration will suffice.

In Acts 10, we see how the Holy Spirit "fell" on Cornelius and his
household. Whether that captain of the Italian cohort and "all his
house" were proselytes to Judaism is uncertain. Even presuming that
they were all godly-minded, they were not yet Christian believers, for
Peter was sent to *tell* them that "whosoever believeth in Him shall
receive remission of sins" (43). As soon as Peter had reached the point
of telling them that very thing, "the Holy Spirit *fell* on all them which
heard the word" (44, 45). Later, when recounting the episode, Peter
said, "And God, who knoweth the hearts, bare them witness, giving
them the Holy Spirit, even as He did unto us; and put no difference
between us and them, purifying their hearts by faith" (Acts 15: 8, 9).
Vigorous-minded scholar, Dr. Daniel Steele, comments: "This text
(Acts 15: 8, 9) is an incontrovertible demonstration that the fulness
of the Spirit is a *synonym for entire sanctification*".

Now *was* that abnormal falling of the Holy Spirit on those hitherto
unregenerated persons the same thing as entire sanctification? If, as
Dr. Steele avers, entire sanctification is "synonymous" with *that*, then
it must always begin with spectacular signs and be accompanied by
speakings in tongues! Did that speaking in tongues continue permanently with Cornelius's household? Was it not rather only a temporary
or (at most) intermittent "sign"? Up to the very moment of its happen-
ing, did that group of uninformed non-Christians have even the vaguest
inkling of any such thing as "entire sanctification" in our evangelical
sense of the word? Is it not simply common sense to distinguish such
sudden descents of the Spirit from His deeper, more blessed and permanent work of inward sanctification? If Christian believers, seeking
the reality of entire sanctification, are told that it is "synonymous"
with such emotional excitements and speakings in tongues as in Acts
10, will they not be brought into bondage?

I am not denying that entire sanctification *may* begin that way; but
I *am* denying the teaching that it must *necessarily* begin that way. I
am not denying that entire sanctification may come instantaneously;
but I *am* denying that it must *always* come with isolated instant-

aneousness. I am not denying that the entrance-point into entire sanctification may *synchronise* with the promised "enduement of power"; but I *am* insisting that we must not *synonymize* any such power-enduement, or periodic enduements, with the underlying and *continuous* experience of *character*-sanctification. In a word, we must distinguish entire sanctification itself from those phenomena which may often accompany it, but which do not *always* accompany it. No such volcanic upheaval of emotion, or supernatural efflorescences, or speaking in tongues, accompanied Frances Ridley Havergal's entrance into the experience of entire sanctification; yet was it real? There are thousands of others, also, to whom the longed-for blessing has come like the gentle suffusion of a heavenly zephyr. No; entire sanctification must not be equated with some glorious power-shock, nor need it necessarily be entered with a kind of electric-flash instantaneousness. We must distinguish between a temporary *"falling"* of the Spirit (*Acts* 10) and the continuous *"filling"* of the Spirit (Eph. 5: 18).

What then?

What, then, are we to conclude? Is entire sanctification instantaneous or gradual? We answer: (1) Since entire sanctification is *not* "eradication" (either in one or more surgical acts) there is no longer sense or reason in arguing its instantaneousness on *that* ground. (2) In its *positive* aspects—the infilling of heart and mind by the life and love and power and purifying energy of the Holy Spirit, there can certainly be *degrees* of sanctification. (3) Where there is *entire* consecration to Christ by the Christian believer, the point of utterness in yielding *must* be a concentrated point of time, and in that sense must be instantaneous. (4) At that instant there is entire sanctification in the sense that what we ourselves then fully yield, God then fully takes, sets apart, and fills.

So, we do not deny that entire sanctification in *that* sense is instantaneous, but, the point of cross-over to utter surrender may be the *last* point of a gradual series. We must distinguish entire sanctification *itself* from the phenomena which often accompany the entrance-point to it. We must distinguish between a temporary "falling" of the Spirit (Acts 10) and the continuous "filling" of the spirit (Eph. 5: 18). The *crisis* only has meaning when it issues in that character-transfiguring *process* which follows it.

NOW UNTO HIM THAT IS ABLE TO DO EXCEEDING ABUNDANTLY ABOVE ALL THAT WE ASK OR THINK, ACCORDING TO THE POWER THAT WORKETH IN US; UNTO HIM BE GLORY IN THE CHURCH BY CHRIST JESUS THROUGHOUT ALL AGES, AGE WITHOUT END: AMEN.

(Eph. 3: 20, 21.)